Every Day Is a Holiday

George Mahood

Copyright © 2014 by George Mahood
All rights reserved. This book or any portion thereof may not be reproduced or used in any manner whatsoever without the express written permission of the author except for the use of brief quotations in a book review.
This edition published 2014 by George Mahood

All of the photographs in this book are available to view in colour on Facebook

www.facebook.com/georgemahood
www.twitter.com/georgemahood
www.georgemahood.com

For Rachel, Layla, Leo and Kitty

JANUARY

January 1st

The zombies didn't attack, but I was ready for them.

There are a few simple steps that you can take to prepare yourself for a zombie invasion. Firstly, you should secure your surroundings by locking all doors and windows. Zombies are persistent creatures though, and will force their way into a locked house in very little time. It is at this stage that you need to prepare a suitable method of defence. Many people confuse zombies with vampires, and assume that wounding a zombie's heart will kill it. Zombies are not afraid of crucifixes either. These are common misconceptions that need to be addressed. The only way to kill a zombie is to destroy its brain. Use whatever method works best for you. I armed myself with a baseball bat, a meat cleaver and two golf clubs (my trusty 5 and 7-irons, as I have a habit of taking air shots with all other clubs).

If both of the above methods fail, it is important to get to a safe place as quickly as possible. Safe places include army bases, prisons or air raid shelters. If none of these are convenient then the local pub will suffice. Despite an absence of zombies, I took refuge in the local pub, just in case. I didn't take my golf clubs, baseball bat or meat cleaver with me, as the locals get a bit funny about things like that.

The reason I was paranoid about a zombie invasion is that January 1st is not just *New Years Day*, it is also known as *Z-day*. *Z-day*, or *Zombie Day*, is a day dedicated to a sudden uprising of the undead, when a battle between them and mankind commences. Why zombies would choose to attack on a day designated to their uprising, I am unsure. I would have thought that even the living dead could appreciate the element of surprise.

Don't worry. This isn't a book about zombies. I won't mention them again, I promise.

As well as being *New Years Day* and *Z-Day*, January 1st is also *New Year's Dishonour List Day* – a day, created by Lake Superior State University in Michigan, on which a list of overused words and phrases that should be banned from the English language is published. This year's list included the words: *Fiscal Cliff*, *YOLO* (you only live once), *Bucket List* and *Superfood*.

The University's website has an option to submit words for consideration next year. I submitted the words: *'anyhoo'*, *'Blue Sky Scenario'* and the suffix *'dot com'*. I don't mean the end of companies' web addresses - most of the internet would collapse if that was abolished. I mean people using the phrase as part of everyday conversation, or on social media. For example, *'I'm hungry.com'* or just simply *'bored.com'*. It doesn't make any sense whatsoever. It's just so pointless.com.

My plan is to spend the first six months of this year celebrating as many of these bizarre, weird and wonderful days, weeks and months as possible.

Recently, I had been feeling that something was missing from my life, but I couldn't work out exactly what. I am still fairly young and healthy. I have a kind, caring, funny, clever, talented and EXTREMELY beautiful wife (who is also editing this book and keeps adding adjectives), and three amazing children. We have our own house. Having been a self-employed layabout for quite a while, my photography work has increased in recent years and we now just about manage to pay the bills each month. I was extremely happy. But I still had that niggling feeling inside. I needed something more. Then the realisation hit me suddenly at the end of last year; I was suffering a mid-life crisis, at the age of 33.

I had my own proper adventure a few years ago when my good friend Ben and I set off to cycle the length of Great Britain, with the slight disadvantage that we didn't have bikes, clothes, shoes or money. It was three of the greatest weeks of my life and the excitement, fear and adrenaline that I felt during that journey would be almost impossible to ever replicate. Life at home then became very different. Nine months after finishing the trip my wife Rachel and I had a baby. Soon after that we had another, and then another, and in the space of four years we had three children. I love being a dad more than anything, and having children is undoubtedly the best thing that has ever happened to me. But I was still restless. I had itchy feet (I'm sure I could have got some cream for them), and a desire to get back out there and have another adventure. I wanted to push and challenge myself again. I was stuck in a routine and something needed to change in order to reignite that spark in me.

I wrote a book about our bike ride which I published, and beyond all my expectations, people seemed to like it. They were envious of my adventure and enjoyed sharing it vicariously. They wanted to know when I was going on my next adventure. When WAS I going on my next adventure? Or was that just a one off?

I was now a mature (debatable) grown-up, with three young children. I couldn't really just disappear for a long period of time on another physical challenge. Adventures don't have to be physical, though. Just learning a new skill or finding a new hobby is an adventure in itself. You can have an adventure just by experiencing something new; trying something different that draws you away, if only briefly, from your normal routine.

The usual cure for a mid-life crisis is a road trip across America on a motorbike, or the spontaneous purchase of a ridiculous sports car. Some men take up a strange uncharacteristic hobby, such as potholing, skateboarding... or Zumba. Me? I chose to treat my mid-life crisis with a celebration of all that is considered important in this world.

The idea hit me one day when I heard on the radio that it was *Talk Like A Pirate Day* or *National Donut Eating Day*, or something like that, which happened to coincide with *Leprechaun Huggers Appreciation Month*, or *International Dog Poo Picker Uppers Week*, or something similarly ridiculous. I did some research and discovered there are literally hundreds of these days throughout the year. I realised that somebody somewhere had created these days. Somebody somewhere felt that these various celebrations were important enough to warrant their own day, week or month. And if these things were significant enough to have entire days set aside for them, then surely I should be more appreciative of their existence. I decided that if I can celebrate as many of these days, weeks and months as possible, then I will be exposing myself to everything that is worthy and important in this world; absorbing new and valuable qualities along the way. At the end of it... who knows? But I hope to maybe be a more rounded, happier and content person.

Why only six months? Why not an entire year? I realise that a full year of holiday celebrations would make more sense. To celebrate only half of them, would mean I was also missing out on 50% of what is considered important in this world.

There are two main reasons for this. Firstly, I wanted to be realistic with my ambitions. A year is a bloody long time, and I know that I would be more likely to give up on the challenge if it felt like it was never going to end. Six months is still a long time, but it would be a lot more manageable.

The other reason was based around the practicalities of me writing a book. This may never even make it as far as a book, but, for me to make it even remotely worth reading (it is, stick with it), I will need to cover each day as thoroughly as I can. If I extended this project to cover an entire year - and still try and make a readable book from it - I would be flitting from day to day far too quickly, without any substance or depth (either that or write a book longer than War and Peace that nobody would ever finish). This whole project will probably be disjointed as it is, with such a weird eclectic mix of holidays to celebrate. Who knows how it will pan out? Your guess is as good as mine.

All of the holidays in this book are genuine. They are all referenced on a variety of holiday listing sites that can be found on the internet. I couldn't possibly make this shit up.

January 2nd

It is just so typical of cats to be too lazy to celebrate *New Year* on January 1st like the rest of us. They simply can't be bothered, so they celebrate their New Year, or *Mew Year*, as some bright spark named it, the following day.

We have two cats: Father Dougal and Batfink. Father Dougal was named after the priest played by Ardal O'Hanlon in the sitcom *Father Ted*. Like his namesake, he had a slightly bemused expression when he was a kitten. Not that Ardal O'Hanlon was ever a kitten. Father Dougal (the cat) is also black with a white bib and so looks like a clergyman. Although, he has never actually been mistaken for a priest. He is after all a cat. But he is as close to a priest as a cat is ever likely to look.

Batfink was named after the cartoon character of the same name. The cartoon character was a male bat, grey, with a yellow costume and wings that were like a shield of steel. Batfink the cat had none of these characteristics. SHE is not even a HE. Still, we thought it suited her and the name stuck.

Batfink was soon shortened to 'Finky' which at least has a slightly more feminine ring to it.

'HAPPY MEW YEAR!' I shouted to the pair of them, as I fired off a party popper whilst they were eating. They both disappeared out of the cat flap before the streamers had a chance to settle. Cats don't like party poppers I discovered.

I had a photography job in Milton Keynes in the afternoon, which is about 20 minutes down the M1 from Northampton. The journey took significantly longer as I was observing *55 MPH Speed Limit Day*.

The 55mph limit was introduced in the USA in 1974 to try and aid the oil crisis that they were experiencing at the time. It was thought that 55mph was the most fuel-economic speed for driving. It was also introduced to reduce road casualties. Despite being extremely popular amongst safety campaigners, this speed limit was eventually scrapped, and each state was given the power to set their own limit. *'Sure, it'll save a few lives, but millions will be late!'* said a teenage Homer Simpson in a Simpsons flashback episode. And he definitely had a point. A queue of angry lorry drivers started to backup behind me, as many of them have limiters that restrict their speed to 56mph. That extra 1mph would have seriously pissed them off. I confess that I was also itching to put my foot on the accelerator but I managed to resist. By the time I arrived in Milton Keynes, however, I felt calm and relaxed, as though I'd arrived by horse and carriage.

Navigating through the supermarket car park at 55mph on the way home, to buy a pint of milk, was an altogether different experience.

It was only January 2nd, but I was already struggling to find the motivation and inspiration for this challenge that I have set myself. Coincidently, it was *National Motivation and Inspiration Day*, so I turned to the day's creator, Kevin McCrudden, for help.

Kevin's *Motivate America* website has videos and snippets that offered the usual motivational bullshit, but he seemed like a likeable guy, and I did feel slightly better after watching his boundless energy and enthusiasm for ten minutes. His three main goals to become more motivated and inspired all seemed incredibly apt for this holiday project, too:

- *BE REALISTIC WITH YOUR GOALS* – I think I have been, Kevin. That's why I have vowed to celebrate as MANY of these holidays as possible, rather than ALL of them.
- DO SOMETHING TOWARDS YOUR GOAL EVERYDAY – That's the plan, Kevin!
- SURROUND YOURSELF WITH INSPIRATIONAL AND MOTIVATIONAL PEOPLE - Throughout the course of these holidays and celebrations, I hope to meet and speak to many motivational and inspirational people. It's only Day 2 and I've already discovered you, Kevin McCrudden.

Feeling motivated and inspired by my new mate Kev (we're not mates. He doesn't know me. I'm basically just his stalker), I strode on confidently, ready to face the challenge of another day.

January 3rd

My wife Rachel and I met at secondary school. She joined in the third year at the age of 13. For the first few years we were not in any of the same classes, so we never spoke to each other. She was way cooler than me and completely out of my league. We then became friends at the age of 16 when we studied some of the same subjects at A-level. She had an infectious laugh that used to sound like a car struggling to start on a winter's morning. We became very good friends and used to talk to each other for hours on the phone each night. My parents, who had not met her at this point, simply referred to her as 'phone girl'. Whilst on a family holiday, I borrowed my mum's BT chargecard to call Rachel for a chat. I had somehow misunderstood the international calling charges and we discovered a month later that this one phone call had cost me £48. My mum was not best pleased. I am still paying it off in installments.

Most of our conversations tended to be based around her boyfriends or - on the rare occasions that I actually had them - my girlfriends. It was really refreshing to have a close female friend for the first time. I realised towards the end of school that my feelings for Rachel were much more than just friendship. We were just about to disappear off to different universities and my timing could not have been worse. But I decided to tell her how I felt anyway. I expected her to laugh at me, but I was delighted when she admitted that she had feelings for me too. She said she had always thought that - in all likelihood - we would eventually end up together. It was unbelievable, and for a brief moment I thought that the rest of my life was sorted, and I would be with Rachel forever.

But there was a 'but'.

We were just about to start student life, at two completely different universities, hours apart from each other, and Rachel didn't think it was the best time to begin a serious relationship. She was right, of course, but it made the following few years incredibly difficult. We managed to continue being good friends, and chatted regularly on the phone and visited each other several times, and I had to smile and act the supporting friend role when she told me her various boyfriend dilemmas.

We both survived university and with a few months left to go in our final year, as neither of us was in a relationship, I suggested again to Rachel that maybe we should give it a go. This time she agreed.

We moved into a rented flat together a year later, then over the following few years we worked together, travelled together, got married (together, obviously) and then bought our first house together. As our relationship began as a friendship, we sort of bypassed the whole lovey-dovey stage. We tease each other incessantly, we bicker, we moan, but we also have a lot of fun together. She's been incredibly supportive over the years of my stupid ideas, and lack of desire to get a 'real' job. She's awesome, and I'm a really lucky man (and no, she has not edited this bit).

I was suffering from a severe case of Man Flu, so spent most of the day on the sofa celebrating the *Festival of Sleep*. You can never be too careful with Man Flu, as even a mild case can be fatal. Rachel had no sympathy for me whatsoever and considered me a nuisance all day.

It was 8.55pm when I realised I had forgotten to celebrate *Chocolate Covered Cherry Day*. I had chocolate, but no cherries. Despite my incredibly serious and potentially life-threatening illness, I bravely put on a pair of jeans and a jumper and ran down to the shop at the end of our road before it closed.

'No, I don't think we've got cherries of any sort in stock,' said Naz, the owner of our local corner shop. 'Nobody buys them.'

'How about tinned cherries or glacé cherries, Naz?' I asked.

'No, sorry. We've got tins of fruit cocktail.'

'How many cherries are in a tin of fruit cocktail?' I asked, getting desperate.

'I don't know, maybe two. Some don't have any. How come you are so desperate for cherries? Is your young lady pregnant again?'

Naz had experienced Rachel's pregnancy cravings many times over the last few years, as I made repeated visits to his shop for bulk purchases of marzipan, dolly mixtures, gherkins and ice cubes.

'Ha! No, she's not pregnant. The cherries are for me. It's *Chocolate Covered Cherry Day*. It's a long story.'

As I was leaving, I noticed a jar of something behind the chutney and piccalilli. It was a single jar of cocktail cherries. Cocktail cherries, or maraschino cherries as they are also known, are cherries preserved in brine and then soaked in sugar syrup. The type that my mother-in-law serves with her speciality – *melon avec cocktail cherry*.

This particular solitary jar had a thick layer of dust on its lid and had obviously been there for a few decades.

'I've no idea where they came from,' said Naz. 'I don't remember ever ordering those.'

I paid for the cherries and walked home, clutching them like a winning lottery ticket, and emptied them into a sieve. I wasn't too sure how to make chocolate covered cherries, but I assumed that it probably involved covering cherries in chocolate.

I melted some dark chocolate in a bowl in the microwave and then mixed the cherries into it. I then laid them on a plate and put them in the fridge to cool.

An hour later, I sat down and read the first few chapters of *The Hobbit* (as it was also *J.R.R.Tolkein Day*), and ate my chocolate covered cherries. They were bloody good. They tasted a bit like cherries that were covered in chocolate.

'I thought you were supposed to be ill?' said Rachel accusingly.

'It's these chocolate covered cherries,' I said. 'I think they must have magical health-giving properties.'

'That's great. I'll remember to make you a bowl next time you're sitting around being useless.'

January 4th

In order to celebrate *Dimpled Chad Day* I needed to first find out what a dimpled chad was. I had expectations of hunting down a boy named Chad, who happened to have dimples, but was relieved to discover that chads can be found much closer to home.

For those, like me, whose knowledge of chads has a few holes, I will fill you in. A chad is the paper circle that is created when a hole is punched through a piece of paper. I had always thought that little consideration is given to those poor little bits of paper, and now here I was with an entire day dedicated to their existence. I was all ready to set about hole punching the shit out of everything I could find, and making a huge mountain of chads, or even sending an envelope full of chads to a far away exotic destination on some sort of 'chad holiday'. Then I realised that this wasn't about the chads. This was about the dimpled chads; the ones that never made it.

A dimpled chad is a chad that is not completely punched through, and is therefore still partially attached to the original piece of paper. Stuck in limbo, the dimpled chad is forced to spend its existence separated from its birthplace, yet not given the freedom to enjoy life on its own.

However, the dimpled chad should not be viewed as insignificant - far from it. The dimpled chad has been one of the most influential players in modern history. It could be argued that the dimpled chad is responsible for the wars in Iraq and Afghanistan, the economic depression, global warming and the general state of modern society.

Let me explain.

The dimpled chad came to prominence during the 2000 presidential election in the United States when George Bush and Al Gore fought over Florida's 25 electoral votes. Dimpled chads were found on ballot papers after voters had failed to fully punch through their papers. They were contentious because some Florida counties accepted dimpled chads as votes, whilst others didn't. Miami-Dade County did, but Broward County did not. Other counties such as Palm Beach were counting some dimpled chads, but not others.

The closeness of the presidential race was such that these dimpled chads had a potentially huge impact on the final result.

Had these chads been punched through correctly, the USA may have had a different president, and the current state of world affairs might be very different.

I tried not to hold too much of a grudge against dimpled chads, seeing as January 4th was their special day. Instead, I decided to help set some free. In order to set some free I needed to create them in the first place. I happened to have my very own *Dimpled Chad Creator Tool*™, which came in the form of a particularly crap hole-punch from Poundland. One of the bars would stick halfway down resulting in a guaranteed dimpled chad every time. To rub salt in these poor chads' wounds, the other half of the hole-punch worked perfectly, cutting a crisp round chad every time. I punched off a load of holes on a piece of paper, and then proceeded to push through the dimpled chads with a blunt pencil, setting them free forever.

It felt really good.

I felt like I had actually achieved something.

I was a saviour.

At that exact moment, as I was basking in my own self-satisfaction, Rachel walked past with the vacuum cleaner.

'Haven't you got a more productive way to spend your day?' she asked, as she sucked up every single one of the chads from the carpet. She sucked them up with the vacuum cleaner, I should add. She's not some sort of paper-sucking weirdo.

I hadn't saved the dimpled chads at all. I had sent them to their death.

January 4th is also *World Braille Day*, and I was keen to try my hand at reading Braille, if you excuse the pun. It was all very well learning from Wikipedia that Louis Braille created the Braille system in 1821, but I needed to experience some Braille first hand (sorry, I did it again).

I decided the best place for me to find some Braille would be at our local blind charity shop, which is rather aptly named The Local Blind Charity Shop.

I had no success there, so I wandered off in the rain towards Northampton town centre, where I hoped for some inspiration. It came in the form of Northampton Central Library. Surely a huge building containing three expansive floors full of books would have some examples of Braille?

'Do you have any Braille books, by any chance?' I asked the man at the enquiries desk.

'I don't think we do, but I'll have a look on the system for you,' he said.

He sat down at the computer and typed the word BRAILLE slowly into the keyword search using one index finger, as though he was using a computer for the very first time.

'Ah, yes! We do have one book. It's a book about governmental policies, published in 1981. I assume it won't be relevant today.'

'That's ok. I just want to see some real-life Braille.'

'Oh, right you are. Well it's a reference only copy but I can go and get it for you if you would like.'

'Yes please, that would be great.'

He returned five minutes later shaking his head.

'No, I'm sorry. It seems to have disappeared. Somebody must have put it back in the wrong place. A blind person perhaps?' he said with a slight giggle. 'Sorry that I can't be more help.'

I then visited both the theatre and the tourist information, and was told by both that they didn't have any of their leaflets in Braille, but that they could be printed to order.

'How long would that take?' I asked.

'Probably a couple of weeks, I guess.'

So, if a visually impaired person visits Northampton and wants to read for themselves about what the town has to offer, they would have to wait two weeks for a leaflet to be printed. To kill this time, they could perhaps pay a visit to the local library where they could read about governmental policies of 1981, but they would first have to search all three floors and locate the book for themselves.

January 5th

We moved into our current house in 2002. Our first encounter with Doug, our neighbour, was a conversation over the garden wall. It was December. He was wearing a vest and whistling a tune that I didn't recognise. Doug was particularly chatty and friendly, with a warm smile and he was eager to know lots about his new neighbours. He was in his early sixties but had taken early retirement to be a full-time carer for his wife Christine (Chris).

Rachel and I had just moved into the house from a small flat which we had lived in for a year. During the whole time we lived at the flat we only ever saw the people who occupied the flats above and below us a handful of times on the shared stairwell. It was quite strange to then have a whistling man in his vest at his kitchen window or in the garden at all times of the day.

We got used to it very quickly though, and we have become extremely close to Doug and Chris over the years. We moved into our house unmarried, with no children. They have seen us grow into a family and have known all three of our children - Layla, Leo and Kitty - since they were each only hours old. Doug and Chris are pretty much perfect neighbours; always there to keep an eye on our house, lend us things, or just discuss the troubles of Northampton Town Football Club over the garden wall. We help them out too, as much as we can; such as picking up Doug's paper from the shop each morning on the way home from the school run, and helping him unload his weekly supermarket shop from the car.

They have also become particularly fond of Father Dougal. They used to have an elderly cat called Lucy (who names a cat Lucy?) and Father Dougal would sneak through their cat flap, beat the crap out of Lucy, eat her food, and then leave. To begin with, Doug would shout at Father Dougal and chase him out. He then started falling for Father Dougal's charm and affection. He began to allow him to come and eat Lucy's food, and soon he was actively encouraging it. We gradually grew to accept the arrangement as it was nice that Father Dougal was getting so much attention. It also reduced our cat food bill significantly.

Doug and Chris then gave Father Dougal a new name. They called him Basil, which we found a little weird to begin with. I'm not sure whether they just thought the name suited him better, or whether, as Christians, they considered it insulting to name a cat after a man of the cloth. Either way, he became know as Basil at their house and Father Dougal at ours.

Doug's garden is immaculate. He devotes a lot of time to it, and it's always depressing to look out of our upstairs window at our ugly, patchy, balding lawn, alongside his magnificent, vibrant, neatly-trimmed garden next door, with turf reminiscent of Augusta National Golf Club. Doug always has nice tubs of different flowers, depending on the time of year - daffodils, bluebells, pansies, roses and tulips. We have a small bay tree, and a scraggy overgrown buddleia.

Birds don't like our garden. They never have. Many times over the years I have hung feeders for them, but they always remain untouched because of the presence of our cats. Doug has a cat, too, but his garden is less overgrown, which allows the birds some prior warning if they are about to have their head chewed off by a cat.

Today was *Bird Day* and I celebrated by giving Doug a bird feeder that we had been given for Christmas. He hung it in his garden, next to the one we gave him last year, and the one from the year before that, and within minutes the birds were tucking in. I then took a few photos of the birds, almost all of which were shit. I'm certainly no wildlife photographer.

There was one photo, however, that I was very pleased with. It was a complete accident, and was the result of a wrong exposure, but after tweaking it on the computer I think it's incredibly striking. I liked it so much that I decided to make it the logo, and potentially cover, for this holiday challenge. It's not a particularly 'party' picture, in fact it is probably the least partyey (that's not even a real word) party photo ever taken. But this project isn't about partying. It's about experiencing new things and seizing opportunities. This bird is perched on the edge of a ledge with the whole world (Doug's garden) ahead of him, and he (or she, I'm no bird expert) has limitless potential with his eyes gazing at a whole wealth of prospects ahead of him. OK, so maybe I am reading too much into this photo, but I'm sticking with it.

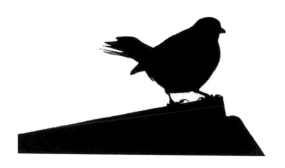

January 6th

I had an epiphany on *Epiphany*. Twelve days of Christmas is WAY too long. Especially as the build up to Christmas seems to start in AUGUST. Traditionally, January 6th - *Epiphany*, or *Twelfth Night* - is the end of Christmas, and the day when you should take down all of your decorations. I had forgotten that *Epiphany* was going to be one of the days I was observing and had already taken our decorations down and put them back in the attic on *New Year's Day*.

'Why are you taking them down already?' Rachel had asked. 'You're being a bit of an old misery.'

'Because Christmas was over six days ago,' I said. 'It's time to move on. New year, new start.'

At this point, Layla, our eldest daughter (aged 5) burst into tears.

'But I don't want Christmas to be over, Daddy,' she sobbed. 'Where are you taking that tree?'

'Into the garden. I'll leave it there until I get a chance to take it to the tip.'

'But it will be sad out there in the cold, without all of its decorations. Can I leave one star on it please, Daddy?' she asked, holding up a solitary silver star with tears still running down her flushed cheeks.

'Ok,' I said, 'just the one.'

Today was my deadline to get rid of the tree, or at least remove that final star. But I couldn't bring myself to do it.

All three of the children had become very attached to the tree, checking on it daily, watering it regularly (despite the rain), and gazing at it every morning and evening from their bedroom window. The tree was in a pot, with roots, and despite the label saying that it wouldn't survive if left outside, a small part of me thought that maybe I could keep it alive until next Christmas.

I felt less guilty about still having a Christmas tree after the twelfth night when I discovered that January 7th is the day on which the Othodox Church celebrates Christmas. They use the Julian calendar, which is 13 days behind the Gregorian calendar that was adopted by most countries in the world. It would at least buy me a few more days.

January 7th

George Mahood thanks God it's Monday

I updated my Facebook status for all to see. People definitely don't say that enough. In fact, I don't think I've ever heard anyone say it. Many of us spend our lives wishing away our week, looking forward to the weekend. The weekend soon passes and then it's just a case of surviving the next few days until it comes around again. I have friends who regularly update their Facebook statuses as such:

OMG can't believe it's only Tuesday. Roll on the weekend.
I hate Mondays! Can't wait for the weekend.
Roll on, death. Friday is too far away.

And then the weekend comes, and by Sunday morning they are already posting again.

Sunday already? Where did the weekend go? Hurry up Friday.

Work tomorrow. Urgh. Can't wait until next weekend.

I had been guilty of this mindset too. But, recently, more than ever, I have started to realise that I want to slow time down as much as possible, not speed it up. The last few years have ghosted by. *Thank God It's Monday Day* is a chance to embrace the start of a new week. Yes, Monday might signify going back to work, school, or college, but make the most of it because every day is extremely precious. *Thank God It's Monday Day* was probably the most sensible day I have celebrated so far.

I had a slight altercation with a vicar at a wedding that I photographed before Christmas. It was at a church I hadn't been to before so I arrived about 45 minutes before the ceremony to introduce myself to the vicar and to ask her policy regarding photos. Rather than saying *hello*, she looked me up and down and then told me I wasn't welcome in her church because of the way I was dressed, despite the fact I was wearing what I always wear to photograph weddings. She took an instant dislike to me and made her feelings known. I was so shocked by the whole thing that I didn't react at the time. I simply smiled and left the church to wait for the arrival of the bridal party. The organist followed me outside and apologised profusely on behalf of the whole church. She gave me the distinct impression that the vicar had no doubt ruffled a few feathers in the parish on other occasions.

The incident made me immensely cross, but I tried to laugh it off and forget about it, but several weeks later it was still bothering me. Today was *I'm Not Going to Take it Anymore Day* so I decided that maybe I should let my feelings be known.

Those of you that have read my other book - *Free Country: A Penniless Adventure the Length of Britain* - might remember a slight run-in that we had with a vicar in Neilston in Scotland.

This is not a regular thing that I do. I don't make a habit of getting into arguments with vicars. As a wedding photographer I work regularly with many vicars and get on really well with all of them. But on this occasion I felt that I couldn't let her abuse her position of power. It needed to be drawn attention to. I sent the following letter to the archdeacon in charge of her diocese, and another copy to her church.

Dear Archdeacon,

I was the official photographer at the wedding of ****** ****** and ****** ********* at St ******* Church in ******* on **[th] ***** last year.

Having spent the morning photographing the bridal preparations at *****'s parents' house, I then arrived at the church to take some photographs of the groom and to meet the vicar. I introduced myself to Revd ***** and politely asked her what her policy was regarding photography during the ceremony. Her response, before even saying 'hello,' was that I was not welcome in the church unless I was wearing a shirt and tie. I explained that I didn't have a shirt and tie and apologised that I was unaware that it was required in her church. I was dressed in smart black shoes, smart black trousers and a black polo shirt, which is what I wear to every wedding that I photograph. She then began a long and aggressive rant towards me, saying that it was appalling that I would consider photographing a wedding dressed in such a manner and that I was being 'disrespectful' to the bride and groom and could potentially spoil their special day. She then told me that she officiated at 20 weddings a year and that no other photographer would ever consider wearing a polo shirt. I photograph 50 weddings a year (all booked from referrals and word-of-mouth) and have never had a single criticism of the way I dress.

I explained to her that the reason that I wear a black polo-shirt is so that I can be easily distinguished as the official photographer. When I first started out I did wear a shirt and tie, but people just assumed that I was a guest with a big camera. She just rolled her eyes at me and told me that it was no excuse.

She then told me that I would have to stand at the back of the church, so as not to be seen by the congregation, and that I would not be welcome back to the church in future.

I am not angry about her opinion that wedding photographers should wear a shirt and tie. I am not even angry that she would only allow me to take photos from the back of the church, as I am always happy to stick to the church's policy. What makes me really angry is the rude, aggressive and self-righteous manner in which she spoke to me. I have photographed over 200 weddings in the last few years and have never had a bad word to say about any of the vicars, registrars, wedding organisers, florists, caterers, bell-ringers, videographers that I have met. I have never been spoken to like that in any area of my professional or personal life.

I was polite and courteous to her throughout as I didn't want to make a scene before the wedding and decided that I would just forget the incident and move on. I even saw the amusing irony in her sermon about how 'God doesn't judge others and loves everyone'. But now, several weeks later, I still find it hard to comprehend how somebody in the position of Revd ***** could treat another person so badly. She was without a doubt the most rude and unpleasant person that I have ever had the misfortune to meet. My only hope is that it was a strange, isolated, personal dislike to me and not representative of her everyday attitude and manner, as she would be doing a huge disservice to the church and its parishioners.

On a positive note, I would like to add that ***** – the organist, and the other young lady who was helping at the church during the wedding were absolutely delightful and both were fine ambassadors of the church.

I have also forwarded a copy of this letter to Revd ****** at St ********.

Yours sincerely,
George Mahood

I didn't know whether the letter would have any effect, but I felt a hell of a lot better for writing it. I was buzzing as I licked the envelope and imagined the vicar's face as she read the letter. I hoped that it would at least be acknowledged.

While I was in the mood for complaining, I wrote a stroppy email to a PR company that are notoriously slow at paying my photography invoices.

Dear Nick,

I have attached an invoice for a job I did for you in early September last year, which has still not been paid. I have forwarded this to you, and the accounts team, THREE times now, and I am getting very frustrated that you have not yet issued payment.

Could you please ensure that payment is issued ASAP, otherwise I will have to take this matter further.

Kind regards
George

I received a reply 12 minutes later...

Dear George,

I am so sorry for the delay in getting this invoice paid for you. For some reason, you slipped through the last couple of payment runs. An emergency cheque has been drawn for you, and will be mailed out first class today.

Apologies again for the inconvenience.
Kind regards
Nick

It had certainly worked. I'm going to start celebrating *I'm Not Going to Take it Anymore Day* more often. No more Mr Nice Guy from me.

January 8th

National English Toffee Day was no hardship. I bought some English toffees, and ate them.

I was excited about the idea of *National Joy Germ Day*, too. I assumed it was a day when I could just spread bacteria for fun - perhaps by not washing my hands after going to the toilet - or sneezing at people just for shits and giggles.

I was disappointed to discover that the day is all about spreading joy, like germs, rather than spreading germs for joy. Meaning that you pass happiness to someone, and it then spreads to someone else, and so on, and so forth.

I thought about posting some of my English toffees through random people's letterboxes, before realising that it would just be a bit creepy.

So, on the way home from a job in Daventry, I let out every person from every junction that I passed. Not just one car, but the whole damn queue at each intersection. I watched those that I let out then let other people out, and in turn those people then let others out. It was beautiful to witness. I could feel the joy instantly. It was spreading, like germs, across the world.

It took fucking hours to get home, mind.

January 9th

Balloon Ascension Day commemorates the date in 1793 on which Frenchman Jean Pierre Blanchard made the first successful balloon flight in North America. Watched on by President George Washington and several future presidents, he successfully flew 15 miles across Philadelphia.

I had been given a voucher for a hot-air balloon ride as a present for photographing a friend's wedding last year. What better way to celebrate *Balloon Ascension Day* than to ascend in a balloon? Frustratingly, the hot-air balloon season in the UK runs roughly from March to October due to the unreliable British weather. Instead, I rubbed a balloon on my head and stuck it to the ceiling. After all, it was also *Static Electricity Day*.

'Wow, coooool. Can I do that?' asked Layla.

'And me!' said Leo.

'MEEEE!' shouted Kitty.

I blew up three more balloons, rubbed them on the children's heads and then stood on a wooden chair and stuck them each in turn to the ceiling. I stuck the balloons to the ceiling, not the children.

'But I want to stick it to the ceiling,' moaned Leo, our second child (aged 3).

'You're not really tall enough, I'm afraid. I can lift you up if you like.'

'That's not fair,' he said. 'But I reeeeeally want to.'

'You're not quite big enough, pal. Look, I can only just reach.'

I passed him his balloon anyway, and he stood on the chair, rubbed the balloon on his head, and threw himself off, arm stretched upwards clutching the balloon. He missed the ceiling by about five feet.

'Oooww!' he shouted.

'Maybe I can reach. I'm bigger than Leo,' said Layla confidently.

'It's too high up for you too, I'm afraid,' I said. 'Why don't we stick them on the walls instead?'

'We want to stick them on the ceiling like YOU,' said Leo.

'I know but I'm much taller than you.'

'MEEEEE!' shouted Kitty, our youngest (aged 1), as she fell off the chair and landed in a heap on the wooden floor.

Thankfully she's pretty tough and stood up and climbed the chair to try again.

Rachel is a teacher and since having children, she has worked between one and two days a week, in between bouts of maternity leave. The majority of my work these days is wedding photography, which means that I tend to be busy most weekends, but quite flexible during the week. Thursday is the day of the week on which Rachel works and I look after the children.

On this occasion, she came home to find all three children sobbing and shouting whilst taking it in turns to jump off a chair in an attempt to stick their balloons to the ceiling.

'Oh dear. Is everyone having fun on Daddy Day?' she asked.

'No! We just want to stick our balloons to the ceiling like Daddy did,' said Layla in between tears.

'We were just celebrating *Balloon Ascension Day* and *Static Electricity Day*,' I said. 'It didn't quite go to plan.'

'And George's pointless holiday project strikes again,' she muttered as she started to tidy up the carnage that Daddy Day had created.

January 10th

I like to think of myself as a fairly energy efficient kind of guy. I hope others think of me that way, too. *'Hey, what do you think of George Mahood?'* I imagine people say. *'Yeah, he sure seems like an energy efficient kind of guy.'*

All of our light bulbs are energy saving. I prefer to wear an extra jumper rather than put the heating on. I take showers not baths. I live by the motto *'if it's yellow let it mellow, if it's brown flush it down'*. I turn lights off when I leave the room. I turn off plugs. I boil enough water in the kettle for what I need. I put bricks in the cistern to reduce the water capacity and I don't use a hosepipe.

I do, however, live with Rachel, who is the complete opposite.

She leaves lights on all day. She would rather wear few clothes and have the heating on full. She takes TWO baths a day. She leaves appliances turned on. She fills the kettle to the brim before boiling, boils it at least TWICE, and then doesn't make tea anyway, and she has a pre-flush before going to the toilet. It is a constant battle between the two of us.

Today was *National Cut Your Energy Costs Day* so I decided to try and cut my energy costs even further.

First of all I put even more bricks in the toilet cistern to reduce the water flow. Flushing now results in the tiniest of trickles, which means that you have to flush it at least twice in order to flush anything down – yellow or brown. It is the thought that counts, though, right?

I also purchased two plug timers as I discovered that we have an *Economy 7* meter, meaning our electricity is cheaper during the night. I put one on the washing machine, as it's in constant use in our house. It's like living in a launderette. But without the random strangers strolling in and doing their washing. That would be weird. The other timer I decided to use for 'miscellaneous' appliances.

'My phone is dead, can I charge it now?' asked Rachel at 6pm.

'No. Plug it in, and it will start charging at 1am when the rate is much cheaper.'

'But I need to use it now.'
'You should've thought of that before.'
'Before what?'
'Exactly. You just don't think.'
'Idiot.'

My resolve lasted about 30 seconds.

'Fine, just plug it in then. Destroy the world why don't you.'

January 11th

It had been raining all day and I was 'working from home'. The pavement was covered in puddles when I went to help Rachel bring the kids in from the car after visiting her sister. I saw my chance and went for it, stamping in a puddle just as she climbed out of the driver's seat.

'What are you doing? I'm soaked,' she shouted.

'It's *Step in a Puddle and Splash Your Friends Day*,' I replied.

'I don't care. You're a dick,' she said, uttering the word 'dick' under her breath so that the children wouldn't hear, which made it sound even more menacing.

'Sorry,' I said.

'Anyway, I'm your wife. Not one of your friends,' she barked, looking genuinely scary.

'I haven't seen any of my friends today, and you may be my wife but you're also my bestest friend in the whole world,' I said, trying to win her over.

'That's not going to work on me. So what have you done today? Productive day?'

'Yes, very. I learnt my name in Morse Code because it's also *Learn Your Name in Morse Code Day*. It's dah-dah-dit, dit, dah-dah-dah, di-dah-dit, dah-dah-dit...'

'Well done you,' she interrupted. 'Another day wasted then.'

January 12th

Fruitcake Toss Day is a strange day. The idea is that you can finally get rid of that fruitcake that has been lurking around since Christmas. Where you toss it, I'm not sure, but it sounded pretty awesome.

The problem is that the fruitcake my mother-in-law makes for us at Christmas is so damn good that it never hangs around until January 12th. It's rare for there to be any left on Boxing Day.

I had to buy a cheap fruitcake from the shop on the way home from a run, which Rachel and I then played catch with in the kitchen. After a while we realised there were no rules and no point to the game. Although, it was surprisingly fun as we started to throw the cake harder and harder, until it got to the stage that we were doing full force baseball-style pitches across the kitchen. I can see it becoming an Olympic event in years to come, and I'm fairly sure I would medal. The packet soon split open and fruitcake crumbs sprayed the entire room.

'Right, game over. You'd better clean the floor now,' said Rachel.

'But it broke when YOU threw it.'

'It was your idea to play the silly game.'

'Fine. I'll clean it up,' I said as I removed my running shorts, socks and t-shirt to put in the washing machine.

'Oh yeah,' she added, as she was leaving the room, 'I see it's also *Feast of Fabulous Wild Men Day* today.'

'Since when have you been interested in what holiday it is?' I asked.

'Since today. I'm off to look at some pictures of some fabulous wild men on the internet.'

'The internet? But you have a fabulous wild man right here,' I said, poised in the middle of the kitchen in my pants, with a pink dustpan and brush in one hand, and a crumbled fruit loaf in the other.

She raised one eyebrow, curled her lip, snorted a laugh and kept on walking.

January 14th

'What holiday is it today?' asked Rachel.
'Ah, nothing really. Just one of those quiet days.'
'So there's nothing to celebrate today?'
'Well, no, not really.'
'Give me the list. What day is it?'

I tried to grab my printed list of all the events from the table, but she was too quick for me. Her eyes scoured the page looking for January 14th.

'Ah ha, *Organize Your Home Day* AND *Clean Off Your Desk Day*. What a day! How are you going to celebrate?'

'No, I... er... I...'

'Well, I think it's important for you to celebrate ALL of these days. I'll make you a list of chores so that you can help organise our home.'

And so she did.

Clean your desk
Clean bathroom (including toilet)
Wash kitchen floor
Clean out overflowing food cupboard
Hoover everywhere (make sure you do stairs and under bed)
Sort out cellar
Put your football stuff in the shed
Clean windows
CLEAN YOUR DESK!!

'That's not organising! That's cleaning!' I snapped.

'It's the same thing. You know what they say *'A clean house is an organised house',*' said Rachel.

'No, THEY don't say that. You just made that up.'

'Well it's true. If you clean the house, then you will feel organised.'

She was right, as usual.

I completed all of the jobs in two hours. The day had given me the motivation to get organised, and I felt much better as a result. I liked the ME that this challenge was creating. Two hours later, my desk was completely trashed again.

My in-laws used to have a dog called Misty that we looked after when they went away on holiday. It was a small Cairn terrier. They provided us with a red tartan waistcoat for it to wear on walks when it was cold. I unfortunately used to 'forget' to put this on the dog before we left the house. The only thing less manly than walking a rat-sized dog in the park, is walking a rat-sized dog wearing a tartan red waistcoat.

Misty sadly died a couple of years ago. Of old age, by the way, and not pneumonia.

Today was *Dress up Your Pet Day*. If I was going to dress up my pets then it needed to be for a purpose. No pet of mine will ever wear a tartan waistcoat. Our cats have fur to keep them warm, and they certainly don't look like the sort of animals that would enjoy dressing up for FUN. I needed to dress them in something that would benefit them. And then I had a brainwave.

HIGH VIS VESTS!

It made perfect sense. Sure, cats might have reflective eyes, but the rest of their body is far from reflective. This simple act of dressing up my pet could potentially save its life.

Father Dougal had other ideas. He was less than impressed with me trying to put a reflective waistcoat on him and thrashed and howled like he was caught in a snare. Within seconds of taking his photo, he broke free from his clothes like the Incredible Hulk and vanished through the cat flap and into the darkness. Unclothed and unprotected.

January 16th

Nothing Day was my kind of day.

The weather outside was horrendous, so, after dropping Layla at school, we spent the day on the sofa watching TV trying to do, well, nothing. However, doing nothing with two young children is physically impossible.

'Why aren't we doing ANYTHING today?' asked Leo, swinging his arms like a sulky teenager.

'Because it's Nothing Day today, which means we can sit and do nothing. We don't have to do anything.'

'Whhhyyyy?'

'It just is. Don't you want to just sit and chill? Sometimes it's fun doing nothing.'

'No. I want to do SOMETHING.'

It was also *Appreciate a Dragon Day*, so Leo, Kitty and I headed into town where I bought them a cuddly toy dragon to share.

'But why can't we have one EACH?' he moaned.

'Because it's *Appreciate a DRAGON Day*, not dragons.'

'Whhhyyyy?'

'It just is.'

At 11pm, when Rachel and the children were all fast asleep, I was still on the sofa doing nothing. I turned over to watch the recorded highlights of the Masters snooker. There's nothing like a bit of snooker to get you in the mood for sleeping.

'Ladies and Gentlemen, please welcome to the table - The Thunder from Down Under - Neil Robertson,' said the announcer, using the traditional pre-match players' nicknames.

The crowd cheered.

Then it was time for the arrival of his opponent, the 25 year old Chinese star Ding Junhui.

'Ladies and Gentlemen, Enter the Dragon, it's Ding Junhui.'

I sat open-mouthed. I need not have gone to the toy shop after all. I had found another dragon, in the form of a geeky-looking Chinese snooker player with the nickname 'Enter the Dragon'. He was leading 5-3 and cruising to victory in a best of 11 frames match. I grabbed a beer from the fridge and sat down to appreciate my dragon.

He lost 6-5. The loser.

January 17th

'Do you want to invent something today?' I asked Layla, as we walked back from school.

'What do you mean, Daddy?'

'Do you want to make up something new, like a new toy or a machine or anything that doesn't already exist?'

'Ok.'

'What would you like to invent?'

'Ermm... a game.'

'Ok, that's a good idea. Today is *Kid Inventors' Day*. Why don't you try and invent a new game and then we can play it later?'

'Ok.'

'Are you ready to play my new game, Daddy?' asked Layla after dinner.

'Yes please. What is it called?'

'It's called Match the... er... Match the... ermm... *Match the Pumpkin.*'

'*Match the Pumpkin*. Cool, that sounds fun.'

I didn't completely understand the rules, but it seemed to involve drawing a pumpkin, and then drawing another pumpkin, and then drawing another pumpkin.

It's only a matter of time before the copyright is snapped up by Hasbro. I'm warning you, *Match the Pumpkin* is going to be HUGE.

January 18th

'It's my granddad's birthday next week. Any ideas what to get him?' asked Rachel.

'What about the usual box of chocolates or something?'

'I suppose. But that's a bit boring, isn't it?'

Rachel's granddad Walter is a remarkable man. He is about to turn 91 and, despite his age, he is still very active. He regularly gets the bus from his village near Kettering to come and visit family members in Northampton. We do of course offer to drive him, but he enjoys the excitement of getting public transport. He is a big Manchester United fan and listens to all of their games on his radio. With our mutual love of football, Walter and I really hit it off from the start and always have great discussions about recent matches. For his 90th birthday last year, we bought him a replica 1920s Manchester United shirt, which was the decade in which he was born. Embroidered on the back we had WALTER and the number 90. It went down very well.

'Is there anything he wants, or needs?' I asked. 'I guess when you get to 91 then you probably have everything.'

'My dad said he wanted a new Thesaurus,' said Rachel.

'Are you taking the piss?'

'No, apparently his other one is falling apart.'

'I mean, are you taking the piss out of me? Are you mocking this holiday project of mine?' I asked, suspiciously.

'No, why?'

'Because it's *Thesaurus Day* today!'

'There's no such thing as *Thesaurus Day*,' she said. 'You're the one taking the piss.'

'Yes, there is. It's today! It's the anniversary of Mr Roget's birth. Or maybe his death, I think. You know, the thesaurus guy?'

'Seriously? That's weird. I promise I had no idea.'

'That is a bizarre coincidence. It all seems to be falling into place nicely. Well that settles it. I think you should definitely buy him a Thesaurus for his birthday.'

So we did.

It was also *Women in Blue Jeans Day*. The only way to celebrate this, I assumed, would be to head into town to stare at women, in blue jeans. It might sound perverted, but it would have all been in the name of research, I can assure you. Just before I left the house, I did a quick internet search to see if there was any more significance to *Women in Blue Jeans Day*. I was disappointed to discover that there was.

Women in Blue Jeans is an American organisation that celebrates women of rural America. Each year they have a conference in South Dakota for women to get together and learn new things and share experiences. According to their mission statement:

'What you'll find at Women in Blue Jeans is a group of feisty women who come together for a variety of reasons. Some come to relax, some to

learn, and some to meet new people or get together with old friends. Come to Women in Blue Jeans and let us celebrate you and your contributions to rural America. Let us entertain and inspire you. You'll be so glad you did.'

I SO wanted to go, but there was no way I could get to South Dakota in time. The fact that I was neither a feisty woman, nor a rural American, didn't even enter my mind.

Instead, I sent an email to Diana, the founder and organiser of *Women in Blue Jeans*.

Hi Diana,

Just a quick email to wish you all happy Women in Blue Jeans Day. I hope that you have a fantastic conference this weekend, and good luck for the rest of the year. I think what you are all doing is brilliant. YOU GO, GIRLS!

I'll be thinking of you all and celebrating Women in Blue Jeans Day over here in England.

Best wishes
George Mahood
Northampton, England

Later in the day I had a reply from Diana. It was short and sweet and was probably the only way that she could have responded to my slightly weird and creepy email. It simply said:

Thank you!

'Today is also *International Fetish Day*,' I said suggestively to Rachel in bed, as I put my arm around her waist.

'Dream on,' she said, and rolled over.

January 19th

I received a letter today on headed notepaper from an archdeacon. That was definitely a first for me. It was a response to my complaint about the vicar that I wrote a couple of weeks ago.

Dear Mr Mahood,

Thank you for your recent letter. I am very sorry to hear that you feel you were treated badly at one of our churches. I have spoken to Revd ***** and to investigate the matter further for you, I have invited the organist in for a meeting with me. I shall report back after the meeting.

Yours sincerely,
Archdeacon *******

This was remarkable. An archdeacon was doing some 'investigating' for ME. I had my own private detective, who also happened to be one of the most senior members of the church. It sounded like Revd ****** (that's not her name by the way) was really in the shit. Ha! That would teach her. Maybe she'd get the sack. Maybe she'd lose her home and all of her friends. Wait a minute... what was I THINKING? I didn't want any of that to happen. All I wanted was for her to know that I felt she didn't have the right to talk to me like she did. I certainly didn't want the organist to have to get involved. She would have to work with Revd ****** on a daily basis and it would put her in a dreadfully awkward position. Also, it happened to be *Week of Christian Unity*. It was time for me to do the right thing and unite those Christians. I knew that a letter might not get to him in time before the meeting, so I sent the Archdeacon a quick email. Yeah, Archdeacons are so down with the kids these days.

Dear Archdeacon,

Thank you very much for your letter regarding my complaint about Revd ******. It is very kind of you to take the matter so seriously.

It was never my intention to cause any discord in the parish, and I hate the idea of the organist being asked to get involved as she would be putting herself in a very difficult position.

All I wanted was for Revd. ****** to realise how unfairly I felt she had treated me, and that she didn't seem to be representing the Christian faith in the most appropriate manner. There is no need for you to pursue the matter any further and I am happy to forget the whole thing.

Thank you once again for taking the time to keep me updated.
Best wishes,
George Mahood

I had a reply a couple of hours later.

Dear Mr Mahood

Thank you for your email. In the light of what you say I do not intend to take the matter any further. I apologise that you experienced a bad reception and I have pointed out where lessons must be learned for the future. The file on this matter is now closed.

With kind regards,
Archdeacon ******

So, what did you do today? Well I just united Christianity, that's all. Not a bad day.

Popcorn has been around for thousands of years. In 1948, they found evidence of popcorn in a cave in New Mexico. Reports vary, but it is estimated that it was between 1500 and 5000 years old. Their cooking method involved heating the kernels in a bowl of sand over a fire. The sand would heat up, causing the kernels to pop and rise to the top above the sand. I imagine their popcorn was also extremely gritty and rank.

Today was *Popcorn Day*, and I prefer mine to be a mixture of sweet and salted, with not too much added sand and grit. Next time you go to the cinema, ask for half and half. Trust me, it's the future. We don't get out much these days, so our popcorn normally comes from the microwave. It was *Tin Can Day*, too. What better accompaniment to a bowl of popcorn than a tin of beer. I deserved it after reuniting Christianity.

Just before I climbed into bed, I pulled back the curtain to look out onto the street. It's a habit that I have always had. I'm not sure why as our street always looks the same. On this occasion, however, I was surprised to see heavy snow falling. The rush of excitement that raced through my body at seeing snow has not dissipated since I was a child. It gets me every single time. I think it's the stealth like silence of snow that causes such a thrill. With a heavy rainfall, or severe wind, you can hear it long before you see it, so the element of surprise disappears. Snow is the ninja of weather types.

The weather forecasters had been warning of snow for a few days, but whilst it had been reported in other parts of the country, it looked like it was going to bypass Northampton.

Rachel claims to be able to smell snow in the air, long before it snows. To her credit, she did once say that she could smell snow and then it did snow a few hours later, but her success rate ever since has been rather questionable. She spends most of the winter saying that she can smell snow, and it very, very rarely does. On this occasion, despite the warnings from the weather forecasters, she stated categorically that it WASN'T going to snow, because she couldn't smell it.

'Come and look. It's snowing!' I said excitedly from the bedroom window.

'Yeah, right. You always do that to try and trick me,' she said.

'I'm not tricking. It really is snowing.'
'I'm not falling for it this time.'
'Fine, don't believe me then.'

'Alright, just to humour you,' she sighed as she climbed out of bed. 'Oh, wow. It really is snowing.'

'How come you didn't smell it this time?'

'I think I have got a bit of a cold.'

January 20th

We had planned to visit my sister and brother-in-law at their new flat in London, but due to the snow, my sister advised us against driving down. There had only been a slight dusting in Northampton overnight, but it was enough to get the kids excited about heading to the park to build a snowman and go sledging. Who am I kidding? I was the one desperate to get to the park!

By lunchtime we had used up the last of the snow, and most of the surrounding roads and pavements had cleared. It was *Penguin Awareness Day*, and I had been promising the kids a visit to the zoo at some point, and today seemed like the perfect opportunity.

'You realise that we close at 4pm?' said the attendant at the entrance gate to Woburn Safari Park. 'It's 2.00pm now, so you won't get very long.'

'That's fine, thanks. We've really only come to see the penguins,' I said.

We raced around the safari drive as quickly as we could, shunting SUV's and tigers off the road as we went by. We got delayed whilst driving through the monkey enclosure as the car in front had monkeys all over its bonnet and roof. The owners had clearly scattered their car with food before entering as a ploy to attract the animals. Either that or they'd had a particularly disastrous picnic.

Woburn doesn't just have a penguin enclosure, it has Penguin WORLD. Penguin World is, well, just a penguin enclosure, really, but it sounds WAY better. We stood and admired the penguins for a while, from above the water and from the underwater viewing window. Kitty was very bemused by it all. The occasional glimpse of a darting black slippery animal, viewed through an underwater window must be an extraordinarily surreal experience for a one year-old.

Most of the penguins at Woburn are Humboldt penguins, found predominantly in South America. These are one of the most endangered species of penguin in the world. They are found on islands off Peru and Chile and their existence is under threat from over-fishing and from the commercial mining of their excrement (guano), which is taken from their nests and used as a natural fertiliser. I wonder what qualifications are required to become a professional shit-stealer?

January 21st

There had been a very heavy snowfall overnight (Rachel hadn't smelt this one coming either) and we checked the County Council website and saw the news that Layla's school was closed for the day.

'YEY! SNOW DAY!! How COOL is that? You get a DAY OFF SCHOOL because of the SNOW,' I said with immense excitement, as if it was me who had the day off school.

'That's not fair. I wanted to go to school today,' said Layla.

'But isn't it better to have an extra day of fun at home? We could go sledging, or build a snowman. Whatever you like!'

'But we did that yesterday.'

'I know we did. But it doesn't snow very often. It's nice to make the most of it when it does. Isn't it?'

'I wanted to go to school and do Art and Maths and reading and see my friends.'

'What sort of child have we created?' I whispered to Rachel.

'Aw, leave her alone. It's great that she likes school so much.'

I bargained with Layla one last time.

'How about we phone your friends and see if they are going to the park too, and then we can all go together and then come back here for hot chocolate?'

'Ok,' she said, with a slight smile that suggested that maybe it was an adequate alternative to a day at school after all.

We all spent the morning at the park with Layla's friends and she finally admitted that perhaps snow days were alright after all. We built a giant snowman, and then at some point whilst we were sledging, someone added a giant snow cock to it.

'Daddy, why has our snowman got a BIG WILLY now?' laughed Leo, as we walked past it on the way home.

'I think some older children were just being a bit silly,' I said.

All of the children giggled for several minutes.

'Daddy. what does T-W-A-T spell?' asked Layla, catching me completely by surprise.

'What? Where did you see that?' I said.

'It says it on that car. Look. T-W-A-T. What does it spell?'

I looked up and, sure enough, one of the cars in our street had the word TWAT written into the snow on its windscreen.

'It's a very rude word, darling. Someone was just being naughty. You shouldn't ever say that word.'

The next car also had been written on. I then looked further ahead and could see that almost every car on our entire street had an expletive written into the snow. I ushered all of the children closer together and tried to distract them with conversation as we walked up the road.

'Daddy?'

'Yes, Layla.'

'What does C-U-N...'

'RIGHT!' interrupted Rachel. 'Who wants a hot-chocolate with MARSHMALLOWS?'

'MEEEEEE!' they all said.

'Did you know it was *Squirrel Appreciation Day today*?' said Rachel, whilst looking on her laptop later in the evening.

'Yes, I know,' I said. 'We fed them at the park earlier, remember?'

'What about me? Couldn't you have appreciated me instead?' she asked.

It was true. Squirrel is the pet name that I call Rachel. I think it stems from her dad telling me she looked like a squirrel when she was born – all grey and furry.

'I might call you squirrel, but you are not technically a squirrel,' I argued. 'And anyway, I appreciate you every day.'

'Aw, sweet. You liar,' she said.

It was also *Hugging Day*. I had hugged Rachel and the children, but I did that everyday. I needed more than that. I logged onto Facebook, and as usual had received several requests from *Candy Crush, FarmVille* and various other annoying Facebook apps. But there was one that caught my eye.

Hug request

Somebody else must be celebrating *Hugging Day*, too. I clicked on the link.

You have received 1 hugs but have not given any! Don't you feel cold?

Well, yes. Yes I did actually. I felt very cold.

Hug someone now.

Ok, I will. I immediately sent several hugs out to my 'friends' and instantly felt much better. This is 2013. Hugging is all virtual these days anyway.

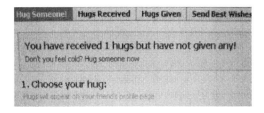

January 22nd

It has become a bit of a tradition that I take all of our children to Layla's school on a sledge during the days that we have snow. It certainly gives the school run an added edge. After the snow starts to melt, it then freezes on the pavement causing it to become one giant sheet of ice. Walking to school with three young children is not easy on a good day, but on icy days it is horrendous. You only need a thin layer of ice for the sledge to work, so it's much easier to squash them all into a sledge and drag them to school, and then I only have to worry about keeping myself upright. On this particular day something looked different. The roads looked clearer and neater for some reason, but I couldn't pinpoint why. I then realised that they had been ploughed and gritted. In the 11 years that we have lived here the streets in our area of Northampton have NEVER been ploughed or gritted. Things were clearly on the up. This was progress. I was thoroughly impressed with Northampton Borough Council.

'Our road has been gritted,' I said to one of the mums in the school playground, by way of making conversation and with a lack of anything interesting to say.

'Yes, they have cleared all of them around here. It's because Prince Charles is coming to visit today.'

'Ha ha!' I laughed.

'He really is. It was on the radio. He's going to have a tour of the Crockett and Jones shoe factory.'

'Really? That's just around the corner from us. You can see if from our upstairs window.'

'He's visiting this afternoon. They're not sure which route he'll take from the station so that's why they have gritted everywhere.'

'Well I wish he would come and visit more often if this is what happens.'

I went home and told Rachel about our neighbourhood's special visitor.

'Shall we go and see him?' she asked.

'You go. I'm not too bothered, to be honest. It will be during Kitty's nap time so I'm happy to stay here.'

'Are you sure? I'll take Leo then. It might be fun,' she said.

'Absolutely.'

It was *Celebration of Life Day*. I feel that through the course of this challenge that I am celebrating life far more than I did before. I am experiencing new things, meeting new people, appreciating things that I have taken for granted. It was all one big celebration of life. I then opened one of the nicest emails that I have ever received. It was from an 82-year old man from Texas, USA, who had just finished reading my first book. He told me about how he used to cycle everyday, all year round, and about his love of photography, and how much he had enjoyed reading about our adventure. He finished with a line that will stay with me forever.

'Thank you for a really fun read. It made me feel young again'

This was the best celebration of life that I could ask for.

January 23rd

Forget the wheel, electricity, penicillin, the internet or sliced bread; the pie is UNDOUBTEDLY the world's greatest invention. They say that pies were first made by the Egyptians in about 2000 BC, although how 'they' know this I have no idea. I doubt the Egyptians painted hieroglyphics of themselves tucking into a Steak Bake or a Fray Bentos.

It is believed that the Greeks then stole the idea of pies from the Egyptians. I find this hard to believe, too. If the Greeks had discovered pies so early on, then why did they start messing around with yoghurt and vine leaves when they had already found food perfection? They should have quit while they were ahead and stuck with pies.

The Romans then jumped on the pie bandwagon in about 100BC, and the first recorded pie recipe was for a rye-crusted goat cheese and honey pie. I wonder why Greggs don't stock those?

Pies eventually reached England in the 12th Century where they have remained a crucial part of our national menu ever since. For many years, the pastry was simply used to hold the filling together and was not eaten as part of the pie. IDIOTS! The pastry is the best bit!

We celebrated *Pie Day*, with a dinner of Steak and Mushroom pie and chips. I'll save the rye-crusted goat cheese and honey pie for another day. In another life.

I measured my feet, too, as it was *Measure Your Feet Day*. They are 27cm, in case you are interested.

January 24th

I stuck a can of beer up a chicken's butt today. It was *Beer Can Day*, and this seemed like an appropriate way to celebrate.

I should probably explain.

The chicken was dead. It was bought from the shop and ready for roasting. The beer can idea was from Jamie Oliver – a new up-and-coming chef, virtually unheard of here in the UK. Keep an eye out for him, though. He's going to be BIG. You heard it here first.

So you open a can of beer, and sit the chicken on it, inside its cavity, and then roast the chicken – or barbeque it, if you'd prefer – in an upright position. The idea is that that the beer keeps the chicken moist, and sort of steams it from the inside.

The chicken did taste particularly good. The can of beer, however, tasted exceptionally chickeny and boiling hot. Still... waste not, want not. After a few sips I decided I quite liked it. I don't think I'll ever be able to drink beer again unless it's been cooked inside a chicken for two hours.

'Ooo-ahh, it's almost time to up them there stairs to the land of bed, me dear,' I said to Rachel, later in the evening.

'Why are you talking like an idiot?' she asked.

'It's *Talk Like a Grizzled Prospector Day*.'

'Of course. How silly of me. And what may I ask is a grizzled prospector?'

'I'm not really sure, me dear. I think it's someone searching for gold in America, who is a bit, y'know, grizzled. Ooo-ahh.'

'And they spoke like that did they?'

'Yes, probably, me dear. Well, I don't know, I wasn't there. Ooo-ahh.'

'Shame it's not *Talk Like a Moron Day*. You've nailed that one.'

January 25th

This challenge has been a lot of fun so far, but almost all of the holidays that I have observed have been temporary. One day it is celebrated, the next it is forgotten, leaving little in the way of a lasting effect. The idea of this whole thing was to try and change me. I wanted the days to have a positive effect on me that would outlast the end of the experiment. That was always the plan. Today I planned to embrace that.

'Why is my teaching stuff piled up in the hall?' asked Rachel when she got back from visiting her sister at lunchtime.

'Today is *A Room of One's Own Day*,' I said.

'And? That doesn't answer my question,' she said, her eyes widening.

'Well, I thought seeing as you only teach one or two days a week and you don't need all of this stuff, maybe I could make the study MY room.'

'And what am I supposed to do with all my stuff?'

'Put your stuff in your room.'

'And which room is MY room?' she asked, looking increasingly irritated.

'You can have the shed if you want.'

'Listen, just put all my stuff back in the study where it was, OK?'

'Why can't it be MY room?' I argued.

'Are you stupid or something? Because, we live in a small house, and we don't have enough rooms for you to claim an entire room as your own. And, if you hadn't already noticed, Kitty's cot is in there too. It's HER room as well. That's where she sleeps! Were you planning on moving her into the shed, too?'

'She sleeps in there at night. It's *A Room of One's Own DAY*. Can I at least move your stuff back in tomorrow, so that I can have my own room just for today?' I pleaded.

'Fine, it can be YOUR room until 7pm this evening, and my stuff had better all be moved back first thing tomorrow morning. This whole holiday thing is getting ridiculous.'

We had haggis, neeps and tatties for dinner as it was *Burns Night*. Since visiting Robert Burns' house in Dumfries, on a cold, wet and windy day during our Lands End to John O'Groats bike ride, when we huddled by an electric heater in the gift shop, I feel like I have a bit of an affinity with ol' Rabbie. Celebrating *Burns Night* properly for the first time brought us even closer together still.

January 26th

On the way back from taking Layla to school in the morning, I picked up Doug's paper from the shop and had a flick though it as I walked down the street. Prince Charles' visit earlier in the week was headline news and there were plenty of photos to accompany the article. Hoards of people were waving union flags, with big grins across their faces. I then spotted Rachel and Leo in the background of one of the photos. Prince Charles was just a few feet away from them and every single person in the photo had their excited eyes glued to him. Everyone, that is apart from Rachel, who was busy chatting to Jason our postman. I rushed back to the shop to buy another copy of the paper so that I could show it to her.

'The future king of our country was standing right next to you and you are chatting to our postman,' I said.

'Ha ha!' laughed Rachel. 'I was just having a good old chat with Jason.'

'You make me laugh. What were you talking about that was more interesting than Prince Charles?'

'You know... this and that - the snow mostly, and how they had cleared the streets.'

'Yes, because of Prince Charles, who was standing RIGHT NEXT TO YOU!'

'Well at least I made the effort to go and see him.'

'Fair point,' I conceded.

Rachel is at the back wearing the cream-coloured peaked hat. (photograph courtesy of Northampton Chronicle and Echo)

Cockroaches are not easy to get hold of in Northampton.

I phoned Northampton Borough Council's pest control department to see if they had any.

'No, we occasionally have to deal with cockroaches, but they are all disposed of,' said the stern man from the council.

'Oh, do you not have any at the moment?' I asked.

'No, as I said, we want to get RID of them, not keep them. Can I ask why you want some cockroaches?'

'It's *Cockroach Race Day*, and I was hoping to race some cockroaches.'

'Riiiiight. Ok. Er, no, I can't help,' he said, putting down the phone.

Cockroach Race Day began 30 years ago in the Story Bridge Hotel in Brisbane, Australia, when two drinkers were arguing about which part of Brisbane had the fastest cockroaches. As you do. They settled the argument with a cockroach race the following day, and the pub has carried on the tradition ever since.

I wasn't going to start scouring the dampest, grimiest parts of Northampton to find my own cockroaches, so I celebrated the day by watching videos online of last year's *Cockroach Race Day* in Brisbane. I had no idea that cockroach racing was so popular over there, or that cockroaches were so damn fast.

January 27th

Thomas Crapper did not, as many people believe, invent the flush toilet. He did however increase its popularity and helped develop the ballcock system (is it possible to say or write the word 'ballcock' without smiling? Just me?). The links between the word 'crap' and Thomas Crapper are purely coincidental. It is believed that the word 'crap' is derived from the Dutch word '*krappen*' meaning 'to cut off', and the Old French word '*crappe*' meaning 'waste or rejected matter'. Today was *Thomas Crapper Day*, and I celebrated the day in the only way that Thomas Crapper would have wanted.

January 28th

Like most people, I always find it hard to resist a few quick pops whenever I have some bubble wrap. But I don't think I've ever fully appreciated its full potential. Too often nowadays, padded envelopes or polystyrene packing are used, leaving bubble wrap sadly neglected.

Seeing as it was *Bubble Wrap Appreciation Day*, I decided to find other ways to appreciate such a versatile product other than the two common uses: packing and popping.

I came across *www.bubblewrapfun.com*, which is a site set up by the original makers of bubble wrap, Sealed Air. Like many inventions, bubble wrap was created by mistake; two engineers - Alfred Fielding and Marc Chavannes – were trying to create textured plastic wallpaper but created a packing revolution instead.

Their website boosts *1001 Uses for Bubble Wrap*, of which only 70 have been discovered so far. 1001 does seem a little ambitious. These uses included such genius ideas as *'Bubble Wrap Insect Repellent'*. The description reads:

'Prevent mosquito bites on arms and legs by covering extremities in bubble wrap. When mosquitoes do try to bite you, the bubble wrap bubble will pop and the tiny explosion of air will send the mosquito spiralling through the air.'

So simple, yet so brilliant.

All we need to do now is bubble wrap the entire population of Africa, Asia and the Americas and we could rid the world of malaria within days.

Another suggested using bubble wrap as *'Christmas wrapping paper'*. I have nothing against this idea, but the reason stated that it will make your gift look like it is *'held in a million tiny snow globes'*. Yes, either that or it will make your gift look like it is wrapped in BUBBLE WRAP!

Other suggestions included: *doghouse insulation*, a *popable tie, beach blanket, bubble wrap suitcase* and *boobie traps*. The site also includes an option to submit your own ideas, and since they were still 931 off their total, I felt it was my duty to try and help them out. I came up with the following three suggestions:

Cell phone protection - don't bother insuring your cell phone. Simply wrap it in bubble wrap and you will greatly reduce the risk of it breaking. It is also unlikely to be stolen when it looks so ridiculous.

Cat safety-wear - they say that cats have nine lives. If you want to extend this indefinitely, then wrap your cat in bubble wrap... and a high vis vest.

And my personal favourite:

Bubble wrap cycling helmet - a cheap, versatile, custom-fitted and incredibly safe and effective* alternative to other cycling helmets

*I have no scientific basis for this claim about its safety. It looks pretty good to me though.

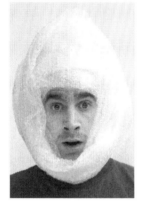

I discovered a thrilling world of bubble wrap that I had been completely unaware of, and that I genuinely felt I had been missing out on. There is an annual award ceremony each year when young inventors are awarded for their best use of bubble wrap. If only I had known about this earlier I might have stood a chance with one of my inventions. Admittedly, I didn't fulfil the criteria of being a young school kid from America, but I'm sure I could have winged it.

A previous winner was a girl who created 'sensory wallpaper' from bubble wrap. WHAT THE FUCK? Sensory wallpaper? That was the reason that bubble wrap was accidentally invented in the first place. The cheating bitch!

And what might you say the prize would be for a poxy competition such as this? $10,000 and a trip to New York sound ok? I'm serious. The prize was TEN THOUSAND DOLLARS and a trip to New York. The world has gone popping crazy.

It was *Data Privacy Day*, so I changed the password on our wireless router and updated my computer's virus protection, because that's how I roll.

It was also *Fun at Work Day* and I couldn't think of a better way to have fun at work than by thanking some plugin developers. Conveniently it was *Thank a Plugin Developer Day*. I wasn't even sure what a plugin was and I certainly didn't know any plugin developers to thank.

A plugin, it turns out, is an additional bit of software that you can add on to another, such as a web browser, photo editing program or blog software. I looked on the internet and found a list of highly regarded plugin developers.

I thought I would share this list with you. These are now OFFICIALLY my favourite plugin developers: I may have made their nicknames up.

Joost de Valk (*'Juicy'*)
Ozh Richard (*'Dicky'*)
Donncha O Caoimh (*'Doc'*)
Lester Chan (*'Lesbo'*)
Mark Jaquith (*'Marko'*)

John Kolbert (*'Johnny Boy'*)
Patrick Altoft (*'Paddy Plugin'*)
Vladimir Prelovac (*'Vlad the Implugin'*)
Viper007Bond (*'Licence to plugin'*)

I would like to thank them all for their hard work, even though I'm not sure exactly what it was that they have developed. Thank you, plugin developers. You ROCK!

January 29th

As it was *National Curmudgeon Day*, I decided not to celebrate any of the other stupid holidays today.

January 30th

This morning I had to photograph some headshots for a firm of solicitors at their offices in the middle of the Northamptonshire countryside. I arrived for the job over 30 minutes early, so sat in my car and looked to see if there were any holidays that I could celebrate whilst I was waiting. It was *Inane Answering Machine Message Day* so I decided to make some phone calls. There was no phone signal so I went for a wander. I soon worked out that I could get one intermittent bar of signal by climbing onto a nearby gate, and then a slightly stronger signal by standing with my arm outstretched towards the sky - the official pose for searching for a phone signal. It was not strong enough to make a proper phone call, and besides, how could I be sure that I would get someone's answering machine?

Instead, I decided to send some voice texts to the landlines of friends of mine. My inane messages could be sent through the ether and then read out by a sexy female robot at the other end. I went for something cryptic:

'The drop-off is scheduled for noon by the bench in the park. 1400 custard creams. And a single chocolate bourbon. Don't let me down.'

I sent this off to a few friends, thinking that it would be left anonymously. I had forgotten that before the message is read out, the sexy female robot divulges the telephone number of the person that sent the message.

I had these text message replies when I checked my phone later in the day.

'Have you gone mental?'
'Eh?'
'Was that meant for me? Why do you need so many biscuits?'
And my favourite response…
'Mission complete. I'll await further instructions.'

January 31st

I have never been much of an artist. Layla is five and her drawings are already far more realistic than mine. My portraiture has never progressed further than stick men, and I am slightly ashamed by my lack of any artistic talent. My sister is a very talented artist, and both my mum and dad have taken art classes and created some lovely artwork. The artistic gene clearly bypassed me. Rachel is a talented artist, too. At least, she is in principle. She has only ever done ONE drawing. I mean one drawing as a grown-up. She wasn't deprived of crayons as a child. Her one drawing was a biro sketch of me that she drew whilst sitting in the passenger seat of a car, as we drove through Minnesota as part of a US road trip in 2000. Despite the difficult working conditions, it's a very good likeness (although she has grossly accentuated my eyebrow) and the picture has sat in a small frame on our mantelpiece ever since. It was Rachel's first proper attempt at a portrait, and she decided to go out on a high, and retire from art there and then. She hasn't drawn since.

Today was *Inspire Your Heart With Art Day*, which also falls on the same day as *Backward Day* - a day when you are encouraged to do things the opposite way to how you normally would; talk backwards, walk backwards, wear your clothes backwards. I decided to combine these two days by drawing with my left hand. It was actually extremely therapeutic and I did feel that my heart was inspired. Using my left hand, I finally had an excuse for why my drawings were so shit. The playing field had been levelled and I was as good a left-handed artist as most people. Apart from other left-handed people, of course. Of which Layla is one. Dammit!

Here is my left-handed effort. A little bit of artistic licence was used on our modest mid-terraced house.

FEBRUARY

February 1st

'What on earth are you doing?' shouted Rachel, as she walked into the study first thing in the morning. 'Why the hell haven't you got any clothes on?'

'It's *Work Naked Day*,' I said. 'So I am working naked.'

'It's February! Aren't you freezing, you freak? And you are supposed to be taking Layla to school in a minute.'

'I'm quite warm thanks, as you insist on the heating being on permanently. Don't worry, I'll put some clothes on when I do the school run.'

Lisa Kanarek, who created *Work Naked Day*, is a home-based business consultant. The day can be interpreted either literally, or figuratively; rather than clothes, working naked could mean *'being stripped of the resources that millions take for granted in the traditional corporate workplace.'* I preferred to take it literally. I have to confess, working naked felt pretty good. I spend many a working day sitting around in my pants, but this notched things up a level. It was certainly something that I could get used to.

'You should try working naked, too,' I suggested to Rachel. 'It's awesome.'

'I'm a primary school teacher. I would get arrested,' she said.

'Ok, fair point. Although it is *Give Kids a Smile Day* as well today.'

Give Kids a Smile Day sounded a little sinister. It was also *Bubble Gum Day*, but smiling at children and offering them bubble gum would probably have got me into some serious trouble.

I was relieved to discover that *Give Kids a Smile Day* is actually a day created by the American Dental Association on which many dentists offer free oral healthcare to children from low-income families. Here in the UK, because of the blessing that is the NHS, children are entitled to free dental care all year round.

Of all the days in the year, it seems ironic that bubble gum – the dentist's nemesis – should have its day, on the exact same day that the American Dental Association encourages kids to get their teeth checked. Perhaps that's the point.

There's no reason that children can't have bubble gum and still have healthy teeth. I had lots of bubble gum when I was a child, and my teeth are perfect now... because they are all made of ACRYLIC. My real teeth rotted away years ago. Not really.

To celebrate the day, I phoned our dentist and booked the whole family in for a check-up as we were long overdue. I chewed some bubble gum whilst on the phone. Ha! I was really sticking it to the dentist! I wasn't sticking the bubble gum to the dentist. They get a bit arsey when I do that.

When Rachel returned home from work later, she was very pleased to see me fully clothed, and was more than happy to celebrate *Hula in the Coola Day*. It's a chance to ignore the cold weather and pretend, for one day, that you are in Hawaii... rather than Northampton. We made piña coladas, donned flower garlands and danced the night away. Well, five minutes of it, at least.

February 2nd

Legend has it that when the groundhog – a beaver-like rodent – emerges from its burrow on February 2nd, if it sees its shadow then it signifies that winter will continue for another six weeks. If, however, no shadow is cast, then it means that spring is just around the corner.

I checked the local press, but surprisingly Northampton didn't have much in the way of *Groundhog Day* celebrations this year. Thankfully, due to the wonder of a new phenomenon called The Internets, I was able to watch a live video of Punxsutawney Phil – the most famous Groundhog in America – emerge from his hole in a place called Gobbler's Knob. (Grow up! There's nothing funny about the name Gobbler's Knob whatsoever.)

It was pretty tense viewing. There were thousands of people gathered in the wind and rain at Gobbler's Knob (stop it!), many with placards saying 'I LOVE PHIL' There was at least ten nerve-wracking minutes of build-up, which consisted of various introductions from the members of the

Punxsutawney Groundhog Club's Inner Circle, who have titles such as Thunder Conductor, Sky Painter and Storm Chaser - I so wanted to be one of them.

Eventually, Phil was woken from his temporary home on Gobbler's Knob (that's the last mention of it, I promise) and presented to the adoring crowd. It was then decided that no shadow had been cast, which meant that spring is nearly here. It was a bit of an anticlimax, to be honest, but certainly more exciting - and definitely as reliable - as checking the long-range weather forecast.

We had crepes for dinner, as it was *Crepe Day*.

February 3rd

Today was *Dump Your Significant Jerk Day*. This is a day when you are encouraged to get out of your bad relationship and dump your other half. Seeing as I am happily married, I thought it unwise to take this day too literally. Perhaps Rachel would have preferred it if I had. Instead I decided to use it as an excuse to remove any deadwood from my circle of friends.

Up until recently, getting rid of a friend would have been a huge ordeal. It would have involved a confrontation of sorts, possible tears, and a bucket-load of guilt. Nowadays, friends are all virtual, and all it takes to end a relationship is a simple click of the mouse.

I had 337 friends on Facebook, which is way more than I would ever need. I looked through them one by one. I had not seen most of them in years. Many of them I could do without, but I didn't consider any of them 'jerks'. I didn't know many jerks. I tend not to become friends with jerks in the first place. It's easier that way.

I settled on Ian Stewart. I went to the same school as Ian. We were never best friends, but we were always civil enough to each other. There was something slightly jerkish about him, though. He oozed smugness, and I never found him particularly endearing. I clicked the '*remove*' button and dumped him from my world.

I had hoped to feel liberated, and cleansed, but all I felt was a huge sense of guilt and sympathy. Ian had never done anything to hurt me. Sure, he was a bit of a dick, but he was a nice enough guy. How could I just delete him like that? Surely he would notice? What would happen if I ever bumped into him?

Rachel regularly has Facebook culls, and feels no remorse. I don't know how she does it. She often then bumps into people that she has deleted and has awkward discussions about what they are up to these days, but it doesn't bother her in the slightest. It stresses me out just thinking about it.

I felt awful for deleting Ian already. I debated asking him to be my 'friend' again straightaway, but it was too late. The damage was done. It was time for me to move on in a life without Ian.

February 4th

Our mailman, or postman as we call them in the UK, is the best. His name is Jason. You've already met him. He was the one chatting with Rachel when Prince Charles came to visit. He is undoubtedly one of the nicest men you could ever meet. Despite living in a terraced street in 'downtown' Northampton, we have got to know him very well over the years.

He always stops and chats on the doorstep. Not just to us, but to many of the people on his round. Often, if we are not in, and he has a parcel for us, he will make a note on the delivery card saying which street he will be on next if we want to come and find him, in order to save us a trip to the sorting office. It is this personal service that makes him such a great person. It's also probably the reason why his round takes so bloody long to deliver and why our post often doesn't arrive until the middle of the afternoon.

Today was *Thank a Mailman Day*. Thank you, Jason, you're the best. Today is for you.

February 5th

Rachel was having a rare lie-in, so I made her Nutella on toast in bed. It was *Nutella Day* after all (other chocolate spreads are available, although none are anywhere near as good).

'I'm happy for you to celebrate *Nutella Day* as often as you like,' she said.

'Well, it only happens once a year, I'm afraid.'

'Oh. So what other days is it today?' she asked.

'*Weatherperson's Day*.'

'So I bet you are going to perv at pictures of that weather girl you fancy?'

'Huh? What do you mean? Which weather girl?' I asked.

'You know, the one who you always stare at when she's doing the weather.'

'I'm probably staring because I am interested in the weather.'

'Well, you are certainly interested in her WARM FRONT.'

'Good one!' I said, gutted that I hadn't come up with that pun first. 'I definitely feel an area of HIGH PRESSURE down south when she's presenting.'

'You are gross. You always have to go one better.'

'You started it! Oh, do you mean Lucy Verasamy or Sian Welby?'

'You mean there's more than one? I didn't even mean either of those ones.'

'I... er... no... you said... er...' I stuttered.

'I meant the one who does the local news.'

'Ah, you mean Wendy Hurrell? I don't think she does our local news anymore,' I said, knowing full well that she left Anglia TV way back in 2008. It was an extremely sad year.

I had planned to try and send Sian Welby and Lucy Verasamy a message wishing them a Happy *Weatherperson's Day*, but now my plans had been scuppered. I decided to try and contact the less glamorous John Kettley instead.

John Kettley has been a respected TV and radio weatherman for over 30 years, and I have certainly never perved at him. He is perhaps most famous for being the subject of a hit single by a band called *A Tribe of Toffs* in 1988. The track, appropriately titled *John Kettley is a Weatherman*, reached number 21 in the UK charts. The song, unsurprisingly, is about John Kettley, and the fact that he is a weatherman.

I found John's contact details on his website and sent him a quick email:

Hi John

As you are probably aware, today is Weatherperson's Day, and as you were my favourite weatherman when I was growing up, I thought I would write to wish you a very Happy Weatherperson's Day! I hope you've had a great day.

Best wishes
George

Later in the evening, I had this reply...

Thanks George, it was news to me but I survived OK!
Kind regards
John

I did also send a sneaky tweet to Lucy Verasamy telling her she was my favourite weatherperson in the world. I then sent another to Sian Welby telling her she was my second. Neither of them replied.

February 6th

Lame Duck Day was created to give recognition to people who are approaching the end of their tenure - usually an elected official in a political position. Politics is FULL of lame ducks but it's not for me to name and shame individuals.

Instead, I got rid of an entire flock of lame rubber ducks. Since buying more on *Rubber Duckie Day* (January 13th. Don't flick back. I deleted that section as it was so boring. YES, more boring than this bit. OK?), the old ones had all gone rank inside. When the kids squeezed the ducks, they shot out a jet of disgusting black gunk into the bath. I would then have to shower each of the children before getting them out, which defeated the object of the bath in the first place. The flock of ducks was reduced from nine to three. Survival of the fittest.

February 7th

Today had been a nice, quiet and fairly uneventful day. I had a short photography job in the morning and then spent a couple of hours catching up on emails and admin in the afternoon. I could not have predicted how the day would end.

It was *Wave All Your Fingers At Your Neighbour Day*, so I gave Doug an extra cheery wave at his window on my way home from school with Layla. Moments later, he appeared at his front door with a concerned look on his face.

'George, have you got a minute?' he said slightly frantically.

'Yes, of course,' I said. Rachel was out with Leo and Kitty so I took Layla by the hand and followed Doug inside.

When I got into the living room, he was talking to someone on the speakerphone.

'He's a male cat. About four years old, we think. His name is Michael,' Doug said to the person on the phone.

'And what exactly is the problem?' asked the lady, who I now understood to be a vet.

'He's not looking well at all. He's been sick. He won't eat his food. He looks like he's struggling to breathe. Can you send someone out urgently?'

'Do you want a vet to come to you?'

'Yes please,' said Doug. 'As soon as possible.'

'Just to let you know that there is a £100 call out charge, and this doesn't take into account any costs involved with treating Michael.'

'Yes, that's fine.'

'Let me just check when a vet will be available.' There was a slight pause. 'They are all in surgery at the moment, so it will be about 5.30pm before we can get anyone out to you. Are you not able to bring Michael in, and then we can take a look at him sooner?'

'No, I'm struggling to walk with my arthritis at the moment, let alone drive.'

'I'll take you,' I said.

'Really? Are you sure, George?' said Doug. 'What about Layla?'

'She can come too.'

Michael was not the most loving of pets. He had turned up on our doorstep as a stray two years previously, and Doug and Chris had adopted him after we had been unable to trace his owner. To be fair, they had transformed him from a malnourished, vicious, unsociable cat into a well-fed, vicious, unsociable cat. And who names a cat Michael?

Michael didn't look in great shape, but it was hopefully something that a dose of antibiotics would sort out. We put him into a cat carrier and onto Doug's lap in the front seat of my car.

'Where are we taking Michael, Daddy?' asked Layla.

'To the vets. He's a bit poorly but the vet will make him better,' I said.

The surgery was less than a mile away, but on the way Michael made an escape attempt from his carrier. Doug struggled with him and managed to get him securely back inside, and then Michael seemed to relax. We reached the vets less than a minute later, and I noticed when we were in the waiting room that Michael seemed to be unusually still.

'Poor thing,' said Doug. 'He must be very tired after the day he's had.'

We were seen by the vet immediately and when he lifted Michael out, he confirmed my suspicion that Michael was dead. The vet suggested that he had probably had a heart attack on the way in.

Doug was distraught. I put my arms around him and gave him a big hug as he sobbed into my shoulder.

'Daddy, why isn't Michael moving?' asked Layla.

'Because he was too poorly, darling, and the vet wasn't able to fix him. He's gone to live in heaven now. He'll be there with Misty - Nana and Granddad's dog,' I said.

'But Misty hated cats, Daddy. And Michael hated dogs,' she said.

That was my reward for waving all my fingers at my neighbour.

February 8th

It was *Laugh and Get Rich Day*. I laughed, but didn't get rich.

The month of February is *National Canned Food Month*. It would be too boring and predictable for me to just eat some canned food. I needed to think of a way to celebrate canned food in a more creative way. I was searching through the cupboards to try and find some form of inspiration from the many tins that we have accumulated, when I discovered at the back of the cupboard, a solitary tin with no label. There was no discernable markings and absolutely no way of identifying its contents.

'I think you should have that for dinner, whatever is inside,' suggested Rachel.

'What if it's cat food?'

'Well, that's part of the fun. It's like a tinned version of Russian Roulette. RushCAN Roulette!'

'That's clever. Well done.'

'Thanks. I'm quite proud of that.'

I opened the can and was relieved, although admittedly slightly disappointed, to discover that it was tinned tomatoes. I used it to cook a delicious, although fairly boring, pasta sauce for dinner. I had got a strange sense of excitement at opening an unlabeled can, and it would have been nice to have had the option to be a little more creative.

Before opening it, I had posted a photo of the unlabelled can on Facebook, with the caption *'I'm having this for dinner. I hope it's not cat food.'*

Dan, a school friend who now lives in Melbourne, responded:

'Here's a challenge for you. Man vs. Can! Each day you have an unlabeled tin of food as the basis of your main meal, improvising what accompanies its contents as you go and documenting your adventures on Facebook. Fill your cupboards with tins, George.'

It was a truly genius idea, and the perfect way to celebrate *National Canned Food Month*. Rachel was equally keen on the idea but added her own element to the challenge.

'I can go to the shops for you and buy lots of different random tins and take all of the labels off, then you will have no idea what is in any of them.'

'Great idea. As long as you promise to only buy human food, ok?'

'Ok, deal. But you have to promise to cook a meal from whatever you open.'

'I promise. Just remember that I'll probably be cooking dinner for ALL of us.'

February 9th

I decided to stop bullying today as it was *Stop Bullying Day*.

That speccy, four-eyed, ugly fat kid, whose lunch I always stole, probably didn't deserve the daily physical torture I was giving him. I pledged to leave him alone from now on.

Instead, I read a book in the bath. Not an entire book, but several pages of one. It was *Read in the Bathtub Day*. People say that the disadvantage of these modern e-book readers is that you can't read them in the bath, because if you dropped them they would break. Have you ever tried dropping a paperback in the bath? They're not particularly fond of it either.

Rachel went off to the supermarket and returned with 20 cans. All of equal size, and she had already removed all of the labels and placed the identical looking cans on the kitchen counter.

'So, the rules are simple. There are enough tins here for you to use one a day for the rest of February,' she said.

'Are they all edible?'

'Yes, they are all edible. They are not all savoury. Some might work better as a dessert, but that's up to you. Are you ready to take your pick?'

I was born ready. This was the most excited I had been for a very long time. Twenty different cans sat in front of me and I didn't have the faintest clue what was in any of them. It was like I was on a surreal version of *Deal or No Deal*, but in this version I was guaranteed to be a winner. I spent a while deliberating which tin to pick, and then realised that it was futile as they all looked the same, and I would be eating them all at some point anyway. I grabbed the nearest tin and excitedly set to work opening it. I could not have anticipated getting such a thrill from using a tin-opener. The tension was unbelievable. The battle of Man vs. Can had commenced.

I lifted off the lid to reveal... beans. But these weren't any old baked beans. They were borlotti beans.

We had some sausages in the fridge, so for dinner I created a delicious sausage and borlotti bean cassoulet, by following one of Jamie Oliver's *'30 Minute Meals'* (see, I told you he was going to be big). As usual, his 30 minute meal took me about 90 minutes as I was missing most of the ingredients and so had to improvise. Also, our oven stopped working halfway through the cooking so I had to use the hob instead. Jamie Oliver doesn't have to put up with shit like this.

'This is delicious,' said Layla.

'Yummy,' said Leo with his mouth full.

Kitty didn't say anything as she was shovelling another spoonful of sausage into her mouth.

'It seems *National Canned Food Month* has been a great success so far,' said Rachel. 'I think it's going to be a fun month.'

February 10th

Samuel Plimsoll was a British politician whose contribution to world shipping cannot be overstated. He developed the 'Plimsoll line', which is the line on a ship's hull that shows the safe legal limit that a ship can be loaded, depending on different temperatures and water conditions.

The plimsoll shoe got its name because of the coloured band on the rubber around the shoe resembling a ship's Plimsoll line. But how would I celebrate such a momentous day as *Plimsoll Day*? I live in Northampton - one of the furthest points from the coast in the whole of the UK.

'Daddy, what are you doing to my boat?' asked Leo.

'I'm drawing a line on it so that you don't overload it in the bath.'

'Why?'

'Because if the line goes under the water then you have put too much on the boat and it will sink.'

'But I don't put too many things on it. I only put Captain Jack and the seagull. Don't worry. It won't sink, Daddy.'

'Not now it won't, thanks to Samuel Plimsoll.'

'Who is Sam Yule Pimp Sol?'

'The youth of today,' I muttered.

I had promised Rachel a Chinese takeaway for dinner to celebrate *Chinese New Year*, but still had to incorporate a can into the day's meals somehow. I picked another can at random and discovered it to be a tin of ratatouille. We had a weird Sunday lunch of leftover sausages from the cassoluet, sautéed potatoes, baby sweet corn and ratatouille. I won't be buying tinned ratatouille again.

In the evening, after the children had gone to bed, I walked down to our local Chinese takeaway only to discover a sign on the door saying it was closed because it was, of course, *Chinese New Year*. I then walked half a mile to our other nearby 'Chinese' takeaway which seems to be run by a Greek family. It was open.

'Happy Chinese New Year,' I blurted enthusiastically when I entered.

'Oh, is that today?' said the young man behind the counter. 'I wondered why it was so busy.'

February 11th

I spent the day editing wedding photos on my computer upstairs. My mum rang later in the afternoon and asked if she could call in to visit and I made up an excuse that we were busy.

'Why did you do that? It would've been nice to see your mum,' said Rachel.

'I can't. It's *Shut-in Visitation Day*. That means I'm not allowed any visitors,' I said.

'Are you sure that's what it means? Is that why you've been hiding upstairs all day?'

'Yep, I have to shut myself in, and shut myself up and shut myself away from visitors.'

'Surely *Shut-in Visitation*, means that you should visit people that are shut in? Like old people who can't leave their house.'

'Oh. Perhaps you're right. Oh well, it's a bit late in the day to be visiting old people,' I said.

'It's funny how you interpret these days so that they suit you. Anyway, if you're not going out today, why are you wearing a shirt?'

'It's *White Shirt Day*.'

'Of course. Silly me.'

My mystery can at dinner was mushy peas. I decided to be a little more creative and tried to turn mushy peas into a fine dining experience. I'm not sure I succeeded.

Mushy peas, five ways
-Pea stuffed mushroom
-Pea and salsa on a bed of cracker
-Pea in a spaghetti nest
-Minted pea parfait with a pretzel crust
-Smeared pea

'Ha! You've excelled yourself this time,' laughed Rachel when I presented it to her, along with my descriptions of the five different elements to the dish.

'Thanks,' I said. 'I'm well chuffed with this creation.'

'I meant with your time-wasting. You spent nearly an hour on THAT.'

'It was worth it. I'm fairly certain that this dish is even beyond Heston Blumenthal.' I said.

'I'm actually quite impressed with how it looks,' she said. 'I'm particularly impressed with the 'smeared pea'.'

'That's my favourite one, too. I did it with the back of a spoon like they do on TV cookery shows.'

'I can tell. It looks, er... really professional.'

'So, how does it taste?' I asked Rachel, as she deliberated, cogitated and digested a mouthful.

'Unfortunately, I think it is back to the development kitchen for this dish.'

February 12th

Today was *Shrove Tuesday*, or *Pancake Day* - a day, traditionally, when all of the unhealthy foods are eaten before the start of Lent. It is also an excuse to eat shit loads of pancakes. We had chocolate and banana pancakes for breakfast, visited a National Trust property during the day (we're so rock 'n' roll) and had pancakes there for lunch. We had pancakes for pudding after dinner, but for the main course we were, of course, restricted by the cans.

Today's offering was a can of chicken and vegetable soup. Our oven had stopped working completely, so I decided to serve the soup in its natural form and not tamper with it.

During *Man vs. Can* I have been uploading my photos daily to Facebook. I know it's not cool to post photos of your dinner on social media (it's even less cool to post them IN A BLOODY BOOK), but I felt that as Facebook was where the *Man vs. Can* project was born then I should keep my friends updated. Dan, the challenge's instigator, even insisted upon it in his original brief. Those who had followed the challenge on Facebook had been positive and enthusiastic so far. After posting a photo of my chicken soup, however, there was a sudden backlash. My 'fans' (both of them) were not happy with my latest creation.

Natasha commented: *'Surely this could have been the sauce for a delicious chicken pie?! 3 out of 10'*

Dan added: *'Not up to your usual standard George, clearly lacking motivation when you opened this can'*

I tried to argue that we had a broken oven and that it wasn't possible to make a chicken pie using a hob, but I knew they were right. I had been lazy. I had let the challenge down. I had let my friends down. I had let myself down. But most importantly, I had let the cans down. They deserved better. I needed to up my game.

February 13th

I used to take Lent quite seriously as a child. My parents are not religious, but they encouraged, actually they insisted, that we give something up. I almost enjoyed the physical and mental challenge of abstaining from something for 40 days and 40 nights. It was usually chocolate, and I always found the whole process extremely tough but ultimately rewarding. As soon as I was old enough to realise that I didn't HAVE to give up anything, I decided not to give up things for lent and then didn't for the next 20 years. If I am to take this project seriously then I cannot overlook *Ash Wednesday*. Giving up chocolate is too predictable. Giving up alcohol is too difficult. A couple of years ago I gave up Facebook for lent. I found it quite tough to begin with, but after a few days I didn't miss it in the slightest. I felt that I had a lot more free time... to devote to other pointless time-wasting activities instead. My plan also backfired because as soon as Easter Sunday arrived, I spent the following 40 days and 40 nights catching up on what I'd missed.

This year I decided to give up caffeine. I drink an awful lot of tea and coffee. Being self-employed, I make tea or coffee at every opportunity to avoid doing any actual work. I have also had a theory for a while that caffeine has an adverse effect on me. After the initial 'buzz' wears off I then just feel tired and lousy. An extreme example of this was a university dissertation that I had to finish. I made myself a coffee with six teaspoons of coffee and six teaspoons of sugar. It was so thick I needed a spoon to drink it. I had a couple of sips and the next thing I knew it was 7am and I was waking up on my desk. Dissertation unfinished.

Giving up caffeine would be a big undertaking for me. I have no idea how much I rely on caffeine, but I know that I rely heavily on tea and coffee. Thankfully, Rachel agreed to try and give it up too. The constant smell of coffee in the house for 40 days would have made it far tougher. We celebrated our resolve with a cup of peppermint tea. Living the dream.

Rachel was asleep by the time I got home from football late in the evening, so I opened one of the unlabeled cans on my own. It was baked beans with mini sausages. I was so tempted to just heat up the contents and serve it on toast, but I needed to use more ingenuity. The fridge was barren. As was the freezer, apart from a bag of frozen Yorkshire puddings. Because we were still without a functioning oven, I had to toast the frozen Yorkshire puddings over the flame of the gas hob like marshmallows. It didn't quite go to plan. Who knew Yorkshire puddings were SO damn flammable?

I uploaded a photo to Facebook, hoping it would silence my critics but immediately Natasha responded with her *Masterchef* inspired citique:

'The problem is, George - at this stage in the competition... we're looking for someone who can consistently deliver inspiring exciting food ... And I'm just not sure that you are doing that yet. Does he intentionally have a black eye?.

Thankfully Dan leapt to my defence this time:

'Sorry Natasha I have to disagree. George had a real slump with the soup but has been very innovative with what are rather drab core ingredients. We can't expect him to create fine dining from tins of beans.'

I explained that I had toasted the frozen Yorkshire puddings on a gas hob and this seemed to win Natasha over:

'Ok - I'll give you extra points for the fact that you still don't have an oven - innovative thinking for the Yorkshire cooking. Let's hope the next can contains something more inspiring and your oven is soon returned to working order. I think you've definitely earned the right to cook again...'

February 14th

You would think that *Valentine's Day* has such a monopoly over February 14th that the creators of other holidays would steer well clear of this date when choosing a day to schedule theirs.

Far from it. It's almost as though people see popular dates such as *Valentine's Day* as an incentive to set something up to counteract it. There are some days of the year that don't have ANY official celebrations, so why people don't use these instead of a day already saturated with symbolism, I am unsure.

As well as *Valentine's Day*, February 14th is also: *Ferris Wheel Day, National Condom Day, Quirky Alone Day, (World) Congenital Heart Defect Awareness Day, League of Women Voters Day, Library Lovers Day, National Women's Heart Day, Call in Single Day* and *Race Relations Day*.

I had a short photography job to do in London in the morning and I broke the news to Rachel that I would be spending most of *Valentine's Day* without her. She seemed delighted by the idea and told me not to hurry back.

I boarded a train to London and, after finishing the job, I thought I would do a bit of sightseeing as it was *Quirky Alone Day*. In order to cross *Ferris Wheel Day* off my list too, I visited the London Eye. For any international readers not familiar with The London Eye, it is a giant Ferris wheel on the bank of the River Thames. It is the biggest Ferris wheel in Europe, and at the time of construction, was the biggest in the world. It has since been overtaken by similar wheels in China and Singapore.

Now for your history lesson.

The first Ferris Wheel was designed, unsurprisingly, by a man named Ferris. George Washington Gale Ferris Jr, a Pennsylvania bridge-builder, built the first wheel in 1893 for the World's Columbian Exposition in Chicago, Illinois.

Being *Valentine's Day*, the London Eye was full of couples. Those that didn't opt for the 'luxury package', which ensured a capsule all to themselves, were squashed into capsules with other couples, and lonely individuals like me. There were 25 of us in the one I was in. Twelve couples and me.

There was an awkward silence throughout most of the trip as each couple was too self-conscious to speak to their other half in front of the others. One particular guy kept fiddling with something in the pocket of his jeans, and I've no doubt that he planned to propose to his girlfriend high above the capital, but bottled in on account of his audience. Either that or he had a particularly itchy crotch.

I stuck my head to the glass and enjoyed the view instead. London is a stunningly beautiful city, and The London Eye is an incredible way to experience it. If, however, you are a singleton in London on *Valentine's Day*, I would avoid it like the plague.

As I was in London and it was *(World) Congenital Heart Defect Awareness Day* and *National Women's Heart Day* I decided that it would be a good idea to head to The Heart Hospital on Westmoreland St. I thought perhaps I could volunteer for a few hours, or just learn a bit about congenital heart defects. I could look at the different treatments, and maybe speak to people who had heart problems. I could even perhaps help raise awareness somehow, or do some fundraising.

But then I realised something incredibly selfish. I simply didn't want to. I know it's bad to ignore holidays that are not 'fun', but I had other priorities. I should not have been spending *Valentine's Day* in London on my own. I needed to be home with Rachel and the children. I headed for the station, stopping briefly to buy condoms on the way, with the hope of celebrating *National Condom Day* in style.

Over the last few weeks, there had been lots of stories in the local news about libraries being threatened with closure because of budget cuts. I remembered reading about an online petition that was doing the rounds, that was going to be sent to the county council as a protest against these planned closures. I found the website on my phone on the way home, and added my name to the list. Just doing my bit for *Library Lovers Day*.

'Not a bloody chance!' said Rachel a split second after I waved the pack of Durex at her with a knowing wink.

'But it's *National Condom Day*. What better way to celebrate?'

'You've spent the afternoon mooching around London, on *Valentine's Day*, so there is absolutely no chance that we will be doing any 'celebrating' of that type this evening.'

'You're right. I'm really sorry. I did have a job in London this morning, though. But I've been an idiot. I promise to make it up to you.'

'It's a bit late for condoms anyway,' she said.

'Why?'

'I'm pregnant.'

'What? Really? But how?' I gasped.

She stared back at me with a completely emotionless face.

'Only kidding,' she said. 'I just wanted to see your face.'

'That wasn't funny.'

'Yeah, it was.'

I opened my anonymous can and was presented with evaporated milk from which I created some delicious fudge, which impressed my Facebook judges and helped go someway to redeem myself to Rachel.

February 15th

The ancient festival of *Lupercalia* begins with the sacrifice of two male goats and a dog.

The blood is then wiped from the knife onto a piece of wool soaked in milk, which is then smeared onto the foreheads of two young people. They are then expected to dress themselves in the skins of the slaughtered animals and proceed to run around the walls of the city whipping young girls and women who had gathered to watch.

It seemed simple enough.

There were a few minor legal, moral and ethical implications to deal with, but I was up for a challenge. I was just about to begin sacrificing animals, smearing blood and whipping young girls, when I realised that we had used the last of the milk at breakfast, so I couldn't celebrate *Lupercalia* after all.

Maybe next year.

For dinner we had Thai red chicken curry that I made from a tin of coconut milk. And some other ingredients, of course. I'm not a wizard.

Just before bed, I had a quick look at the website of our local newspaper. At the top of the page was the following article:

BREAKING NEWS: Council u-turn will see all libraries in Northamptonshire saved from closure

My signature had worked. I had single-handedly saved all of the county's libraries. I was a hero. Admittedly, this decision had probably been made long before I had added my name to the petition, but still, I like to feel that I contributed.

February 16th

I was photographing a wedding at an opulent stately home just outside of Northampton. One of the disadvantages of the room that they use for the majority of their weddings is that it is fully enclosed with no natural light. The ambient light is all from chandeliers and candelabras, which is all very nice if you are a guest, but not so great if you are the photographer. It means I'm fairly reliant on my camera flash. I have two flashes, one of them significantly better than the other, but on this occasion the good one was having a small issue in that it wasn't staying on the camera. Part of the bracket had got loose and whenever the camera deviated from a non-horizontal position it slid right off. The obvious solution would be for me to just use the slightly crapper flash. But today was *Innovation Day*. I wasn't going to take the easy option; I was going to innovate. I tried tying some string around the flash but there was nothing for the string to grip to. I tried keeping my right thumb on the back of the flash to hold it in place but this was completely impractical and made me look like it was the first time I'd picked up a camera, which is not the best impression to give at a wedding. I then stumbled upon the perfect innovation. Chewing gum! I chewed up one piece and then moulded it around the hotshoe in between the flash and the camera. It held the flash perfectly tight. Admittedly it was going to be a real bastard to clean off when I removed the flash, but I would worry about that later. For today at least, I was an innovator.

I got home very late from the wedding and opened a can. It was spicy bean soup. After the uproar from the last time I had soup, I had to be creative. I also needed something substantial having worked all day, and so mixed it together with the remains of the Thai red curry and the rice from yesterday to form some sort of Thai Bean Risotto Curry Fusion. It was fairly disgusting, but took me less than two minutes to concoct.

You may, quite rightly, be wondering why all of these food photos in this book are so crap. I am supposedly a photographer after all. Firstly, I'm not a food photographer and have no experience of how to present and photograph food. Secondly, and most importantly, I get ridiculously grumpy when I'm hungry. The last thing I want to do when I've cooked a meal is to start faffing around with lighting and presentation in order to take a decent photograph. I just take a quick snap with my mobile phone, and then a couple of minutes later the plate is empty. It's as simple as that. I'm sorry.

February 17th

My sister and her husband had moved into a new flat in London before Christmas and we still hadn't seen it. We cancelled a visit in January because of the snow, and today was our rearranged trip.

'Sat nav says it will only take us an hour and 15 minutes to get there,' said Rachel as she frantically tried to locate the sat nav's charger and fiddle with the connecters at each end to get it charging before its battery died.

'You can put the sat nav away. We won't need it. Today we are going my way,' I said.

'What do you mean? You've never been to their new place before.'

'I know, but I'll find it. It can't be that hard.'

'Are you serious? You don't have a clue where to go. You hate driving in London, and you usually use sat nav just to get to the shop at the end of the road.'

'Well not today. Because today is *My Way Day*.'

'Oh bloody hell. I should have known.'

'I took a quick look at the map before we left home. We just have to follow the M1 until the end, and then onto the North Circular - I think - and then through Kilburn and then we're sort of there. But I think I know a shortcut!'

'Oh joy. This is going to be fun,' said Rachel.

'Are we nearly there yet, Mummy?' asked Leo, five minutes into the journey.

'It might be an idea to have a sleep back there, kids. It's going to be a very long journey. Daddy is being a wally,' responded Rachel.

We did get there eventually. Admittedly, I did have to phone my brother-in-law (twice) just to clarify their address and what other notable landmarks were in the vicinity. But it only took us 1 hour and 55 minutes. We followed sat nav on the way home. 2 hours 5 minutes. IN YOUR FACE, SAT NAV! My way rules!

I know that this *Man vs. Can* food diary is possibly the most mind-numbing thing you have ever read. It's not great literature, I agree, but I have found the whole challenge ridiculously exciting. It has been quite cathartic writing about a daily meal too. It brings with it a strange sense of familiarity. Every morning at primary school, we had to write a short diary about what we did the previous evening. It was a way to encourage us to practise our hand-writing and grammar, and presumably for the teacher to have 15 minutes peace and quiet at the start of the day. The diary only needed to be about three lines long, and I soon worked out that I could pad out about 1.5 of those lines by mentioning what we had for dinner. So, every single day, for several years at primary school, my daily diary would say something along the lines of:

Last night I played football with Mark. Then we had a go-cart race. For tea we had sausages, beans and chips.

I like to think that my teacher looked forward to finding out what I'd had for dinner, but I think it is highly unlikely. Man vs. Can is basically just an extension of this primary school food diary. Not that I am in anyway suggesting that it is purely a device to pad out this book. How dare you! I guess a small part of me naively hopes that you might look forward to finding out what I've had for dinner each day. I admit it's highly unlikely, too. Failing that, at least in another 25 years time I'll be able to look back at this, with a mixture of intrigue and embarrassment, and laugh at myself in the way that I do reading through my old school diaries now.

Man vs. Can has forced me to think of new ways to make meals out of basic ingredients, and to cook dishes I would not otherwise have considered. The fact that I have uploaded the photos onto Facebook each day has also meant that, despite my hunger rage, I have spent a little more time than I normally would on presentation.

Take tonight's meal, for example. We had a late lunch at my sister's in London so neither Rachel nor I was hungry when we got home. By 10pm we were both a bit more peckish, so we opened a can. It was boring tomato soup. We didn't want tomato soup. Our eyes were on the giant pork pie that we had bought at the farmer's market in London. It was time to innovate.

Pork encased in crispy pastry, served with a cream of tomato jus*.
*Yes, I used the back of my spoon again for that smear. I think I nailed it this time.

February 18th

There are some official days that are simply not feasible or practical to celebrate. *Cow Milked While Flying In An Airplane Day* was certainly one of those. As much as I wanted to experience milking a cow in an aeroplane, unfortunately I didn't have access to a cow nor an aeroplane.

The date celebrates the anniversary of the day in 1930 when Elm Farm Ollie became the first cow to fly in an aeroplane. Elm Farm Ollie was then, bizarrely, milked during the flight and the milk was sealed in containers and then parachuted over St. Louis, Missouri. What anyone gained from this experiment I have no idea.

I did, however, pretend to milk a toy plastic cow, that I put into the back of a toy plastic helicopter (I didn't have a toy aeroplane). Rachel caught me mid-act.

'I'm not even going to ask,' she said.
'Wait! I can explain,' I said.

'Please don't. So, what gastronomic experience do you have planned for tonight? How are you going to top last night's pork pie?'

'I don't know. Let's go and see,' I said.

The contents of the can looked and smelt like dog food.

'Is this dog food?' I asked, showing it to Rachel.

'I don't know what that is. It looks revolting.'

I prodded it with a fork and broke through the fatty, jelly surface to reveal what looked like some sort of mince.

'Is this mince? Can you even get tinned mince?'

'Yes. I think I did get tinned mince actually. It smells disgusting. I think I might just have a bowl of cereal for dinner tonight. You're on your own with that, I'm afraid.'

'Are you sure? It can't be that bad, can it? I think I'll have it with a tortilla and make it a sort of burrito.'

'Enjoy!' said Rachel sarcastically.

It was every bit as repulsive as it looked and smelt. To make matters worse, I burnt my hand on the bowl as I removed it from the microwave and slopped some of the contents onto the kitchen floor. Batfink the cat walked up to it, took a sniff and then walked off.

'Daddy, is that poo on the floor?' asked Leo. 'Did you do it?'

'No, it's not poo,' I said, at which point Layla came to see what was going on.

'Mummy, Daddy did a poo all over the kitchen floor. It looks like he's got diarrhoea,' she said.

'IT'S NOT POO! That's my DINNER!' I said.

'Ewww, gross,' said Leo.

'Daddy's having poo for dinner,' added Layla.

February 19th

Being self-employed, I usually have many things on the go at a time, and in theory plenty of time to do them. In reality, I do bits and pieces of everything all at the same time and rarely get anything done at all.

On this particular day, for example, I had photos from Saturday's wedding to sort out, album amendments to make to another recent wedding, a website to update, invoices to send, a book to write, another to promote, a house to be cleaned and children to be entertained. *Single Tasking Day* completely cleared my mind.

I ignored all but one of the things that I had planned, and spent the day completely focused on one. I spent the day with Layla, Leo and Kitty. It was half-term so I wanted to spend as much of it as possible with Layla whilst she was off school. Holidays are a bit rubbish when you're self-employed as any unproductive days are laced with guilt about having not earned any money.

I remember fondly the days of contracted employment - not that I want to go back to them - but it did make paid time-off infinitely more enjoyable. It even made breaks during the working day more pleasing. I used to have some software on my computer when I worked in an office called a *'poo timer'*. You entered in your salary and then clicked *'start poo'* when you went off to the bathroom, and *'finish poo'* when you returned. It told you PRECISELY how much money you had earned whilst sitting on the toilet. It kept me amused for several years. There are no such luxuries when you are self-employed. Time is precious. I am much more time-efficient with my toilet breaks these days. I'm in and out before the poo timer has even clocked up its first second.

But on days that I specifically set aside to look after the children - such as when Rachel is working - I don't feel guilty. Because I know on those days, that is my only job. *Single Tasking Day* was extremely rewarding, as it gave me the excuse to simplify things and focus on what was important. I even spent a decent amount of time on the toilet, even though it didn't earn me a penny.

Dinner was a triumph, too. I opened a tin of hotdog sausages and served them with French bread, fried onions, mustard and ketchup. Everyone was very happy.

February 20th

Every now and again, a holiday in the future would catch my eye but I would try to resist the temptation to discover too much about it before the big day arrived. One such day was *Northern Hemisphere Hoodie Hoo Day*. Whatever it was, it sounded better than the previous few days of camera repairs, sat nav journeys and milking cows in aeroplanes.

Northern Hemisphere Hoodie Hoo Day, as it transpired, always falls on February 20th. It is a day during which people in the northern hemisphere are encouraged to go outside at noon and shout *'Hoodie Hoo'* at the top of their voices. The point? Supposedly, to chase winter away in order to make way for spring in a month's time.

So that's what I did.

In the pouring rain, I walked down to the local park, stood in the middle and shouted *'Hoodie Hoo'* as loudly as I could.

The rain continued.

I shouted it again and a big dog started barking at me. I scurried home feeling like a complete fool for even humouring the creators of this stupid day. Apparently it is quite popular in small town America, where they have nothing else to do. I can't see it catching on in Northampton anytime soon.

I discovered a new favourite food of mine today; something that I had never heard of, let alone cooked before: chimichurri. The can I opened was black-eyed beans, and as we had a chorizo in the fridge I Googled 'black-eyed beans chorizo recipe' and found a recipe for black-eyed beans with chorizo and chimichurri. Chimichurri is basically grilled red peppers with olive oil, vinegar, herbs and a few other ingredients. *Man vs. Can* was a success yet again.

February 21st

Up until a few months ago we were a one car family. It suited us absolutely fine. We are lucky enough to live within walking distance from two great parks, plenty of regular mums and tots groups, and Northampton town centre. If Rachel or I had to work, the other would just stay somewhere local with the children. Over the last five years I have got into the almost autonomous habit of heading to the park for the morning of Rachel's work day, whatever the weather.

Our one car then started falling apart in every possible way. It would take about eight or nine attempts to get it to start each morning. The windscreen wipers stopped working. The central locking failed, which was a little inconvenient with three children. One of the rear-windows had become detached from its mechanism so that every time we closed the door, the window dropped down by itself and we had to manually push the glass up from the outside. It would soon slip down again and the inside of the car would get soaked whenever it rained. The car was worth almost nothing, but it still had 10 months tax and MOT, so we decided to keep it until we were forced to spend more money on it.

It was a car that we bought from my Dad several years ago. In an act of defiance, and to make a point of not being nepotistic, he charged us more than the recommended retail price for the car. When I questioned this, he argued that he was doing us a favour by allowing us to pay in several 'interest-free' instalments. I pointed out that they weren't really 'interest free' if we were paying more than the RRP. He then told us he was including a *Beach Boys Greatest Hits* cassette as part of the deal (which he had left in the tape player by mistake), and, as a BONUS, a FREE cassette entitled *Intermediate Level French - Part 2* (which he had accidently left in the glove box). How could we possibly turn down an offer like that?

So we recently bought a new car. When I say 'new', I mean slightly less crap. We stayed well clear of one that my Dad was trying to flog us this time. The new car gives me added freedom on Thursdays when Rachel works. There is a whole world of potential dad activities on offer. Today, rather than our usual trip to the local park, I decided to take Leo and Kitty to a local indoor soft play centre. Soft play centres are basically buildings where you pay money to let your children crawl around in other children's vomit and urine. They are incredibly popular. Today was *Introduce a Girl to Engineering Day*, so Leo and I tried to show Kitty how to build a house from large spongy bricks. Each time we stacked the bricks more than two high, Kitty - aged 17 months - walked over and trashed the entire structure. We persevered for while but it proved impossible to introduce engineering to a girl so intent on destruction.

'Can we just go to the park next time?' cried Leo. 'I don't like it here.'

'Ok,' I said. 'Let's stick to the park from now on.'

I haven't deliberately blurred Leo's face out, by the way. He's just mid-tantrum whilst Kitty destroys his creation.

My *can of surprise* (I'm finding it increasingly difficult to describe the can each night) contained a tin of peaches. I was in the mood for something a little lighter and fresher than what we had been eating for the previous few nights, so I made a peach and feta salad. As you do.

'That looks really weird,' said Rachel. 'Is peach and feta even a thing?'

'It is now. It does taste quite strange,' I said after having my first mouthful. I tried to put a positive spin on it like a food critic would: 'The first thing you get is the sweetness of the peach. Then the saltiness of the feta and the sharpness of the spring onions cut through, before being hit by a wave of balsamic and black pepper and finally the earthiness of the spinach and cucumber. All brought together by the smooth, delicate subtlety of the velvety olive oil.'

'You're still not really selling it to me. I think I'll just stick with the wine thanks,' said Rachel.

February 22nd

One of the best nights of my life was at a small little wood shack of a place called the Moskkito Bar, in a town called Rurrenabaque in the Bolivian jungle. It had a pool table, friendly staff, great food, and an affordable cocktail menu. Rachel and I spent a couple of nights there during a trip to South America, and worked our way through most of the cocktails. We tried all sorts, but kept coming back to the classic margarita. I have a strong dislike of tequila on its own, but when disguised in a margarita I'm converted. That was way back in 2005 and I had not had a margarita since.

It was therefore very exciting to be able to celebrate *Margarita Day* - the sacred combination of tequila, triple sec and lime, served over crushed ice. Rachel and I drank several glasses between us as we looked through an old photo album of our time in South America.

The evening was made even better by the addition of some homemade Portuguese custard tarts (pastel de nata), which I made using a tin of custard.

February 23rd

During our Land's End to John O'Groats bike ride we called into the Glenmorangie Whisky distillery in Scotland. We took a tour of the site and then had a couple of whisky tasting sessions. As a goodwill gesture, the staff presented us with a rare bottle of whisky. They said that we could either drink it on the road or save it to enjoy when we had finished the bike ride. Several years had passed and the bottle still sat - in its slightly battered box - on the shelf in the kitchen.

Tonight was *Open That Bottle Night*. The day (or night) was created by *'Tastings'* columnists Dorothy J. Gaiter and John Brecher to encourage people to finally open and enjoy THAT bottle that they considered too special for everyday consumption.

The Glenmorangie Truffle Oak Reserve seemed to more than qualify for 'that bottle' status. I retrieved it from the shelf, dusted the bottle off and got a couple of whisky tumblers from the kitchen cupboard. I should explain why I own a couple of whisky tumblers considering that I don't even like whisky, and if I did, I don't think I'm the sort of person that would buy a specific glass dedicated to the one drink.

Several years ago I took part in a charity golf tournament with my mum. A huge thunder and lightning storm interrupted proceedings halfway through and the tournament was abandoned because the course was no longer considered safe. There had been a *Longest Drive* competition planned for the 14th hole, but none of the pairings had got as far as this hole before the storm hit. Rather than let the prize go to waste they picked a name out of a hat and I was the lucky winner. I won a *Longest Drive* trophy and a couple of cut glass whisky tumblers. The trophy has sat proudly on the mantelpiece ever since. It was the first and last golf prize I will ever win.

'How much is that bottle worth?' asked Rachel, as I removed it from the box.

'I'm not sure. I think it was selling for about £30 in the shop.'

'But doesn't whisky increase its value the older it gets?'

'Probably, but I doubt by much,' I said as Rachel frantically tapped away on her laptop next to me.

I settled down on the sofa and was just about to break the seal when she interrupted me.

'STOP!' she shouted. 'An identical bottle of that £30 whisky that you are about to open recently sold at auction for nearly £400.'

'Yeah right,' I laughed. 'Let me see.'

She was telling the truth. A little deeper research discovered another identical one that sold last year for over £600.

'Wow,' I said. 'That's crazy. Well we better make sure we savour it even more then.'

'You're not still planning on opening it are you?'

'I have to. It's *Open That Bottle Night*.'

'But you don't even like whisky. I thought you were planning on selling it for charity. Think of what a charity could do with all that money.'

She was right. How could I possibly consider wasting an expensive bottle of whisky just for the sake of a stupid holiday celebration, when the money could be put to far better use by a charity? I put the whisky back in the box, and instead opened an expensive-looking - but probably fairly cheap - bottle of champagne that we had been given for Christmas. It's a hard life.

The champagne was marred only slightly by the strange desert that I concocted from today's secret surprise can which contained prunes.

Following the success (?) of *Mushy Peas - five ways*, I decided to create another experimental tasting platter.

Tastings of Prune.
- prune avec cheerios
- prune carpaccio
- Nutella infused prune
- prune and strawberry yoghurt
- smeared prune

Food critic Natasha had mixed feelings...

'This looks like a bush tucker trial!! The can of prunes was an evil can of poo-like filling. I won't be trying ANY of these recipes anytime soon.... Nice presentation though so marks for trying!!

I especially like the little white nipple you've given the prune in yoghurt!! Lovely little extra finishing touch.'

I should add that *Tastings of Prune* has to be accompanied by champagne in order to fully appreciate the complexity of the flavour combinations.

February 24th

It was a fairly uneventful day today, as all of my planned celebrations happened at night. It was *Academy Awards Night* and *Daytona 500*. I'm not sure either of these technically counts as a 'holiday', but they were on my list so I felt a duty to watch them.

Daytona 500 started at 6.30pm, so I made sure the children were in bed before it started, rather than the usual 7pm. We'd had an eventful day going swimming and to the park so there was little protest.

There is little interest in NASCAR in the UK so the race was not being shown live on any TV channels, but I located a dodgy internet stream - purely for research purposes of course - and settled down to see what all the fuss was about. The race went ahead as planned, despite a horrific NASCAR crash yesterday in which 33 fans were injured by flying debris, including a wheel and an engine that found their way into the spectators' area. The start of the race was certainly thrilling. 38 cars all racing at ridiculous speeds just inches from each other's bumpers. The screeching of the engines and the roar of the fans made it an entertaining spectacle. As it's on an oval track, the cars only have to turn left, which makes it extremely repetitive but strangely hypotonic and enjoyable. I was instantly hooked. NASCAR was awesome! And then I realised that the race lasts for FOUR HOURS! Four hours going around the same two corners. I felt dizzy after the first four minutes.

The problem, for me, is not so much in the tedium of the actual sport (I can hardly talk as I quite enjoy watching a five day cricket match, which often ends in a draw), but because the enjoyment of motor racing seems to be based solely on the morbid fascination that you are hoping to witness a crash. I don't think I'm alone in thinking this. I obviously don't want to see people injured, let alone killed, but when they are just cars racing around a track (rather than people inside those cars) then the excitement and anticipation is built around the fact that one tiny mistake could end in a catastrophic crash. It's for the same reason that I don't like boxing. People would much rather see a brutal knock-out that a dreary points victory

I lasted the full four hours, though. Rachel made me plug headphones into my laptop after about five minutes and chose to watch some property programme on TV instead. The time passed fairly quickly thanks to several hundred advert breaks, and two giant bags of Doritos. It was also *Tortilla Chip Day*.

To accompany the tortilla chips I made some houmous from some weird-looking black chickpea type things found in today's can. They weren't chickpeas but Rachel couldn't remember what they were. I put them in the food processor with garlic, olive oil, salt and pepper and lemon juice. It was just a quick way to use up the tin, so I was delighted to discover that it tasted better than normal houmous. Listen to me, describing radical houmous experiments. I'm such a boring wanker.

Daytona had left me physically and emotionally exhausted and I knew that I was not going to be able to stay awake for another four hours until the start of the *Academy Awards*. I tried to keep my eyes open, but I slowly drifted off to sleep. I woke up at frequent intervals to a LOT of clapping, and I think I got the gist of what was happening. Absolutely bugger all.

February 25th

Today was *Pistol Patent Day*. The day commemorates the day in 1836 on which Samuel Colt was granted the patent on his Colt Revolver. I'm not a fan of guns; in fact I hate the fucking things. But now is not the time for venting my views on gun control. Now is the time for patenting pistol designs. Woo hoo!

My gun still gives the user the satisfaction of firing a gun, and whomever or whatever the gun is pointing at still has the possibility of being shot. But the risk is greatly reduced, due to the fact that the barrel points to the sky. If the person being fired at is still unable to dodge the falling bullet, then frankly they deserve to get shot.

That's a bullet exiting the gun, by the way. Not a little campfire. I told you I was bad at drawing.

For dinner I cooked a delicious Spaghetti Bolognese using a tin of carrots.

February 26th

I tend to do the majority of the cooking in our house. I'm not a great cook but what I lack in skill I make up for in enthusiasm. I particularly like the challenge of trying to create a meal out of whatever meagre ingredients we have lying around. It makes me feel like I am on *Ready Steady Cook*.

Several years ago, before we had children, the contents of our cupboards and fridge always looked particularly bleak and depressing. I was out one night drinking with a friend and we got back to my house, having not had enough money for a kebab, with the intention of making some feast from the provisions on offer. We opened the fridge to discover that literally all we had was a jar of pickled onions and some milk. In our drunken state, and not to be deterred, we set about creating some form of gourmet meal from these two simple ingredients. We brought a pan of milk up to a gentle simmer and then emptied the pickled onions (with the vinegar) into the pan with the intention of poaching them. I'm not sure why we thought these pickled onions needed poaching, but it seemed like a great idea at the time. The vinegar from the onions reacted with the milk causing it to foam ferociously for a few seconds before reverting back to a gentle simmer.

After a few minutes we decided that the onions were done and fished them out with a slotted spoon. We noticed that the milk had curdled into a congealed gloopy mush. It seemed a shame to waste it, so we plated up our dish of *'poached pickled onions, served with a milk jus'*. The milk had the exact consistency, and almost the same taste, as mozzarella cheese. It was strangely enjoyable, although I am yet to try and replicate the recipe whilst sober.

I later discovered that milk and vinegar are the only two ingredients required in a recipe to make homemade plastic. It was suddenly not so appealing.

Where was I? Ah yes, so I enjoy cooking. Rachel also enjoys cooking but doesn't have the same confidence with ingredients. She would, quite rightly, never mix pickled onions and milk. Last year she cut the stalks off my entire spring onion crop thinking they were chives, and then roasted some potatoes with almost all of the leaves from our bay tree, thinking it was sage. It was certainly one of the most potent meals I've ever tasted.

Today was *National Personal Chef's Day* and Rachel had kindly offered to be my personal chef for the day.

'That's exciting. What are you going to cook for me?' I asked.

'What would you like? The specials today are... er... macaroni cheese, or cauliflower cheese.'

Rachel's repertoire doesn't extend much beyond these two dishes. They are both very good, but to me they are side dishes rather than meals in their own right. Rachel disagrees.

'You chose. I am happy to eat anything,' I said.

'But you don't think cauliflower cheese is a meal, do you?'

'Well... I... it's just that... I do love your cauliflower cheese.'

'I've got an idea. Just you wait. You're in for a treat tonight.'

'What about the cans? You'll need to open a can too and include that in the meal somehow. It's only fair.'

'No problem. Go and sit down. I've got this covered,' she said.

My mouth salivated at the prospect of what she might create. There were so many possibilities. I was ridiculously excited. I could see a lot of stirring going on in the kitchen, and there were at least THREE pots on the go, which was definitely a good sign. I was in for quite the feast. A while later she arrived at the table carrying two plates, both piled high with cauliflower cheese AND macaroni cheese. It was undoubtedly the cheesiest, beigest meal I've ever eaten, but very tasty though. And just when I thought the meal couldn't get any more beige, she brought us each a bowl of banana and tinned custard for pudding.

'But we've already had a tin of custard in Man vs. Can, haven't we? I made those custard tarts, remember?' I said.

'Ah, yes. The custard was buy-one-get-one free.'

February 27th

Today it was *Inconvenience Yourself Day* so rather than turn on my laptop to write this entry, I typed it all on my phone with my own big fat fingers. Most of the words that I am writing now are being auto-corrected to something completely different, so that when I email it to myself to add to the rest of the manuscript, I will have to go through it word for word and try and decipher what it was I was trying to say. It was certainly inconvenient.

The day was made a lot better by a plate of fiery hot chilli con carne, using a can of red kidney beans.

February 28th

My cousins run a craft business and are in the process of launching their own range of greetings cards. They approached me - as a photographer - to ask if I wanted to design a range of cards for them. At first I was extremely eager, and then I realised I had absolutely no idea of what photographs would make attractive greeting cards. When I buy cards, I find it immensely frustrating when a nice looking card is ruined by a horribly cheesy message, or occasion-specific greeting inside. ALL greeting cards should be left blank, in my opinion. Without exception. It's not difficult to write your own *'Happy Birthday'* or *'Congratulations'*, and not only does it make the card seem more personal to the receiver, but it makes the choice of cards so much more diverse for the sender.

It was *Floral Design Day* so it seemed appropriate for me to design the cards based on a floral theme. Everyone likes flowers, right? I walked to the florist at the end of our road and bought some individual flowers. I would tell you what type, but I haven't a clue what they were. There was a pink flower, a blue flower, a sunflower (I know that one) and a giant daisy-type flower. I then photographed each of them in turn and cut the flower shape out in Photoshop before repeating each flower as a pattern across a brightly coloured background in an Andy Warhol style. I was delighted with the results. They were fresh, modern, universal, and appropriate for any occasion. Also, as they were patterns, rather than pictures, they could also be printed as wrapping paper. So versatile. I was on to something here. My cousins were going to be delighted. I could envisage my designs becoming THE latest must have wrapping paper and card design.

I eagerly attached them to an email and sent them off, smug with the knowledge that I was now a 'designer'.

I had a reply soon after:

'Thanks George. We'll be in touch. Ben.'

I've not heard from him since.

Here are my four cards, in all their glory. If you are reading this in paperback or on a black and white device then they are going to look particularly shit. If anyone out there is interested in using these UNBELIEVABLY attractive, universal and extremely multipurpose card designs then please get in touch.

Man vs. Can came to an end today. It finished in style with a can of stewing steak, from which I made an awesome beef, Guinness and mushroom pie, served with mash and peas. Pie and mash is up there as one of my all time favourite dinners, and this was a more than adequate rendition.

It was a fitting tribute to a brilliant challenge. I had no idea that 20 unlabelled cans could have provided me with so much fun, and caused me to cook and try new things that I would never have previously considered; such as homemade fudge, Chimichurri or mushy peas - five ways. I was slightly sad that it had come to an end. Not that I would necessarily miss eating tinned food, but I would certainly miss the excitement of the challenge. The end of Canned Food Month was definitely going to leave a can shaped hole in my life.

MARCH

March 1st

March 1st is confusingly *Dress in Blue Day* AND *Wear Yellow Day*. *Dress in Blue Day* was created by Colon Cancer Alliance to show support and help raise awareness about colon cancer. Whereas *Wear Yellow Day* forms part of *Endometriosis Awareness Month*.

I didn't know too much about Endometriosis, other than it was a female 'thing' and I didn't want to get into a debate about whether it was more or less important than colon cancer *('there's only one way to find out... FIIIIIGGGHHT')*. I had to compromise. I wore a yellow t-shirt and blue trousers.

It was also *Horse Protection Day* as well as *Pig Day*. Could I kill two birds with one stone again and get a pig to protect a horse? It seemed unlikely.

March 3rd

There are probably several George Mahoods in the world, but only two of us feature with any regularity if you Google the name. My photography website and my book have several listings, and then there is the DJ George Mahood who sounds WAY cooler than me. He appears to own an online record store and be the former editor of a music magazine called *Big Daddy*. I occasionally get friend requests on Facebook from other DJs or people that are clearly looking for this George Mahood instead. I have often wondered what he is like. Would we have anything in common? Did he ever wonder what I was like? Probably not, but it was *Namesake Day* so I decided to get in touch.

I found the contact details for his online record store and sent him an email.

Dear George Mahood
My name is George Mahood, too.
It's Namesake Day today, so I thought I would get in touch to say hello. HELLO!
Maybe we could meet for a beer one day?
George Mahood

It was exciting to think about all the fun we could have together and of all the HILARIOUS conversations we would have.
'*Hey, George Mahood. Do you fancy another beer?*'
'*Why yes, thank you very much, George Mahood.*'
'*It's my pleasure, George Mahood.*'
Oh how we would have laughed and laughed and laughed.
It was probably for his own good that he didn't reply.

March 4th

Something was missing from my day-to-day life this week and it was bothering me. I felt like this holiday challenge had stagnated somewhat. I have just been plodding along on a day-by-day basis, lacking in inspiration and enthusiasm. I then realised that I was still in mourning for *Man vs. Can*. The absence of my daily food challenge had sapped my fervour. Despite only being four days since the final can, I had already become lazy with my cooking again. I had resorted to the same old dinners that I made before and I had lost the creative and inventive flare that had been the driving force behind *Man vs. Can*. It was time for another food challenge already.

When I posted the final photo of all of the empty cans on Facebook, lots of people (about six) seemed keen for me to try another challenge and suggested possible scenarios for the next one.

Kris: *'Well done, George. You are a truly inspirational challenger. How about Man vs. Pan next. No oven. No microwave. All done in a pan.'*

Natasha: *'What about if we get hold of someone called 'Pam' and you could cook off against her in the battle of Man vs Pam? We could vote on the winning dish each day. And whoever got the most 'likes' would win that challenge?'*

James: *'Man v Lamb. You get a whole lamb from the butcher and have to find uses for all of it nose to tail.'*

Al: *'Man vs. Spam'*

Damian: *'I think the lamb should come alive. Then you can knit a jumper and kill it as part of the challenge.'*

James (again): *'Maybe George should be present when the lamb is born, getting right in there with those really long rubber gloves that vets wear. Then he has to nurture the lamb, bring it up in his own back garden, name it. Then, once it's big enough, kill it and just wear the pelt like a Neolithic warrior.'*

Andrew: *'How about Man vs Jam & Spam, cooked in a Pan by Pam?'*

Tristan: *'George - you need some serious help mate'*

All of the suggestions were good. Tristan's was particularly apt. But none of them jumped out at me as being 'the one'. As our oven had been broken for a few weeks, most of *Man vs. Can* had been done in a pan, so that ruled out *Man vs. Pan*. I didn't know ANY Pams, let alone a Pam that would be willing to enter a daily food challenge against me. I liked the lamb idea (not the nurturing, killing and wearing the pelt bit), but our freezer isn't big enough to house an entire lamb, and buying it daily from the shops would be very impractical and expensive. I also needed something that fitted into a holiday celebration. February had been *National Canned Food Month*, which was the whole point of *Man vs. Can* in the first place. I checked my listings.

It was *Bell Peppers* and *Broccoli Month* and also *Berries and Cherries Month*. All were potential candidates, but they didn't sound particularly exciting. How many ways are there to cook broccoli? I then noticed that March is also *National Pig Month*. That certainly had potential. I'm not sure that eating a pig is necessarily how a pig would chose to be honoured or celebrated, but the idea did have something going for it. But I faced the same issue that I did with the lamb regarding freezer space. And then, from out of nowhere, the ultimate idea hit me. *Man vs. HAM!* It was PERFECT. Most importantly, it rhymed (sort of).

I wouldn't just use any old packet ham, though. I would buy a proper leg of Iberian smoked ham like they have in tapas bars. They don't have to be kept in the fridge, which solved my space issue, and I could be reasonably sure that the pig had been treated well, up until the point that it had its leg cut off. I was therefore celebrating pigs, as well as eating them. Well, it sounded good in my head, although it looks less convincing when written down.

I phoned a local deli in Northampton and they said they were able to order me one for tomorrow.

March 5th

As soon as I had dropped Layla at school, I headed into town on my bike to pick up my ham. I had completely underestimated the size and weight of it. I managed to squash the big end into my rucksack, with the thin end of the leg poking out of the top. It also came with a 'ham stand' (there is probably a more technical name for it), in order to hold the ham still whilst being thinly sliced. I had to dangle this in a carrier bag from the handlebars and then cycle home with the weight of my rucksack bending me back into an almost horizontal position. It was like I was riding an extremely large recumbent bicycle. My bike's front wheel kept bouncing off the road surface as the heavy load pulled me backwards. I did sporadic wheelies the entire way home.

'What is that, Daddy?' asked Leo.

'It's a ham.'

'That's not ham! Ham comes from a packet. Silly Daddy.'

'Yes, but before that, it actually comes from a pig.'

'Is that a pig?'

'Well it's a bit of a pig. It's a pig's leg,' I said.

'Ugh, that's gross.'

I couldn't leave my ham on the side for the duration of *Man vs Ham* as it had a very potent smell, and I didn't want the cats to eat it. Instead, I cleared out one of the kitchen cupboards in order to provide the ham with its own entire space. It's what the pig deserved.

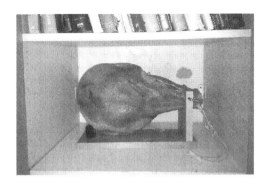

March 6th

The rules were simple: *One ham. One man. One plan.*

I would eat the ham as part of a meal EVERY DAY, until it was all gone.

I don't want to bore you senseless with reports of my dinner each night for the duration, because I am sure many of you would find that extremely tedious. I also don't want those that do like the idea of *Man vs. Ham* to feel like they are missing out on all the fun, so, as a compromise, I will include a picture each day of the ham in various incarnations with a brief title of the dish. If you are vegetarian, then I am very sorry about the rest of this month.

Macaroni cheese with ham, and Greek salad

March 7th

I studied English Literature as part of my degree. Yet I somehow managed to get through the entire three years of my university course without reading a single book. We had to read at least a book a week for each of our English modules, and then we would spend just ONE HOUR in a seminar discussing it. At the start of each seminar, some pretentious young tosser would raise some deep and philosophical bullshit about a tiny insignificant element of the book, that the rest of the class would then be forced to discuss for the duration. The seminar would then end, the book would be quickly forgotten, and we would be required to complete another by the following week.

I used to sit through these seminars dreading that I would ever be asked a direct question. On the occasions that I was, I would utter some vague meaningless drivel about how so-and-so in the book was 'misunderstood' or how the book provided an interesting angle on the 'nature versus nurture' debate, even if it did nothing of the sort. The rest of the group would sit and nod along in agreement.

Towards the end of term, our tutor for the American Literature module decided that we would all take it in turns to do a weekly presentation to the rest of the class on a different book, and an aspect of that book that he chose. For example, discussing materialism in *The Go-between* or prose structure in *On the Road*. I thought my time was up and I was actually going to have to READ a book. Then one week our tutor announced the following seminar's topic:

'Next week I want someone to talk about the first page of *Huckleberry Finn* and how it sets up the rest of the novel.'

My hand was up in the air quicker than a school child needing the toilet.

My presentation went brilliantly. I only read the first page, and made the point that I felt it would taint my judgement of how the start set up the rest of the novel if I knew what happened later.

The tutor said he was impressed by my restraint. Little did he know that it took me most of the week just to finish the first page.

Not that I have anything against *Huckleberry Finn*, or books in general, but I've always felt intimidated by being told what to read, and when to read it by, and then a little intimidated by the expectation of what you are supposed to interpret from a book.

My phobia stems back from GCSE English Literature when we seemed to spend an entire YEAR analysing every goddamn syllable of Wilfred Owen's *Dulce et Decorum Est*. We found depth in that poem that had never even entered Owen's mind.

I bloody LOVE books now. They are awesome. Once I realised that I could choose to read what I liked, when I liked, I discovered that books didn't have to be seen as a chore. Getting my first Kindle a year ago changed everything. I no longer felt obliged to finish reading a book, just because I had started it (please finish this one, though - there's a dramatic twist at the end), and I could dip in and out of several books at the same time. It also meant that I started reading books that I would not have even considered had I been browsing in a book shop. I imagine, for many of you, this book falls into that category for you. If so, then thanks for taking a gamble!

Today was *World Book Day*. Well, in the UK and Ireland, at least. The rest of the world celebrates *World Book Day* on April 23rd (a notable date because - according to the *World Book and Copyright Day* website - '*Cervantes, Shakespeare and Inca Garcilaso de la Vega all died. It is also the date of birth or death of other prominent authors such as Maurice Druon, Haldor K.Laxness, Vladimir*

Nabokov, Josep Pla and Manuel Mejía Vallejo' - no, apart from Shakespeare I haven't heard of any of those either).

World Book Day in the UK and Ireland is a charity event, organised by UNESCO, on which all children in full-time education are given a £1 book token. The token can be spent at any participating bookshop, or, as with Layla's school, a school book sale. Many of the books are priced at £1 so they are technically free. It's a really brilliant idea and Layla was extremely excited about spending her token.

'Daddy, can I buy this one please?' she said, holding up the book she'd chosen after at least 20 minutes of consideration.

'*My Sister the Vampire*? Really? Are you sure that's the one you want?' I said, taking a look at the cover blurb.

'Yes, DEFINITELY!'

'It says it is 'a vampire book for girls who want to read about young love and innocent romance'. I think it might be a bit grownup for you, darling.'

'But it's in a children's book sale,' she argued

'I know, but it says here that it's suitable for children aged 9+. You are 5.'

'Oh, pleeeeeasseee!'

Normally I would have stuck to my instincts and got her to buy something more appropriate, but I realised how my love of books had developed after I had the freedom to read what I wanted. I know these rules don't necessarily apply when you are five, but the book didn't look TOO bad. And if it's suitable for a nine year old to read, then it can't be that inappropriate for a five year old, surely? It's not as if I was buying her *50 Shades of Grey*. Plus, I really wanted to find out what happened with Olivia and Ivy, the vampire twins, when one of them got a new boyfriend.

'Ok,' I said, 'but don't show it to Mummy.'

Microwaved Singapore noodles (from the petrol station), with added ham.

March 8th

My middle name is Meredith. George Meredith Mahood. There, I've said it. Yes, I know that Meredith is a fairly common girl's name. I didn't choose it. I admit I have always been slightly embarrassed about my middle name. Even nowadays when I have to give my full name to someone official I give a slight wince as I say the word and use a slightly muffled voice, which always backfires as I then have to repeat it. I then watch the person who is writing my name stifle a smirk. Even when saying it on the phone, I always hear a muted giggle on the other end of the line.

At school, once people had got bored of the *Georgie Porgie* rhyme, they then moved onto Meredith which provided years of entertainment for them. It's supposedly a Mahood family name, but it is one that has unfortunately died out with me. My dad was an only child, and I decided not to pass on the Meredith moniker to Leo.

But today I am proud of the name. Today I'm glad of being called Meredith. Today is *Middle Name Pride Day*. And, finally, at the age of 33, I genuinely do have pride in my middle name. I wouldn't change it if I could. Yes, it's a stupid name. Yes, it's a girl's name. But at least it's got character. I feel a bit like Johnny Cash's *A Boy Named Sue*. I suppose I should probably thank my dad for the gravel in ma guts and the spit in ma eye.

Middle Name Pride Day was established in 1997 by an American onomatology hobbyist named Jerry Hill. Ironically, Jerry Hill is not quoted with HIS middle name. Ashamed of it are you, Jerry? George Meredith Mahood is very disappointed in you.

Chicken, stuffed with Boursin (other garlic and herb soft cheeses are available), and wrapped in ham.

March 9th

As a non-American, you can't hear the phrase 'fanny pack' without laughing. The American name for a 'bum bag' provides a great deal of amusement to most English speaking nations outside of America. The word 'fanny', of course, is slang for 'vagina', but in America it is slang for bottom. I imagine that most Americans are amused by the term 'bum bag', too. The confusing thing is that they are more commonly worn on the front of the body, rather than the back, so in fact 'fanny pack', but with the British meaning, is actually more accurate.

Today was *International Fanny Pack Day*. I think fanny packs, or bum bags, or whatever you want to call them, are underrated. I know they went out of fashion in the 1980s, but they are incredibly practical. My trouser pockets are always bulging with a phone, wallet and keys (and girl's pants occasionally, but I'll get to that later). A fanny pack would be so much more practical. I'm going to start campaigning for a fanny pack revival. It's time to make fanny packs cool again. How about a range of fanny packs exclusively for men, as an alternative to a Man Bag? Let's call it a *Manny Pack*. That's it! Genius! I think I might be able to retire as the inventor of the Manny Pack.

Oh, bollocks. I've just checked and Manny Packs already exist. I'm too slow again. I'm definitely going to order one for myself, though. No more bulging trousers for me. Oh, behave!

Ham croquettes with aioli.

March 10th

The Christmas tree in the garden had taken a turn for the worst. For most of January and some of February it was looking ok, and still sort of Christmas-tree-like. But then its deep green needles started to turn brown and crisp up. I had to break the news to the children. It was dead.

'Will we bury it?' asked Layla.

'No, I don't think so. People don't tend to bury trees when they die.'

'What will we do with it then?'

'Well, I'll probably just take it to the tip.'

'Oh, that's so sad. Poor tree.'

'Or we could chop it up and burn it?' I suggested.

'A fire in our house?' she asked excitedly.

'Yes, would that be good?'

'AWESOME!' she shouted.

'Yeah! F-F-FIRE!' shouted Leo.

'Yeeeeahhhh!' screamed Kitty, having no idea what she was getting excited about.

Kids sure love fire. We cut the tree up using some broken secateurs and a rusty saw and then had a ceremonial burning in the living room. We have a fireplace, by the way. I'm not stupid.

Ham, egg and chips.

March 11th

'Why don't the taps in the bathroom work?' asked Rachel just before lunch.

'It's *World Plumbing Day* so I thought I would try and fix the taps. They didn't work properly.'

'Now they don't work at all.'

'I know. I'm sorry about that. Water started spurting everywhere so I had to turn the stop tap off to fix them.'

'So what happened about *World Plumbing Day*?'

'I stopped the water spraying everywhere. That counts as plumbing.'

'But it wasn't spraying everywhere before you started. When will we be able to use the bath again? You're off to London for the rest of the day and tomorrow.'

'Don't worry. I'll sort it out as soon as I get back. All of the other taps work fine. Showers are more economical anyway. That's what plumbing has taught me. Do you have any staplers that need filling?'

'What? No. Why?'

'It's *Fill Your Staplers Day*. I've done the broken one in my study, but do we have any others?'

'No,' she said hastily. 'Just go to London.'

I headed off to the station and boarded a train to London. I was going to stay with my friend Ben for the night. Ben was my companion during my Land's End to John O'Groats trip. It had been a while since I had last seen him and I was really looking forward to catching up. I tried to sleep on the train as it was *Napping Day* and finally managed to fall asleep just as the announcer welcomed our arrival to Euston.

I then got another train to Ben's house in Hackney where we ate Ben's 'special' Mexican lasagne and played a board game. Do we know how to party, or WHAT?

The main reason for my visit was that we had tickets to an event in Leicester Square in the evening called *Night of Adventure*. It was organised by adventurer, author, speaker, round-the-world cyclist and hero of mine Alastair Humphreys. The evening consisted of a series of 14 talks by adventurers, including cyclists, sailors, urban explorers and many other inspirational people. I had seen the event mentioned on Twitter and asked Ben if he wanted to come along with me. He jumped at the chance.

'We should be doing these talks about our bike ride,' said Ben in between speakers.

'I don't think our bike ride is quite in the same league as these guys,' I said, terrified at the thought.

'Of course it is. Just because we didn't spend ages planning our trip, or take thousands of pounds worth of equipment, it's still a worthy adventure.'

'Maybe. But what would be the point in us doing it?'

'Think of all the chicks at the after-party,' said Ben with a laugh.

I spat half a mouthful of beer out and glanced around the room which was made up, almost exclusively, of middle-aged men.

'Yeah, good luck with that one, mate.'

We both felt incredibly inspired by the talks and afterwards went and had a few beers in Soho.

'Let's do another bike ride like *Free Country*,' said Ben, grabbing me excitedly by both shoulders.

'But you hated the last bike ride,' I said.

'I didn't. I fucking LOVED it. I know I moaned an awful lot, but it was one of the best things I've ever done. I'd do it all again in a heartbeat.'

'I'd love to do another one, too. It might be a bit difficult with three young children now though. Maybe in a few years when they are all at school.'

'That's fair enough. Are you up for going on some microadventures like they were talking about earlier?' he asked.

A microadventure (or a #microadventure, as they are referred to on social media) is a concept championed by

Alastair Humphreys that promotes the idea that adventures don't have to be well-planned, long-distance, expensive, money-sapping, time-consuming expeditions that happen on the other side of the world. They can still fit around a normal working day. The idea being that although you might work 9-5, that means that you still have the 5-9 which can be fully embraced. A #microadventure might include going for a long walk and camping out, cycling to the coast and sleeping on a beach, or climbing a hill and sleeping out beneath the stars.

'I'm definitely up for doing some hashtag microadventures,' I said.

'Maybe one of them will turn into your next book,' he said.

'I'm not sure one microadventure would warrant a book. It would be more of a pamphlet. I'm actually sort of writing another book at the moment,' I said.

'Seriously? What about?'

I tried to explain the whole concept of *Every Day Is a Holiday* to Ben and did a really bad job of it. The beers certainly hadn't helped, but I also realised that I still don't fully know where I'm going with this challenge, and whether it will ever even make it as far as a book.

'So, give me an example of a day?' he said.

'Well, there's loads. Literally HUNDREDS. There are several different events for each day.'

'Such as?'

'Well, there's... er... let me think...' I said, unable to think of a single one, '...there's *55mph Speed Limit Day* when I had to drive at 55mph all day. And there's... errr... it's really hard to think off the top of my head. It's *Fill Your Staplers Day* today. Do you need any staplers filling?'

'No thanks,' he said. 'It sounds like a bit of a shit book, if I'm honest.'

'I think you are probably right. I'm not just doing it to write a book, though. It's more of a personal challenge because I was just a bit bored with everything and wanted to have some new experiences. If I can write a book about the whole thing then that would obviously be a bonus, but I'm just keen to have a bit of fun for a few months.'

'That's cool. It does sound like a fun idea. I just don't know how the book would work. It might just be a bit disjointed, and, well, a little pointless maybe? Would the days all be connected or would it just be a list of things? "I did this, and then I did that, etcetera, etcetera".'

'I don't know. I guess it probably will be a bit disjointed.'

'You should stick at it though, mate. I'm sure you'll get it to work out.'

'Yeah, I'll definitely see the challenge out. As for the book... who knows? I appreciate your advice though.'

'Anytime!'

'I'm really hungry,' I said. 'Shall we get a kebab?'

'Sounds good. If we get the bus back to Hackney there's a good kebab shop near mine.'

'Do you have any ham at home, by any chance?'

'Yes, why?'

'It's *National Pig Month* and to celebrate I am eating ham every day this month.'

'I'm a little bit worried about you.'

'You're not the first person to say that.'

Shish kebab (with added ham) and chips.

March 12th

I woke up at 7.00am, having gone to bed at 3.00am. I got dressed, folded up the futon and the sleeping bag on Ben's floor and prodded him to say goodbye.

'How come you're leaving this early?' he groaned.

'I'm going to walk to Euston. How long do you think it will take me?'

'What the hell? Why are you going to walk to Euston? It's bloody miles. It will take you at least two hours. Why not just get the tube?'

'I thought it could be my first microadventure,' I said.

'You mean hashtag microadventure. Get it right,' he yawned.

'Yeah, sorry. Do you want to come on this hashtag microadventure with me?'

'Thanks, but I think I'm going to go back to sleep. Great to see you, mate. We'll definitely meet up for a hashtag microadventure soon.'

'Cheers for letting me stay last night. It was awesome to see you. How do I get to Euston?'

'Turn right out the front door. Follow the road all the way to the end, turn left and then keep heading in that sort of direction. You'll find it. It's the big building with all the trains.'

I don't go to London very often, and when I do I'm always desperate to leave as quickly as possible. I get frustrated if I am crossing London in a car because of the traffic. I get claustrophobic crossing London on public transport because of all the people, and I always look and feel like a sad lost tourist.

As I walked through London with the commuters at 7.30am on this Tuesday morning, I found a new love for the city. I had nearly three hours until my train so was in no rush whatsoever. I muddled my way through the quiet backstreets of Hackney, stumbled upon London Fields, and then walked through bustling Broadway Market (although it was not a market day). I bought a chocolate croissant from a bakery and then asked somebody for directions to Euston.

'The nearest underground is just down this road, and then...' he said.

'Sorry, I'm walking,' I interrupted.

'Walking?' he said in surprise, as though it was a completely new concept to him. 'It's a very long way.'

'That's ok,' I said. 'I'm in no hurry.'

'Ok, well I guess you could just follow Regents Canal for most of the way then. You can meet it at the end of this road. Just turn right and keep walking.'

'Perfect. Thank you.'

I followed the canal for a couple of miles and had an unexpected feeling that I finally 'got' London. Yes, people were buzzing all around me. Yes, even in the middle of the park, and along the canal towpath, you could hear the hum of cars, trains and city life. But it was incredibly exciting. Walking along the canal at a fairly slow pace is an amazing way to travel. I know that time is precious to London commuters, but there really is no better way to appreciate your surroundings than at walking speed. The air was cold but the sun was out and burning away the morning mist. The canal was perfectly still and provided a faultless reflection of the vibrant colours of London life.

I reached the end of the canal and then stopped for a quick Sausage and Egg McMuffin (other breakfast sandwiches are available) near King's Cross and arrived at Euston in plenty of time for my train home. I estimate that I probably only walked about six miles. It was certainly not the most exceptional or daring of microadventures, but it was definitely a start, and was a damn fine way to begin my day. This microadventure had allowed me to see a side of London than I had never experienced, and helped me to almost understand for the first time, the magic of the city.

The afternoon was spent in a far less glamorous way. It was *Organize Your Home Office Day*. My home office needed some serious organising. As I have said, I share my study with Kitty, our 18-month old daughter, which is not the greatest of arrangements, and the room is so small that the desk has become a dumping ground for all of my paperwork and camera equipment. I do all my work on a tiny sofa squashed next to the cot. Our WiFi router is downstairs, and for me to get a decent signal to check my email, upload wedding galleries or waste time on the internet, I have to perch on the edge of the sofa with my laptop balanced on my knees. It's not the most ideal working environment.

It was time to clear the desk.

After a couple of hours of organising, which involved moving the piles of stuff from the desk to the sofa, I set up my laptop on the nice clear work surface. I then tried to do some work, and remembered that I couldn't get any WiFi signal from my desk, which was why I had relocated to the sofa in the first place. I then moved all of the piles of stuff back onto the desk and resumed my position on the sofa. It was a pretty unproductive afternoon.

Sea bass wrapped (sort of) in ham, with patatas bravas and green beans.

March 13th

Superstitions are horrible things. We know they are little more than mythical traditions, but there is still something sinister about them. I dropped a mirror in the sink a year ago and a part of me did think that maybe the following seven years would be filled with bad luck.

What purpose do superstitions serve other than to distress people? Admittedly, there are some positive superstitions, but most seem to exist solely to cause anxiety. Take walking under a ladder, for example. The most innocent and natural of acts is considered to be bad luck. It can't be a health and safety issue, as it seems far more dangerous walking around a ladder than under it. Surely stepping out in front of a car as you negotiate a ladder is more of a danger than having a wet sponge dropped on your head as you pass underneath?

Religion is partly to blame. A ladder leaning against a wall forms a triangle with the ground. This triangle is said to represent the Holy Trinity, and walking through this sacred area desecrates God.

National Open An Umbrella Indoors Day was my chance to rebel against superstitions.

This superstition is thought to stem from the umbrella's sacred relationship with the sun. It is therefore considered an insult to open an umbrella indoors.

It felt liberating to hold an open umbrella indoors. I pranced around the room like Gene Kelly would have done, had he had to balls to open an umbrella inside. I was mid twirl when the edge of the umbrella caught a vase on the mantelpiece and sent it crashing to the floor. I have a habit of smashing Rachel's vases. By accident, of course.

'What was that?' called Rachel in her teacher voice from upstairs.

'Just a beer bottle. I'll clear it up.'

'Hmmm. It better not have been another one of my vases.'

Fish, chips, mushy peas... and ham.

March 14th

Breakfast - Eggs Benedict 'ham-style'.

MOTH-er Day was one that I couldn't pass up.

A moth-er is someone who likes or collects moths. I had never met a moth-er before. A quick call to a local moth group (yes, such groups do exist), put me in touch with a local moth-er. I gave him a call and he agreed to let me go and see his moth collection.

My initial excitement soon wore off when I remembered the moth-collecting serial killer Buffalo Bill in *The Silence of the Lambs*. Even Buffalo Bill might have been a member of a moth group. I told Rachel where I was going and asked her to call Clarice Starling if I was gone for more than two hours.

Jonathan Greaver, the moth-er, was a lovely man, and he fortunately didn't try to skin me or throw me into a pit, which was a relief. He was in his early 70s and lost his wife to cancer five years ago. He'd had a small collection of moths that he bought from an antique fair many years ago, but had only become a serious collector following the death of his wife. They were kept tidily in display boxes, and a few were framed on the wall. His house was bright, clean and uncluttered. Quite the opposite of what I had expected from a moth-er.

'Why do you like moths so much?' I asked.

'They're really fascinating creatures, and the fact that they are nocturnal makes them so much more mysterious than butterflies,' he said.

'Butterflies are much prettier though,' I said, hoping I wouldn't offend him.

'Nonsense! Butterflies are the whores of the air,' he said with a cheeky smile. 'Besides, beauty is only wing-deep. Sorry, that's just a favourite joke of mine.'

I humoured him with a laugh.

'If moths are so obsessed with lights, then why don't they just live during the day like butterflies?' I asked. 'Surely they would be much happier?'

'Ah! Very good question. When you see a moth fluttering around a light bulb, it is not because they like the light as such, but because they use moonlight to help them navigate, and an artificial light confuses their navigational sense.'

Aside from the serial killer associations, I had anticipated the fluttering of moths in all corners of the house, and boxes of chrysalises stacked everywhere. Jonathan treated mothing like collecting stamps, or football stickers. No mess, no hassle, and no holes in clothes. They even play swapsies at Moth-er Club.

'So how many moths do you have in your collection?' I asked.

'Oooh, I'd say about 80 different types. It's only a relatively small collection, considering there are thousands of different varieties.'

'Where do you get them from?' I asked, expecting him to tell me that he scoured woodlands at night with a torch and a jam jar.

'eBay mostly,' he said.

I said goodbye to Jonathan and left with a whole new respect for moths and moth-ers.

Second Life is an online virtual world in which you create an avatar and then interact with others, build and trade homes and commodities, socialise, explore, and take part in all sorts of activities. I didn't know much about it, but the idea fascinated, confused, scared and bored me in equal measures. My dad once had to attend a seminar that took place in *Second Life* as part of his Open University degree. When he arrived (virtually) at the designated place, the room was full, and he and a group of other 'virtual' students, had to hang around on the street corner outside the building. He went back to the venue the following day and was able to enter the room and see the aftermath of the seminar with the used flipchart complete with annotations from the discussions that he had missed. The whole concept is very bizarre. I also read about a case of a woman who filed for divorce after catching her husband's *Second Life* character having an affair with another character. The woman even went as far as hiring a virtual private detective to investigate her husband's antics. He went on to virtually marry his virtual mistress, and his real-life wife then met a new partner via another online role-playing game - *World of Warcraft* - and they all lived happily ever after. Virtually.

It was *Pi Day* - the mathematical constant - and a big *Pi Day* celebration was planned at the Exploratorium in San Francisco. I couldn't afford to fly over for the occasion but I noticed on their website that they were also hosting a special *Pi Day* event on *Second Life*. It looked intriguing so I downloaded the *Second Life* software and chose my avatar - a well-built black man - and a few minutes later I walked (virtually, of course) into a large conference room with a giant *Pi* sign on the wall.

The Exploratorium's *Pi* website promised *'exhibits, fireworks, a sky dancer and DJ'* but I seemed to be either too early or - more likely - too late as the building was deserted. Techno music blasted from my computer as I tried to get my avatar to explore the building. Being unfamiliar with the controls - or computer games in general, for that matter - my avatar did a mixture of bunny-hops, erratic hand gestures and crab-like side-steps around the room. It's a good job that nobody was there to witness it. To make matters worse, I received a notification when I installed the software saying that my avatar's clothing was still being downloaded, so he was strutting his stuff half-naked.

I had seen enough of the Exploratorium, but I was sure there must be more to *Second Life*. I wanted to go somewhere exciting, so I typed *'New York City'* into the destination bar, and I was warned that *'this location contains adult content'*. HELL YEAH! That's more like it! Seconds later I was standing on a street in virtual Manhattan with a different techno track blaring out of my speakers. The streets were deserted. Where was everyone? I wondered if *Second Life* is perhaps 'sooo last year' and whether everyone is playing *Candy Crush* instead these days. I headed to the nearest building - which was called *Erotic Xstacy Estate* - and it took me nearly ten minutes to get my well-built black persona to navigate through the revolving door, still dressed in just my vest and pants. I was greeted with yet another empty room, save for a lone barman. I ordered a bag of crisps to celebrate *Potato Chip Day* and then sat at a nearby piano where my character demonstrated no musical ability whatsoever.

Despite not seeing a single person, other than the barman, I was still slightly intrigued by my *Second Life* experience. But I was adamant that I didn't want to get sucked in. I waste far too much of my first life on the computer, and I don't have time for another. To resist the temptation to pursue it, I quit the application and removed it from my computer.

I had far more exciting reasons to celebrate my first life. It was *Steak and Blowjob Day*, which was - needless to say - the highlight of the challenge so far.

Steak, homemade chips and salad... and ham.

March 15th

The *Ides of March* always falls on March 15th and is best known, in modern times, as the anniversary of the date on which Gaius Julius Caesar was killed in 44 BC. The assassination plot of the Roman General is of course most famously known from William Shakespeare's play. According to the ancient historian Flavius Eutropius, more than 60 people took part in the assassination and he was stabbed 23 times.

Somewhat insensitively, March 15th is also *Brutus Day*, in recognition of the man widely claimed to be integral to the assassination plot. The idea of *Brutus Day* is to recognise that betrayal, dirty politics and back stabbing (not literal back stabbing, though) are as common in our modern lives as they were in Ancient Rome.

Having worked in an office for many years, I can confirm that this is the case. During my time working in many different office jobs I witnessed more back stabbings, attempts at usurpation and dirty political tactics than in the rest of Ancient Rome combined. It was brutal.

Being self-employed, any betrayal, dirty politics and back stabbings take place in my own head. But they still do happen. I have been known to talk about myself behind my own back on many occasions. It's only a matter of time before I file an official complaint.

Pickled onions wrapped in ham and served on a bed of Pringle.

March 16th

The legend of St Urho was invented by a Finnish-American named Richard Mattson in 1956. I had never heard of him before today. St Urho, that is, not Richard Mattson. Although, I had never heard of him either. *St Urho's Day* was created on March 16th in a deliberate attempt to upstage the celebration of the more famous Saint Patrick the following day.

The legend of St Urho - the patron saint of the Finnish vineyard worker - states that he drove away all of the grasshoppers from Finland using the incantation *'Heinäsirkka, heinäsirkka, mene täältä hiiteen!'* which translates (I think, as my Finnish is just a little bit rusty) as *'Grasshopper, grasshopper, go from hence to Hell!'*. He is credited with saving the Finnish grape crops. This was all pre-ice age, presumably, when Finland actually had any grape crops.

St Urho has gained a bit of a cult following in the USA, Canada and even his 'native' Finland where he has a statue in his honour. Ironically, 82.5% of the Finnish population is connected to the Lutheran Church, which does not recognise the feasts of Saints.

To celebrate this mythical Finnish-American hero I was to stand on top of a hill dressed in green (to represent the grasshoppers) and chant the chant. After the grasshoppers dispersed I was then required to change into royal purple (presumably to represent the grapes). It probably didn't have the same effect when standing on my own in a wet and windy Northampton park, but I gave it a damn good go. It was the second time in a few weeks that I had to stand in the rain in a Northampton park chanting a weird chant. I'm going to get a bit of a reputation around here. If the grapes of Northampton (surely there must be some) have a particularly good year, then it will all be down to me.

Broad beans with ham.

March 17th

St Patrick, the patron saint of Ireland, is one of the world's most popular saints. According to legend, he drove away all the snakes from Ireland. So how do we celebrate all of his good work? By getting shitfaced on Guinness and Irish whiskey, of course. It's what he would have wanted.

The horrendous weather over the last few days had given us all cabin fever. Rachel and I decided to kit the kids out in their waterproofs and head to the local park. We were the only people there. We played on the swings, slides and roundabout (the kids did, too) for half an hour and then headed home via the local pub so that we could toast St Patrick.

A little over a year ago, Ye Olde England opened at the end of our road. It was an independently run pub serving beer, cider and wine from local breweries. They had no big pub sign, and a small note on the door warned customers that *'sorry we do not sell lager here'*. Instead of quiz machines, the long wooden tables were scattered with Scrabble, Monopoly, Jenga and packs of cards. And instead of a traditional bar of any sort, the beer was served through a hatch in the wall; a bit like a school tuck shop. It sounded like my ideal pub, but I didn't know how it would fit into Northampton's largely 'laddish' drinking scene, and its location, directly opposite one of the town's most popular drinking spots, didn't work in its favour. I confess that I did have my doubts about whether the pub would survive for long.

I am delighted to say that I was completely wrong. Ye Olde England has been incredibly popular and is always busy. It often opens for breakfast, serves lunch, and has expanded downstairs with more seating and a proper bar - although the tuck shop still serves drinks upstairs, too.

It was therefore a big surprise to see the pub completely empty on *St Patricks Day* - one of the busiest drinking days of the year, and also a Sunday. We got a large table by the door, in case we needed to make a rapid escape, due to an errant child. I soon discovered why the pub was so quiet. They don't serve Guinness. They are probably the only pub in Northampton - possibly the world - not to serve it. As Guinness is not produced by a micro-brewery, Ye Olde England were not interested, and I respected them even more for this. Instead I settled for a pint of Solstice Stout - which, although not Irish, was the closest equivalent, but brewed by Hoggleys Brewery in Northampton. We raised a glass to St Patrick and I enjoyed my pint whilst wearing my lime-green hoodie, looking like the world's worst Irish leprechaun.

Sausages, mash, beans... and ham.

March 18th

Awkward Moments Day is a chance to celebrate and recognise those times in life that you find uncomfortable or embarrassing. They happen fairly frequently to me.

There has been a trend over the last few years for people to post a Facebook status or a tweet that begins *'That awkward moment when...'* and then the person mentions a not very awkward moment. I'm not quite sure why, but I find it one of the most irritating things in the world. It's not even a complete sentence. What about that awkward moment? Tell me how it affected you? Don't just mention it, you moron.

I own a t-shirt with the simple message 'Well, this is awkward' on it. I got it free with a book but have never worn it. If ever there was an occasion to wear it, *Awkward Moments Day* was undoubtedly it. But, as the famous saying goes, *'wearing an awkward t-shirt, does not an awkward day make'*. Actually that's not a famous saying at all. I just made it up, and it sounds more like something Yoda would say.

I wore it all day, despite the cold, which was fairly awkward in itself, but I knew I wouldn't have to plan too hard for an awkward moment to present itself. I could not have predicted the awkward moment that would occur.

I was at the supermarket, just deciding whether to buy *Thomas the Tank Engine* or *Hello Kitty* pasta shapes, when I looked up to see a man perusing the soups, a little further down aisle three. He was wearing a grey t-shirt. But it was not just any old grey t-shirt. It was a t-shirt with the phrase *'Well, this is awkward'* printed on it. It was identical to mine. I stared at him in disbelief. He looked up, mulligatawny in hand, and then spotted me and my t-shirt. We both looked at each other, eyebrows raised, clumsy smiles, and gave a self-conscious point to our own t-shirts. Not a word was spoken, and we both hurried off in different directions. Well, that was awkward.

Who was that guy? Was it just a coincidence that he was wearing his t-shirt too, on such a cold day? Maybe he too was celebrating *Awkward Moments Day*? Maybe he is celebrating ALL of the holidays? Maybe he is writing a book about it? Maybe his book will be better than mine? *'That wouldn't be hard,'* I can hear you mutter. Fine! Go and read his then! See if I care (I do!).

I paid for the pasta shapes and left the shop as quickly as I could.

Thomas the Tank Engine pasta shapes, with added ham.

March 19th

There is a Spanish mission in the town of San Juan Capistrano in Orange Country, California that has been used as a religious and military outpost since 1776. Part of the mission - Serra's Chapel - is the oldest building in California still in use today. Despite the thousands of people who have occupied the mission over the years, the one constant residents - even despite its now ruinous state - are a flock of American cliff swallows that nest below the mission's eaves and archways during the warm spring and summer. Every winter they make the epic 6000 mile trip to Goya, Argentina.

Today was *Swallows Return to San Juan Capistrano Day*. Every year, almost to the day, the swallows make their return journey to the mission. The city thoughtfully celebrates their arrival with a large parade and street party.

In recent years the number of swallows returning has decreased. Reasons suggested for this are the reduction in the number of insects at the nearby rivers on which they feed, and an increase in development of the area giving them more options for places to nest. Having watched videos of the parade on YouTube, I think it's extremely likely they have been put off by the racket. A steel band, fog horns and cheering crowd would be enough to encourage anyone to settle elsewhere. Nobody likes an over-enthusiastic welcome party.

Tagliatelle with mushrooms, spinach and ham.

March 20th

Birthday breakfast - scrambled eggs on toast, with crispy ham.

March 20th was one of the busiest days of the year so far: *Atheist Pride Day*, *Bed-in For Peace Day*, *Great American Meat Out Day*, *International Astrology Day*, *Kick Butts Day*, *Kiss Your Fiancée Day*, *National Jump Out Day*, *National Native HIV Awareness Day*, *Proposal Day*, *National Agriculture Day*, *Persian New Year*, *Snowman Burning Day*, *Vernal Equinox*, *Won't You Be My Neighbour Day* and *Extraterrestrial Abductions Day*.

I didn't know where to start. Fortunately, there was one other important event to celebrate which made the rest of the events insignificant. Rachel's birthday.

'What would you like to do today?' I asked. 'We could bed-in for peace all day, like John and Yoko did.'

'I would love to do that. I don't think John and Yoko had to do their 'bed in' with a 3 year-old and a 1 year-old, though.'

'True. We could burn a snowman? Kick some butt? Read about extraterrestrial abductions? Go to a farm for *Agriculture Day*?'

'Let's go to the ffffaaaarm,' said Leo proudly, now that he can say the 'f' sound.

'Ffffaaaarm,' repeated Kitty.

'It is *National Jump Out Day*, too,' I said. 'We're supposed to encourage the kids to be more active.'

'Ffffarm sounds good to me then,' said Rachel.

'Yey, we are going to the farm,' shouted Layla.

'Ah, no, not you I'm afraid, sweetie. You've got to go to school,' I said.

'But that's so unfair. You get to do all of these fun things when I'm at school,' she sobbed.

'I know it doesn't seem fair. But before you went to school we used to do fun things all the time with you. We still do loads of fun things with you. But it's not fair for Leo and Kitty to miss out just because you are at school. We'll do something fun when you get back from school.'

'Like what, Daddy?'

'We'll make a giant snowman out of paper. How does that sound?'

'Ok,' she conceded.

After dropping Layla at school - a treat in itself, as we always walk (the lucky girl) - we drove to a farm/indoor play centre the other side of Milton Keynes. We fed lambs, stroked rabbits, petted goats and marvelled at Highland cattle. I got a friction burn down the length of my left leg from one of the big slides, but the day was a great success and Rachel thoroughly enjoyed her celebration of *National Agriculture Day*.

Snowman Burning Day marks the change in the seasons from winter to spring. The holiday was first created in 1971 by the Unicorn Hunters - a campus club at Lake Superior State University. Every year they have a symbolic burning of a giant paper snowman to welcome in the spring. The winter has been uncharacteristically miserable so I was more than willing to see the back of it. I also built a giant (well, fairly small) paper snowman with Layla, Leo and Kitty once Layla was home from school.

'Right, now it's time to BURN IT!' I announced.

'What do you mean, Daddy? We're not going to burn it,' said Layla. 'We've only just made it.'

'Yes we are. It's *Snowman Burning Day*,' I said, realising I had forgotten to mention this fairly crucial detail in my plans.

Many tears followed, but these soon dispersed when they saw the flames. First the Christmas tree, and now the snowman; both issues resolved by fire.

In the evening my parents came over to babysit and Rachel and I went out for dinner to celebrate her birthday with her sister and husband. We had chosen a tapas restaurant, and in the spirit of *Great American Meat Out Day* we ordered 12 different dishes, mostly meat; slow-roast pork belly, Spanish morcilla sausage, chorizo, meatballs, steak, lamb, chicken and of course some Spanish ham. It felt so wrong eating ham that wasn't mine (I had also been unfaithful with my ham eating when I stayed with Ben in London, but I was too drunk to care then). I felt so dirty but it tasted so good. I later owned up to my ham affair on Facebook. The critics were out in force once again.

James: *Strike this from the records. I, for one, will not be an enabler to your sordid ham infidelity George.*
Owen: *Traitor*
Jimmy: *Pervert*

March 21st

'Which one of our children is your favourite?' I asked Rachel.

'What do you mean? I love them all the same.'

'Yes, I know, but one of them must be your favourite.'

'Of course not. Why? Do you have a favourite?'

'No, but it's *Absolutely Incredible Kid Day*. That's 'kid' not 'kids'.'

'Well then you'll have to decide. It's got nothing to do with me.'

I couldn't choose either, but I then discovered that I didn't need to. *Absolutely Incredible Kid Day* is a letter-writing campaign day during which adults are encouraged to write letters of love and support to their children. I didn't need to decide which of my children was the MOST incredible. I just needed to write to them to tell them what a most incredible kid they each were.

Layla writes me cards and letters all the time, thanking me for something, or, more likely, saying sorry for something. To be fair, almost all of the time they are written just *'To Mummy'* before Rachel kindly prompts her to try and squash in an *'and Daddy'* on the edge of the page. Still, it's the thought that counts.

I have never really written to my children. Mostly because two of them can't read. Although, I know they would all love to receive a letter. During a break in the wedding that I was photographing, I wrote each of them a letter, telling them how incredible I thought they were, and rather than just giving the letters to them, I posted them. In an actual post-box. Despite the speed and convenience of emails, text messages and phone calls, there is still nothing more exciting than receiving a proper letter from someone. It was a really enjoyable experience and something that I plan to do more often.

Club sandwich with chicken and ham.

March 22nd

It was *International Goof-off Day* today and I strongly considered goofing off the rest of this challenge. For the first time I really felt like I had taken it as far as I could. My holiday mojo had gradually disappeared. It wasn't going quite as I planned and I seemed to have become more preoccupied with ham and canned food than anything else, which was never something I envisaged when it began.

I decided to phone Ben to see what he had to say. Ben is one of the most honest, genuine people that I know and he always has a habit of saying the right thing. It might not necessarily be what you want to hear but it's usually right.

'Do you remember that holiday challenge I was doing?' I said.

'Oh yeah, that thing about filling staplers? How's it going?'

'Not great, to be honest. I'm struggling to find the motivation to continue.'

'Really? Why?'

'I don't know. I think maybe you were right. It's all just a bit pointless really. I shouldn't have bothered starting it in the first place.'

'Did I really say that? I didn't mean it. I was only joking. You can't give up on it now.'

'I don't know if I can stick at this one.'

'Come on, man up, you big gaylord. If you can drag that stupid bike from Land's End to John O'Groats then you can definitely finish this challenge. I have every faith in you.'

'It's just that sometimes I find myself just writing about some completely irrelevant and pointless anecdote that leads nowhere but I just keep on writing and then it tends to peter out into absolutely nothing. It's not even in the remotest bit interesting or funny.'

'Yes, I've heard you tell plenty of stories like that.'

'Cheers for the support, mate!'

'I'm only kidding. Anyway, I think I can help you out with that problem.'

'Really?'

'Definitely. I learnt a technique for that recently that can save you when you get into that sort of situation.'

'What is it?'

'Well, whenever you are telling someone a story and you realise that it hasn't worked out how it sounded in your head and you can tell the person is getting bored and will be disappointed by the ending, you just end the story with the words: *'...and then I found fifty quid!'*

I laughed at the absurdity of it.

'And then I found fifty quid?' I repeated.

'Yes, it's genius. It can render even the most boring and mundane of stories to be really exciting and interesting. It has saved me on many occasions since I learnt it. You should definitely try it.'

'Haha, thanks. I'll bear that in mind. I appreciate the advice. Thanks very much. I'll try and stick at it a bit longer and see how I get on.'

'You'd better. Don't let me down, Dordie Wardie.'

'You said you wouldn't call me that anymore.'

'Sorry, Dord. What holiday is it today anyway?'

'It's *International Goof-off Day*.'

'Sounds like a great one. Well, Happy *International Goof-off Day* to you. See you soon, mate.'

Ham and chorizo potato rosti.

March 23rd

'So, today is *Puppy Day*,' said Rachel. 'Does that mean we can get a puppy?'

'Yes!' shouted Layla. 'Are we getting a puppy? Can we, Daddy? Can we? Can we?'

'We want a PUPPY!' said Leo.

'PUPPY!' shouted Kitty.

'I wish we could get a puppy but I don't think we've really got the room or time for one at the moment, though,' I said.

'Puppies don't take up much space though. They're really small,' said Layla.

'Yes, but they then turn into dogs, which are generally much bigger,' I said.

'It depends on the breed,' said Rachel. 'They don't have to be that big.'

'We are not going to get a puppy, I'm afraid,' I said.

'Oooooh. That's not fair,' said Leo.

'Meany Daddy,' said Layla.

'Meany,' laughed Kitty, poking me in the leg.

I've never had a dog, but I love the idea of having something that wants to go out for a run or a walk in the park every day. Actually, I've got three people that want to do that. But they soon get tired, cold, hungry, or a combination of all three. A dog wouldn't complain or whine nearly as much as children do.

I seriously debated celebrating puppy day in the ultimate way. But I knew that an impulse decision like that wouldn't be fair on the dog. In order to consider it properly I found an online quiz on *dogtime.com* called *'Am I ready for a dog?'* and Rachel and I answered the 15 questions about our lifestyle and expectations honestly and realistically. The results came in.

Are you ready for a dog?

You're close, but not quite ready.

Getting a dog requires a little more work than you may have expected, but your lifestyle needs only a few minor adjustments before you're truly ready.

'Does it say what those adjustments are?' asked Rachel.

'No, it doesn't. Maybe by the end of this holiday project we can take the quiz again and see if anything has changed.'

'Are you really going to take advice from an online quiz?' she asked.

'Well, it's not just any old quiz. It's a proper, honest evaluation on an official-looking dog website,' I said.

'So you agree with it that we are not responsible enough to own a dog?'

'Well, yes, if that's what the results say.'

'Then how on earth are we somehow able to look after three young children?' asked Rachel with her eyebrows raised.

'Perhaps we should have taken one of these quizzes before having children, too,' I said with a smirk, sensing I'd won the argument.

'Perhaps I should have taken an online quiz before marrying you,' said Rachel with a grin that confirmed that she was victorious.

It was also *Near Miss Day* which signifies the date in 1989 when a huge asteroid nearly collided with earth. Impact would have had the same force as 40,000 hydrogen bombs and created a crater the size of the District of Columbia and devastated everything in a 100 mile radius.

It passed within 500,000 miles of Earth. According to NASA this is considered a near miss.

Not getting a puppy because of an internet quiz? Now that was a near miss.

Paella (aka packet of Batchelors Savoury Rice - bit rank) with added ham, chorizo and stuff.

March 24th

Today I was supposed to be taking part in the Oakley 20 - a 20-mile running race around the hilly Bedfordshire countryside. Some running events offer a souvenir t-shirt as a reward for taking part. Some offer a hat or a sweatband. The Oakley 20 gives competitors a HOODIE! This is genuinely the only reason that I enter the event. I have taken part for the last two years and the hoodies have become my clothing of choice for pretty much the entire winter. These hoodies are not just your average hoodies, though. Bedford Harriers, who organise the race, are trendsetters in the world of fashion. They like to be bold with their colour choices. In 2011 they went for a vibrant lime-green colour - the one I wore on *St Patricks Day*. It made me feel ill to look at when I first saw it, but I grew to love it and soon afterwards all the high-street stores were stocking lime-green clothing. Then in 2012, they introduced a bright fluorescent orange hoodie, which again became the high-street colour of the year (probably).

Apart from the hoodie, I was dreading the actual race. The furthest I have run since last May is 6.5 miles. Last year the Oakley 20 nearly killed me, and I had to walk most of the way, promising myself that I would never enter another long-distance run ever again. But the lure of the hoodie was too great, and when the closing date for applications loomed I sent off my payment and planned to get fit. Due to a combination of bad weather, too much work, children, celebrating holidays, writing this book, but most of all laziness, the training didn't happen and I got more and more unfit. I had a horrendous cold too, but still planned on doing the run, even if it ended up being more of a walk. Such was the appeal of the hoodie. This year's design was kept a closely guarded secret and I needed to finish the race to find out what this season's trend-setting colour would be.

I woke on the morning of the race to one of the most exciting text messages I have ever received:

Bedford Harriers regrets to advise that the Oakley 20 has been cancelled. Prevailing weather conditions have made the run route and its environs unacceptably perilous.
The memento hoodies will be mailed to all entrants.

I could not have hoped for a better result. Not only did I not have to run 20 miles, but more importantly, I was still getting the hoodie.

I am trying to think of a way to tie this momentous occasion into *National Chocolate Covered Raisins Day, World Tuberculoses Day* or *Palm Sunday* but I am struggling. I just wanted to share this exciting news with you.

Palm Sunday is the Christian festival that commemorates Jesus' entry into Jerusalem. It was customary to cover the path of somebody considered worthy of the highest honour. The palm branch symbolised, in different cultures, triumph, victory and eternal life.

I consider Rachel worthy of the highest honour, but she didn't take too kindly to me laying a branch that I found in the garden in front of her each time she tried to walk around the house.

'Can't you just go and run 20 miles anyway,' she said.

Pancakes filled with mushrooms, cheese and ham, with spicy tomatoes.

March 25th

Tolkein Reading Day? Haven't we already had *J.R.R. Tolkein Day*? It seems a bit egotistical for him to have another day already, and we're not yet a quarter of the way through the year. Oh well, I don't make the rules.

Last time, I read The Hobbit with some chocolate covered cherries. Today I read The Hobbit (it's the only Tolkein book I own) with some pecans. It was *Pecan Day*.

It was also *Våffeldagen* - Waffle Day. *Våffeldagen* is a Swedish holiday during which people get out their waffle irons and make waffles served with jam and whipped cream. This day came about because of a mistake. The original Christian celebration was called *Vårfrudagen*, which is *Lady Day*. Somewhere along the line it was mistranslated and the Swedes started celebrating waffles instead of ladies. I can't really blame them.

I was feeling smug because we own two waffle iron inserts that came with a cheese toastie maker. They have never been used but I had saved them for a day when they would come in useful and BY GOLLY that day had arrived. I located the inserts but then struggled to find the actual toastie machine.

'Do you know where the toastie maker is?' I asked Rachel.

'In the cupboard, where it usually is?'

'Sorry, not the new one. The one that the waffle inserts fit into?'

'What that gross thing which leaked grease everywhere?'

'Yes.'

'We threw it away years ago. It was disgusting.'

'Did we? Then why do we still have the waffle inserts?'

'You tell me. I've always wondered what those were for.'

Instead, I cooked potato waffles and served them with jam and cream. They were surprisingly good and it turned out potato waffles are waffely versatile. I'm surprised they never mentioned jam and cream as a serving suggestion in the adverts.

Late night snack - gherkins filled with ham, cheese and broken crackers. Don't judge me.

March 26th

Finally, after enduring three months of celebrating what other people think I should celebrate, I had the opportunity to create my own day. Today was *Make Up Your Own Holiday Day*.

The one thing I've noticed during this experiment is that almost all of the holidays are based around the daytime. A significant proportion of each day is obviously night-time but very little consideration is given to the night-time hours when it comes to holiday celebrating. Admittedly, it's quite difficult to celebrate a holiday when you are asleep, but still.

I enjoy the night-time. My days are usually fairly full on, and the evenings are therefore even more important as I get the chance to sit down, watch rubbish TV and do absolutely nothing. I always want this part of the day to last as long as possible, so regularly stay up much later than I should.

The night-time should be celebrated more. Think of all those potential hours which are wasted with sleep. Think of what we could achieve by staying up all night, if only for one night a year. You would, in a sense, gain an extra day. I decided I would create a holiday when people are encouraged to miss their regular night's sleep and instead, for one night of the year only, stay up all night. I would call it *Stay Up All Night Night*.

But when would my holiday take place? I liked the idea of it being commemorated on my birthday so that in years to come people could talk about the holiday's 'founder'. But it was also unfair to expect people to stay up all night on a weekday when they have work the next day. As a compromise, I decided to make it a 'moveable feast' and it could be celebrated on the second Saturday of May, therefore always falling near to my birthday.

I did some extensive research (Google) and discovered that you don't necessarily have to register your day anywhere for it to become a 'day'; you simply need to declare it. But unless it is recognised by other organisations, then nobody will find out about it - which is really the whole point of a holiday anyway. There seems to be one main organisation - *Chase's Calender of Events*, which was established in 1957 by two brothers, William D. Chase, a publisher and journalist, and Harrison V. Chase, a social scientist from Florida. They decided to create a single reference source for calendar dates and holidays.

The submission process was fairly simple but it included fields like the holiday's official website, and the origin. There was only one thing for it. I had to create a website and make it look official. I built my photography website myself, after learning how to use some web design software but it took me months and months, and I managed to create it more by trial and error rather than skill. The whole site is so clumsily built that I haven't dared touch it since. I tried updating the photos a couple of years ago, but the entire thing went a bit wonky so I decided not to meddle with it.

I took a photo of myself with matchsticks propping open my eyes and then added it to a hastily built page and included my day's new slogan *'Night is the new day'*, which I was extremely proud of until I discovered that it is also the name of a Katatonia album from 2009.

I then added a brief blurb about the holiday and included a 'gallery' that had precisely zero photos in it, and I was ready to go. I filled in all the details and clicked 'submit' and *Stay Up All Night Night* was official.

Ham, mozzarella and sun-dried tomatoes.

March 27th

The only music my family listened to when I was growing up was The Beatles, Chris de Burgh and country music. Until I discovered Michael Jackson at the age of eight, that was all I knew. I don't mean to suggest I was the first to discover Michael Jackson. I'm fairly sure others had spotted his potential before I did.

I still have a love for all of this music today (Chris de Burgh only in secret), but it is country music that has had the biggest effect on me. It inspired me to learn to play the guitar, it inspired me to sing in a band when I was a teenager and it inspired me to spend nine months driving around small-town America with a friend after I left university. Driving across America took this love of country music to a different level. Listening to local radio in the Southern United States, we were treated to a constant stream of country songs during our every waking moment.

I even wooed my wife Rachel by inviting her to watch Kenny Rogers at London's Royal Albert Hall many years ago. We were the youngest in the audience by about 30 years. It was all going so well and then, halfway through the support act, the sound was cut and a red light started flashing at the side of the stage. A public announcement told us that we all needed to evacuate the building. We all assembled on the edge of Hyde Park, before being told that there had been a bomb scare and the concert was cancelled. We never did get to see Kenny Rogers as it was the last date of his tour and he buggered off back to Texas. But even this didn't halt my love of country music.

Country music is notorious for its slightly corny lyrics and often absurd song titles; mostly concerning the themes of love and loss, hardship and despair.

It was *Quirky Country Music Song Titles Day* and a chance for me to relive some of the classics. A particular favourite of mine that I remember from our US road trip was *My Wife Ran Off With My Best Friend and I Sure Do Miss Him.*

Then there is the all-time classic *Kissing You Goodbye*, by John Denver, which isn't particularly funny as a title on its own, but when heard in the context of such a sombre and beautiful song, it is one of the finest lyrics in musical history:

'*Get your tongue out of my mouth because I'm kissing you goodbye.*'

These are some of my other favourites titles that I unearthed::

I Sold A Car To A Guy Who Stole My Girl, But It Don't Run So We're Even.
I Don't Know Whether To Kill Myself or Go Bowling
If The Phone Don't Ring, You'll Know It's Me
She's Actin' Single and I'm Drinkin' Doubles
How Can I Miss You If You Won't Go Away.
I Keep Forgettin' I Forgot About You.

Viagra, the little blue pill that has changed millions of lives around the world, has its own special day. *Viagra Day* falls on March 27th as it commemorates the date in 1998 on which it was given approval by the Food and Drug Administration (FDA).

Thankfully, I don't suffer from erectile dysfunction, but part of me did want to see what all the fuss was about. No, not THAT part of me.

I did some research online and found that Viagra is still a prescription-only drug in the UK but that you no longer have to get a prescription from your GP. Many pharmacies are able to prescribe it by the consumer answering a short questionnaire - or 'consultation' as they call it, in order for them to get around a legal loophole.

There was no way I could ask my GP to prescribe it. And I couldn't handle the idea of a face-to-face meeting with a pharmacist to try and convince them that I had a problem.

The Viagra itself was fairly expensive in the first place - £22 for four - but it was not possible to order it without paying for the consultation, which cost an extra £25. As it was *Viagra Day* today, I needed it TODAY. My local pharmacy had a *'click and collect'* option, which didn't appeal to me. I have to go to the pharmacy regularly to pick up prescriptions for the rest of the family and their various ailments, and they now know my face. I then noticed a *'Same Day delivery'* courier option from a pharmacy outside of Northampton which was available for an additional £23. It would be completely anonymous, and I would not have to look a pharmacist in the eye with my sad, erectile dysfunctional face. The consultation was all done online. It's basically a medical version of the *'Am I ready for a dog?'* quiz. I was going to make a cheap joke involving bones and boners, but I won't.

A total cost of £70 was a ridiculous amount of money to spend on a drug to cure a problem that I didn't have. I couldn't justify it. I had hardly spent any money on this challenge so far, so to blow £70 on some Viagra just for the sake of it was completely impractical.

I then realised that perhaps I needed to make this financial investment to convince myself that I was taking the challenge seriously. Until now, I had only invested time in celebrating the holidays; sat at my computer, sending emails and looking up things on Wikipedia. Rarely have I actually had to buy anything. If I decided to give up on the challenge, then the wasted time would be all I would lose. If I spent the £70 then I would, in a sense, have a financial motivation to see the project through. This all seemed logical in my head anyway when I filled in the short questionnaire and clicked the 'order' button.

'Are you mental? What the hell did you order Viagra for?' shouted Rachel when I showed her the packet that arrived later in the day.

I explained my reasons whilst she shook her head.

'And how much did it cost? £20?'

'Not quite. A little bit more,' I said sheepishly.

'£30?'

'Yes, 30-something,' I said, not daring to tell her the full cost. 'But it's an investment!'

'An investment? You moan at me if I spend more than £1 on a bottle of shampoo, and at least I have a need for that.'

'Wait and see. You might think it a very worthwhile investment later.'

Once the children were in bed I took one of the little blue pills and waited. I'm not going to go into too much detail, but sure enough, half an hour later things started to happen.

I walked up to Rachel who was sitting on the sofa and gave her a suggestive wink.

'Ha! You must be joking? No chance.'

'What? Oh, come on. That's what I took the pill for. It was all for YOU.'

'Well, unlucky. Anyway, hadn't you better get ready for football?'

'No, it's cancelled because of the snow.'

'Oh, you obviously didn't get the answer phone message then. It's on.'

'No. What message? How can I go to football like THIS?'

'Good job it's so cold out there.'

I put on three tight pairs of pants and a pair of the baggiest shorts that I could find. I then put on last year's Oakley 20 hoodie which hung just below my waist, and I ventured out into the cold, dark night.

'You alright?' asked Mark on the floodlit astroturf pitch. 'You're running strangely today.'

'Yeah, I'm fine thanks. Just a bit stiff.'

Slow-cooked lamb, sweet potato mash... and ham.

March 28th

Weeds get a bit of a hard time. Just because of an outdated classification system, some plants are condemned as weeds forever. Others, often more ugly, are deemed 'flowers' and are given all the care and attention.

Rachel and I are fairly rubbish gardeners. Actually, scrap that, we are awful. Most of the time we can't tell the difference between weeds and plants so we just leave the ones that look the nicest.

Weed Appreciation Day is when weeds finally get their moment. Dandelions are one of the most notorious weeds. They have a habit of appearing everywhere. All over the lawn, in flowerbeds, between patio cracks. We even have one that appears each year from a crack in our windowsill. Despite their beautiful yellow flowers and hypnotic dandelion clock they are still considered pests and people go out of their way to dig them up or spray them with pesticide.

Every part of a dandelion is edible, however, and they have lots of health-giving benefits, as well as medicinal and culinary uses. They are rich in potassium, antioxidants, and vitamins A and C. You can make wine, salads, jellies, fritters. The list is endless. I didn't know any of this before today, by the way, but I sure do now.

I dashed out into the garden with hearty enthusiasm and planned to make a delicious dandelion salad for dinner. My excitement was soon diminished when I discovered that there were no dandelions. It was the end of March, but there was still a slight covering of snow on the ground and it had been unseasonably cold for weeks. I scoured around the patches of grass and found a few old leaves and a couple of new shoots which I thought could potentially be dandelions, and decided they would have to do.

We shared a three-leaf dandelion salad for dinner, served with chicken kebabs as it was *On-a-stick Day*.

My Oakley 20 hoodie arrived in the post today. It was a luscious (do people still use that word?) bright blue colour with yellow writing and a yellow seam on the hood. Definitely the best one yet. I did feel slightly fraudulent wearing it considering I hadn't run the 20 miles, but that wasn't my fault. I pulled it on over my head, where it will now remain until spring has finally sprung. I might wash it occasionally.

Lunch - croque-monsieur.

March 29th

I always get confused by the different days around Easter: *Palm Sunday, Easter Sunday, Ash Wednesday, Shrove Tuesday, Good Friday. Moody Monday. Thirsty Thursday. Snoozy Saturday.*

Good Friday is a slightly ambiguous name for a day that commemorates the crucifixion of Jesus. A crucifixion is not usually, by anyone's standard, considered 'good'. There are a couple of possible theories as to the origin of the word. Some suggest 'good' used to mean holy, and other's claim the word came about from 'God's'.

Good Friday isn't really a day to celebrate, as such, but many Christians observe this day by fasting or with prayer, mediation or repentance.

It was an exciting day for me as I was due to photograph my first ever outdoor wedding. And what exotic faraway destination would be the location for this outdoor wedding? The Bahamas? The Italian Riviera? Not quite. Kettering. A hotel on a dual-carriageway just outside of Kettering, to be precise. Still, they were a lovely couple and it was still an outdoor wedding so I was immensely excited at the prospect. It was bitterly cold but the sun was out and the sky was blue. It was definitely going to be a good Friday.

An hour before the wedding was due to start, it began to snow. Heavily. On March 29th. The bride debated going ahead with the outdoor wedding, but then decided it would not really be possible, so opted for the hotel's contingency indoor plan instead.

The wedding was a great success and the bride and groom were not too disappointed that they had been unable to have the wedding they had dreamt of. I have no idea why I am telling you this story. Ah yes... and then I found £50.

After the wedding I called into Tesco to pick up a frozen pizza to have for dinner. I planned to cook it first, of course. It was 9pm and I had been fasting for the entire day. This was partly to observe *Good Friday*, but mostly because I woke up late and didn't have time for breakfast, and then forgot to take any food with me for lunch.

I was about to buy my pizza when I remembered that it was *Mom and Pop Business Owner's Day*. No disrespect to Tesco, but it is about as far from a Mom and Pop Business as it is possible to get. I put the pizza back and spent 20 minutes driving around Kettering trying to find an independent grocery shop that was open. I then bought the exact same pizza for nearly twice the price, but definitely felt a greater sense of satisfaction. I also purchased a Banoffee Pie Easter egg for Rachel. My good friend claims that his grandma invented banoffee pie. Despite the fact that I don't believe him, a part of me feels a duty to order it or buy banoffee pie whenever I have the opportunity. I like to think his family are benefitting in some way, through royalties, for each bannoffe pie related transaction.

Ham and Mushroom pizza, with added ham.

March 30th

I am a big fan of pencils. We have drawers and drawers full of pens. Most of which don't work. And of those that do work, most of them leak. And of those that do work and don't leak, most of them only work for the first half of whatever I want to write. You don't have those issues with a pencil. Pencils don't leak. They don't run out, and they don't stop working mid sentence.

Pencil Day celebrates the day in 1858 that the United States Patent and Trademark Office gave the first patent for a pencil with an eraser attached to it. I wanted to celebrate *Pencil Day* by visiting the Pencil Museum in Keswick in the Lake District but couldn't for two reasons. Firstly, I had another wedding to photograph, and my contract only covers *'extreme circumstances'* for non-attendance. I don't think a visit to the Pencil Museum fulfils this criterion. Secondly, I've already been to the Pencil Museum. As I said, I'm a BIG fan of pencils. It's a surprisingly brilliant museum - up there with the Northampton Shoe Museum - and has all sorts of activities and exhibits about, well, pencils obviously.

I always carry a pencil with me when photographing a wedding as I use them to make notes of specific shots that have been requested, and cross them off once they have been taken. A pencil has never let me down.

Today was also *The Grass is Always Browner on the Other Side Day* - a day to celebrate what you have, and not to be envious of others. How could I be envious of others when I have just rediscovered my love of pencils? I set off to photograph another snowy wedding, with hope in my heart and a pencil in my pocket.

The bride's mother approached me before the speeches.

'Would it be possible for you to take a picture later this evening of me with all of my brothers and sisters and Great Aunt Mary and cousins Julie and Martin and their grandchildren and my sister Brenda's two godchildren with their mum's sister and her husband and their children and...'

'Hold on, just one second. I'm just going to make a note of these people with my trusty pencil,' I said, as I started to scribble down a list of names. The lead snapped.

'Stupid fucking pencil,' I said under my breath. 'I don't suppose you have a pen I could borrow?'

Post-wedding snack - ham and pineapple encased in a bbq beef flavoured crispy potato parcel.

March 31st

Easter Sunday is also an ambiguous day. It celebrates the resurrection of Jesus, and so we express this joy by binge eating chocolate. I'm sure it's what Jesus would have wanted (?). What is even more confusing is the idea of an egg-laying MAMMAL in the form of the Easter bunny. Apparently eggs and bunnies are supposed to symbolise rebirth and spring. It's quite a tenuous link, but people seem happy to go along with it.

I had been up until 2am on both Friday and Saturday night trying to get on top of the photo editing for both weddings before we headed down to Devon for a few days during the Easter holidays. I then spent most of *Easter Sunday* putting together the wedding albums to ease some of the burden of having work hanging over me whilst we were away. I celebrated *Easter Sunday* in the usual way - by stuffing my face with chocolate.

Today was also *She's Funny That Way Day*; a day when you are encouraged to make a list of five reasons why a favourite female in your life makes you laugh. It's a really great idea. Rachel makes me laugh more than anyone else I know. That's one of the main reasons I fell in love with her. But I have never sat down and thought about the reasons why she does make me laugh. Here goes...

1. She lacks any form of basic common sense. For example, she genuinely doesn't know the difference between a helicopter and an aeroplane. She's convinced that the only difference is that aeroplanes fly higher.

2. She has an amazing knack for confusing famous people who either share the same first name or surname, or even a vague physical similarity such as hair colour. She refuses to believe that Kevin Bacon and Kevin Spacey are different people, and for years she was convinced that Patrick Swayze and David Hasselhoff were the same person.

3. We share an identical sense of humour. Things that make her laugh make me laugh too, and vice versa. It means we usually laugh at the same time. Unless, of course, one of us is laughing AT the other.

4. She can watch an episode of *Friends* that she has already seen about a dozen times before, and still chuckle away as if it's the first time.

5. I have known Rachel for 20 years and been best friends with her for 17 of those. That's HALF of my life. Having spent so much time with each other over the years, we have both gained a wealth of shared experiences, memories and 'in jokes' from which to keep us both amused for a lifetime. She is the only person that gets all of my jokes. I'm the only person who gets all of hers.

Pea and ham soup.

In the battle of Man vs. Ham. MAN WON!

APRIL

April 1st

April Fools' Day is one of the most famous 'quirky' holidays that does not have a religious basis. Its origin is slightly unclear, but the earliest reference to practical jokes being played on April 1st is in Chaucer's *Canterbury Tales* (1392). In Italy, France and Belgium people traditionally stick paper fishes to each other's backs and shout *'April Fish'*. I tried this first thing in the morning but just got a very strange look from Rachel and the kids.

'Are you feeling ok?' asked Rachel.

'Why are you saying *April Fish*?' asked Layla.

'Because you have got a fish on your back. And it's April.'

'Why did you stick a fish on my back?'

'Because it's *April Fools' Day* and that's what they do in France and Italy.'

'But we are not in France or Italy,' said Layla.

'What is *April Fools' Day*?' asked Leo.

'You don't know what *April Fools' Day* is?'

'No.'

'It's a day when you can play tricks on people and then shout *'April Fool'* when you want to tell them it was just a joke.'

'Cool. Can we play?' asked Layla.

'Of course.'

'Ok... errr.... Daddy?'

'Yes, Layla.'

'There's a big dragon on your head.'

'Where? Get it off. Quick!' I shouted, flapping around the room.

'April Fool!' she shouted and they all laughed.

'Oh, you got me there,' I said. 'Nice one.'

'Mummy?'

'Yes, Leo.'

'There's a... there's a... err... there's a robot in your ear.'

'Arghhhh, a robot in my ear? Get it out! Get it out!' she shouted.

'April Fool!' they all shouted, and then burst out laughing.

'Daddy?'

'Yes, Layla.'

'There's a... errmmm...'

'Oh God, what have I started,' I whispered to Rachel.

'They'll be at this for hours now,' she laughed.

After breakfast I loaded all of our bags into the car for our trip down to Devon.

'Daddy, there's a shark in that bag,' she said as I squashed a suitcase into the boot.

'A shark? Arghhh,' I said half-heartedly.

'April Fool!'

The drive down to Devon was one of the longest five hours of my life. There was a constant stream of April Fools' jokes from the back seat, as Rachel and I kept up our laughter charade for as long as possible and then slowly zoned out.

'April Fools' jokes can only be done in the morning. It's bad luck to do them after 12 o'clock,' I said.

'What do you mean it's bad luck?' asked Layla.

'It's considered tradition that if you do an April Fool after midday then something bad might happen to you.'

'What time is it now?'

'12 o'cock,' I said, looking at the clock on the dashboard which said 10.55am.

'Oooooh, that's not fair.'

I was tempted to announce this as an April Fool, but then realised we would have to endure another hour of theirs so I let it lie.

My granddad used to say a rhyme to my sister and me when we were children if we did an April Fool after midday.

'Three potatoes in the pot, you're the fool and I'm not.'

Even now, as a fully grown adult, I am still no closer to understanding what it means. I knew that it signified the fact that you couldn't play April Fools' pranks after midday, but what the hell did that have to do with potatoes? Perhaps it was simply because 'pot' rhymes with 'not', or maybe just because cooking potatoes signifies lunchtime.

Coincidentally, it was also *Tater Day*. *Tater Day* is a festival in Benton, Kentucky that is a celebration of spring. It started in 1843 as a day on which people from the town would trade their sweet potato sprouts (slips) for growing. The festival has expanded and now includes a parade, floats, marching band and all sorts of other activities. It is also the oldest continuous trade day in the US. It doesn't always fall on April 1st so has no significance to the origin of the *'three potatoes'* rhyme. Still, I traded some sweet potatoes at a shop near to where we were staying for two pieces of gold coloured metal that I had worked hard to earn. Disappointingly there was no parade or marching band to celebrate my transaction.

I have to confess I did slightly neglect my holiday celebrations during our few days in Devon. I wanted to enjoy our holiday and although I am not suggesting that my holiday challenge can be considered 'work' in anyway, I did also want to be able to take a slight break from it. I wanted to enjoy the holiday for what it was, rather than have the restrictions of the additional celebrations thrust upon us.

It was particularly cold, but beautifully sunny all week. We made regular trips to the beach (wearing hats and gloves), we went on a steam train ride, we played in the garden, we went to the pub, we played boules, went crab fishing and we ate and drank way too much.

I also managed to successfully photobomb a picture that Rachel was taking of all three children playing in the garden together. This is up there with the greatest achievements of my life.

As Lent had come to an end, Rachel and I also drank an obscene amount of tea and coffee. Giving up caffeine had been a lot easier than we thought. The first few days had been tough and we both did miss it. But the cravings soon disappeared and we quickly got used to going without. I even grew to like decaf tea by the end of the 40 days. This was something that I didn't think was physically possible.

It also disproved my theory about caffeine having an adverse effect on me and contributing to my tiredness. Giving it up made no difference whatsoever. I concluded that, rather than caffeine, the reason that I get tired is because I go to bed way too late and get up way too early. It seems obvious now I think about it.

I didn't neglect the holiday celebrations completely whilst in Devon. We still flew kites on the beach (*National Kite Month*), ordered deep dish pizza instead of my preferred thin and crispy (*Deep Dish Pizza Day*) and, on Friday - just before driving back to Northampton - I wrote my own epitaph to 'celebrate', in the most morbid possible way, *Plan Your Epitaph Day*.

Here lies George Mahood.
Loving father. Loyal husband. Devoted son. Faithful friend.
Bit of a dick.

April 6th

'But, Daddy. You are always telling me and Leo not to hit each other,' said Layla when I tried to explain the rules of a pillow fight.

'I know I did. And normally it is very, very bad to hit other people. Pillow fights are a bit different, though. They are just for fun and because pillows are nice and soft they don't hurt people.'

This wasn't strictly true either. The last time I was involved in a pillow fight was in a youth hostel in a small village in Austria. Two friends and I spent three weeks inter-railing around Europe at the age of 19 and somehow ended up in a hostel in the middle of nowhere, where the three of us shared a dormitory for 30 people. We were the only guests in the entire building. Even the owner decided to stay elsewhere. To make the most of this vacuous space that we had at our disposal, we celebrated, for some reason, with a pillow fight. It started jovially enough, but soon got out hand as we subconsciously vented our tensions from the previous few weeks. It ended with three grown men in tears; one with a swollen, bruised ear, another with a bloody nose and the third with a cut lip and torn shoulder ligament. There were feathers everywhere.

Fourteen years later and I was armed with a pillow again and raring to go. It was *Pillow Fight Day* - sorry, I probably should have mentioned that earlier - and this time my opposition was a five year old, three year old and a one year old. It was every man for himself, and I fancied my chances. It was also *Love Our Children Day*, and there is no doubting that I do, but this was a fight I wanted to win.

It started fairly innocently until they conspired against me. Layla threw herself around my ankles whilst I struggled to remain upright to avoid squashing Kitty. At which point Leo, who had decided to tactically swap his pillow for a wooden sword, struck me at full-force in the bollocks. I doubled over and then Kitty grabbed hold of my hair with one hand and poked me in the eye with her other. I rolled on the floor, with one hand over my stinging eye and the other clutching my balls and admitted defeat.

I received a text message later in the day from Ben.

'Did you go to that big pillow fight in London today?'

'What pillow fight?' I replied.

'It's *Pillow Fight Day*. I thought you knew. There was a massive pillow fight in Trafalgar Square. Just seen it on BBC News.'

I checked the BBC website and sure enough, thousands of people had attended an organised pillow fight in London. There was even some video footage. It looked awesome, and I had missed it.

It had never occurred to me that *Pillow Fight Day* was actually a proper thing. There I was having the shit kicked out of me by three tiny children, when I could have been having the shit kicked out of me by thousands of fully-grown adults. This wasn't the first time that I had missed out on a bigger or better celebration of the day I was supposed to be observing. So far, I had only really been checking the listings on the day itself, which didn't really allow any time for planning or preparation. I needed to be a bit more pro-active and to start looking further ahead.

It was the day of the *Grand National* and the only day of the year when you can walk into a betting shop without having to look both ways before entering. I'm not really interested in horse racing for the rest of the year, but I've been excited by the *Grand National* from a very early age. There are now more and more moral arguments against it and I find it increasingly difficult to justify my love of it, other than it's just so damn exciting.

I chose my horses based on today's holiday celebrations, by trying to find a tenuous link from their name. I put £1 each way on Tatenen at 100-1, because it sounded a bit like 'tartan'. It was *Tartan Day*. And to celebrate *Army Day*, I also backed Imperial Commander at 11-1 as it sounded like a sort of army horse, albeit a 19th century Japanese one.

Neither horse finished the race.

When I was a child, my late-grandfather, who lived in Belfast, used a technique to help us select our horses. He cut each individual horse name from the form guide in the paper, screwed it into a tiny ball, gathered all of the balls together and threw them across the floor. The horse which travelled the furthest was the 'winner'. I remember this whole process being almost as exciting as the race itself and have continued it every year since. I have used this technique in recent years to pick a horse for the children. It's basically just an excuse to back more horses and increase the chances of a win.

The technique has been surprisingly successful over the years and Kitty's 'pick' this year - Auroras Encore - came in at 66-1 winning her £84.50 from a £1 each-way bet. She was delighted that her horse won. Not as happy as her agent (me), who charged her an astronomical commission rate of 95% which left her with just over £4.

April 7th

I had a family photo shoot to do at noon and then decided we should do very little all afternoon.

'Why are you cleaning the kitchen?' I asked Rachel.

'Because it needs cleaning.'

'But it's *No Housework Day*. Leave it, the kitchen can wait.'

'Ok,' she said, without any more persuasion.

'It's also *National Beer Day* and *Caramel Popcorn Day*.'

'It gets better.'

We spent the afternoon on the sofa watching films (all chosen by the children unfortunately), drinking beer and eating caramel popcorn.

April 8th

Draw a Picture of a Bird Day. Ok, I will.

This is GENUINELY my best effort, and I spent a considerable amount of time on it. Yet somehow it looks more like a pig than a bird. How is that even possible? Do birds have pointy ears? I can't remember. Also, its legs are so far back on its weirdly-shaped body that I am sure it would topple forwards and smash its pretty little face on that branch.

April 9th

My mum gave me a broken vase for Christmas last year. It was one of the strangest Christmas presents I have ever received.

A few weeks before Christmas, Leo knocked the small ornamental vase off the shelf (he's just like his Dad) at my parents' house whilst playing a game of long jump on the sofa. It smashed on the hard floor into several pieces. My mum was very calm about the whole thing and told Leo it was only an accident. She then muttered under her breath, as she collected the pieces together, that she had always thought that it might be worth something. She bought it from a car boot sale years ago, but secretly thought it was extremely valuable.

It was then a bit of a surprise when I unwrapped my Christmas present to discover the gathered pieces of said vase all wrapped in bubble wrap and placed in a shoebox.

'Er, thank you,' I said. 'A broken vase. Just what I've always wanted.'

'I thought you could get it valued and then if it's worth something you can keep the money,' she said.

'Thanks, that's really kind of you. But it's broken. Won't that be annoying if it really is worth something? Wouldn't you rather not know?'

'I'm sure it could probably be repaired, and it might be worth something even in its current state.'

'Ok, great. Thanks, I guess.'

The vase had remained in its shoe box and sat cluttering up my desk ever since. Today was *National Cherish an Antique Day* so this seemed like an appropriate day to finally get the vase valued. I phoned a couple of antique shops in town but one didn't offer valuations, and the other said that they didn't specialise in china. I remembered seeing an idea on *Dragon's Den* for an online company that would value anything within

48 hours. I searched on the internet and found *ValueMyStuff.com*. The cost for a single valuation was £7.50 but if the vase turned out to be valuable then it was a worthy investment. I had to fill in a form, upload a few photos and then submit my payment. Five hours later I received the following valuation report:

Description:
A Chinese porcelain vase of baluster form with cylindrical neck and flared foot, the body decorated beneath a crackled glaze in underglaze cobalt blue with sages in a garden, the foot and shoulder with a moulded, bronzed band of stylised flowers, the foot bears a spurious seal 'Hsuan-te Nien Ho'. Meaning made in the reign of the Emperor Hsuan-te (1426-1435).

HOLY SHIT! It had a seal suggesting it was nearly 600 years old! This was incredible. I was going to be RICH!

Measurements:
Height: 130 cm, Width: 70 cm, Depth: 70 cm
Date: mid 20th century.

What the fuck? Mid 20th Century? But what about Emperor Hsuan-te?

Value:
£5 - £10

Oh.

Additional Comments:
Even had the present piece been in undamaged condition, as a modern, mass-produced, cheaply and rather crudely made piece it would command little commercial interest. In its damaged condition it is virtually worthless.

ALRIGHT! I get the message! No need to rub it in.

Thanks a lot, Mum. It cost me £7.50 to discover that the vase was virtually worthless.

I sellotaped the pieces back together and gave it back to her as a present, along with a copy of the valuation certificate. She was delighted.

April 10th

'Have you seen Basil this morning? Sorry, I mean Father Dougal,' asked Doug over the garden wall.

'No, I don't think I have. He popped in early evening yesterday but I haven't seen him since. Have you not?'

'No, I haven't seen him since yesterday. I think he's gone missing again. I've got a bad feeling,' he said.

'He'll be ok. You know what he's like. He's probably just gone for a wander or maybe he's been shut inside someone's house. I'm sure he'll be back soon.'

'I hope you're right, George. I hope you're right. We miss him already.'

Father Dougal had gone missing once before. He disappeared just before Christmas a few years ago. There were no sightings of him for several weeks and we had almost given up hope of seeing him again, when he was found wandering the streets about half a mile away. It's unclear how or why he went missing. Our house is a mid-terrace and there are no access points into the back gardens other than through the houses. Father Dougal has a habit of nosing through neighbours' back doors to see if there is any food on offer, because being fed at two houses is clearly not enough.

The couple that used to be our neighbours on the other side to Doug also had a cat. It was called Nigel (who names a cat Nigel?). This cat was very old and Father Dougal used to take full advantage and sneak through the cat flap and eat his food, knowing full well that poor old Nigel would not be able to retaliate. Our neighbours quite rightly hated Father Dougal. I was sitting outside in the garden one morning, drinking a cup of tea, when I heard shouting from next door.

'YOU FUCKING CAT!' and then a blur of black fur leapt over the wall as Father Dougal made a dash for it. Then Andy, our neighbour, reached the doorway still shouting and swearing at the cat, and threw a pint glass full of water towards Father Dougal. Andy didn't have time to notice me sitting by our back door as the water skimmed inches away from my face.

'Oh my gosh, I'm so sorry,' he said, completely mortified. 'I didn't know you were there. It was just... your cat... and Nigel... you know.... sorry!'

'Don't worry at all. It sounds like he deserved it. I'm sorry that he keeps coming into your house,' I said.

So, the problem with living in a mid-terrace house, and having a cat that likes to visit other people's houses, is that you have to rely on him coming back out the same way that he went in. If he went into a house through the back door, and was then chased out the front door onto the street, there would be no way for him to get back around to the garden. I hoped that on this occasion he had just gone on a hashtag microadventure.

April 11th

There was still no sign of Father Dougal when I went downstairs in the morning and Batfink was sat staring out of the cat flap, clearly a little confused about her brother's whereabouts.

Ironically it was *National Pet Day*.

I knocked on a few doors either side of our house to ask if anyone had seen Father Dougal. I then phoned the local vets and animal shelters to see if there had been any reports. I also registered with a few online missing pet websites but nothing yielded any success.

I then had to photograph a wedding - my second Thursday wedding of the year (Thursday is the new Saturday). Rachel and the children were all very upset about Father Dougal when I left in the morning, and I tried to reassure them that he would return soon.

There was still no news of his whereabouts when I got back home at about 9.30pm. I unloaded my camera equipment into the house and then spent half an hour walking the surrounding streets doing a special whistle that we use when we are giving the cats their food. I'm not sure how you spell the noise of a whistle. It was sort of a *'thew-ee, thew-ee, twew-eeee'*, if that helps set the scene at all. At every parked car I passed I expected him to poke his head out, or appear at the top of a fence or wall on hearing my call. Nothing.

April 12th

I was up until 2am uploading photos from the wedding and doing a basic first edit. I then couldn't sleep because I was thinking about where Father Dougal might be.

On the way back from dropping Layla at school Doug was on his doorstep.

'Any sign of Basil?' he asked.

'No, not yet, I'm afraid. I walked around the streets late last night but no luck. He'll come back soon.'

'Remember last time, he was gone for over a month.'

'Was it really that long?'

'Yes, it was. Four weeks to the day. It felt like forever, though. I don't know what we would do if he didn't come back. Chris and I didn't sleep a wink last night.'

'Me neither. It's a horrible feeling, isn't it?'

'Awful. Just the worst.'

I could empathise with how Doug felt. The previous time Father Dougal had gone missing was before we had children. The cats were very important to us. Then children came along and our priorities changed slightly, and although they were still a part of our lives, both cats had slipped further down the order of precedence. It also felt as though Father Dougal was choosing to distance himself from us. He was spending more and more time at Doug and Chris's house and exploring further and further afield. It was no wonder that he had got himself lost.

It was incredibly important for me to try and get Father Dougal back, though. If anything, I felt an even greater sense of duty and responsibility because now it was no longer just Rachel and I that would miss him, but Layla, Leo and Kitty, and almost more importantly, Doug and Chris.

I never intended to write a soppy cat book. I'm not sure what is happening to me. When I started out on this challenge I didn't expect the cats to feature at all. Little did I know how many 'official' days are devoted to cats, and I had no idea how these months were going to unfold. I know it probably comes across as though Rachel and I are some sort of freaky cat couple, but that's not the case, I promise. At least, I don't think we are. Although, maybe we have just been in denial all this time.

April 13th

I don't usually take many photographs of my pets either, but thanks to this holiday challenge, I had a selection to choose from when I put together a MISSING poster for Father Dougal on my computer. I was torn between the one with him wearing a high-vis vest and another of him covered in party popper streamers. I opted for the party popper one as I thought people might be on the lookout for a bright yellow, reflective cat otherwise.

I printed off 30 copies and the five of us then walked around the neighbourhood attaching the posters to lampposts and telegraph poles.

April 14th

My first book has sold more copies than I ever expected it to. I thought I might sell a few copies to friends and family and maybe the occasional cycling obsessive who had read every other book remotely connected to cycling until they were left with just mine. But I didn't think people would actually like it. I mean, of course I hoped they would. But I'm not a writer. I just had an adventure that I wanted to share with people and the book just followed. Now that lots of people have read my book, and enjoyed it, I obviously want even more people to read it.

Today was *Reach As High As You Can Day* and I didn't feel that I had yet with *Free Country*. One tactic that I had not yet used was a free giveaway of the e-book version of my book. When I first heard about free giveaways I couldn't understand why any author would want to give away copies of their book for FREE. It didn't make any sense.

Then I started hearing success stories from others. Everybody loves a freebie, and if a promotion is done successfully, then several thousand copies of your book will be downloaded in a couple of days. As they are free, you don't make a penny from these downloads, and most of these people will probably never even read the book anyway. But some of them will. Some of those that read it might like it and might recommend it to a friend, or even leave a review. But, perhaps more importantly, it helps your book get more visibility on Amazon through its *'People who bought this, also bought this...'* listings. It also opens your book up to people that would not normally have bought it. The theory is that there should be a big increase in paid sales after the free promotion ends. And if that fails then at least lots of new people with have got a copy of my book. At the end of the day, I want as many people as possible to read it, regardless of whether they have paid for it or not.

This is all probably immensely boring for you, but as a self-published author I spend a vast amount of my time debating and considering stuff like this (with myself). It's not the most rock 'n' roll lifestyle.

I had been meaning to experiment with one of these free promotions but the right time never seemed to materialise. *Reach As High As You Can Day* gave me the perfect incentive to just go ahead and do it. I hadn't prepared. It was a Sunday (NEVER run a promo on a Sunday, claim some authors). Wait until sales have died considerably (mine had slowed, but I was still selling at a steady rate). Contact e-book deal websites at least a month in advance (I can't even plan more than a day ahead). But there was always going to be an excuse. I decided to just go for it. I sent off as many emails as I could to various freebie listing sites. I then posted a few things on Facebook and Twitter and took Layla and Leo swimming whilst the promo hopefully worked its magic.

When I returned two hours later, my book's Amazon ranking had disappeared completely and I had received a grand total of 8 downloads. Not the thousands I was hoping for.

I started cursing Amazon and getting angry with myself for trying to reach as high as I could, when I was probably already as high as I was ever going to be, and should have just been content with that. I risked my book disappearing into obscurity altogether, and if it never made it back into the travel and cycling charts after the promotion, then nobody would ever stumble across my book again. Stupid fucking Amazon and stupid greedy me.

Later in the evening I sat down in front of the TV to watch *The Masters* golf at Augusta, as all European hopefuls slowly fell by the wayside, and, to make matters worse, three Australians were dominating the competition. The day had turned to shit.

At around midnight I checked my sales again, just to prove how pointless the whole experiment had been. My book had been downloaded 1600 times and I was ranked #42 in the overall Free Kindle chart. I pressed F5 as I assumed it was a glitch. No, it was definitely correct. Things were definitely looking good. Getting into the Top 100 of the free chart is considered a great achievement because then people browsing for free books start to notice it too.

My favourite non-British golfer, Ángel Cabrera, lost the play-off to Australian Adam Scott, but I went to bed with a smile on my face

April 15th

By morning, my ranking in the free chart had jumped to #8 and my book had been downloaded over 4000 times.

My excitement then briefly turned to panic when I discovered that it was *Income Tax Pay Day*. I then remembered that the majority of the holidays that I am observing are American, so the same deadline didn't apply to me. After the realisation set in that I didn't legally have to complete my tax return for another nine months, I then remembered that I was supposed to be observing these holidays, regardless of the fact that they were not necessarily relevant to the UK. It had not stopped me joining the *Red Hat Society* or honouring *St Urho* - the patron saint of Finnish vineyard workers. Today would have to be the day that I filed my tax return, whether I liked it or not.

Rachel was over the moon. She has been desperate to move house for several years. I have too, but I am more realistic than her and understand that we can't afford a bigger place. I am self-employed and Rachel works one day a week so we are not mortgage brokers' favourite candidates. For several years I have used the excuse of 'once I've done my next tax return we'll be in a better position to get a mortgage' and it usually buys me a few more months. There is no delaying it this year. Rachel has decided that SHE is moving house this year, with or without me.

I spent a frustrating few hours compiling a spreadsheet of figures and then I discovered that it was *Take a Wild Guess Day*. I couldn't, could I? I'm not sure if it is a bizarre coincidence, or whether the creator of *Take a Wild Guess Day* just had a wicked sense of humour.

To any readers that work for HMRC or the IRS, I certainly did not pluck a random figure from the air for my income tax in order to celebrate this ridiculous holiday. I filled it in completely honestly and accurately and every last penny was accounted for.

Patriots' Day is a civic holiday in Massachusetts and Maine which commemorates the anniversary of the Battles of Lexington and Concord. The Boston Marathon - the world's oldest - has been held every year on *Patriots' Day* since 1897. It's a race I would love to compete in one day, but it is one of the few public events in the world that have required qualifying times. I have completed four marathons in the last four years; my first was London in 2009, followed by Berlin, Chester, and the not-so-glamorous Milton Keynes. Since completing my first marathon, Boston has always been a distant aim, but I am nowhere near quick enough. My most recent marathon time of 4h 17m would qualify me for the Boston Marathon... in the 70-74 age group category. So, providing I can keep my current level of fitness up for the next 40 years, and hope that the average qualifying time doesn't quicken, then I should be able to qualify when I'm in my 70s. My current time is also fast enough to qualify me as a 60-64 year old female. It would mean that I would have to have a sex change, but I would only have 30 years to wait. It's very tempting.

I checked my book's Amazon listing after we had put the children to bed. I had hit the No.1 spot in the free chart. I was absolutely delighted. There are literally tens of thousands of free books available each day on Amazon, and my little story was occupying the top spot. It was an incredible feeling. And then I switched on the television and caught the 9pm news and I suddenly realised how trivial and insignificant this achievement was.

Two bombs had exploded next to the finish line of the Boston Marathon. It was utterly devastating. I could not comprehend what I was seeing. Any form of terrorism is obviously unthinkable, but to target a marathon? It defied belief. Not that marathon runners are any more special than other people, but these were all good, honest people, most of whom would be raising lots of money for worthy causes. And what about the spectators? These are often more heroic than the runners. Giving up their time and energy, fighting for a space by the barrier, cheering and clapping at thousands of people they don't even know, shouting encouragement, many just managing to get a fleeting glance at their family member or loved-one as they completed their gruelling 26.2 mile run. At the time, there was no indication of who was responsible for the bombings, but no cause or justification could ever be given for such an atrocious act.

Tragic events like this remind you of the fragility of life, and they certainly put life's other worries into perspective. But during times like this you also get to see the best of humanity; courageous rescue stories, strangers teaming together to help others, communities becoming stronger; then, later, the incredible stories of survivors rebuilding their lives. There is always a dichotomy of emotions with news stories such as this. On one hand we are shown how cruel and evil some representatives of mankind can be, and on the other we are reminded just how brave, resilient and compassionate the human race is.

April 16th

One Day Without Shoes is a day designed to help bring global awareness to children's health and education by not wearing shoes. The day was created by the Californian shoe company TOMS. For every pair bought, a pair is given to a child in the developing world. Going without shoes for an entire day seemed like a simple enough idea. I could do that.

It was all going smoothly until Rachel reminded me at 3pm that I had to go and collect Layla from school and take her to her swimming lesson.

Walking down our dog-poo ridden street barefoot was a challenge that I have braved many times before. I often nip out to get something from the car with no shoes on, and then remember that the car is parked down the far end of our street. I expected to get a few strange looks in the school playground whilst I waited for Layla, but nobody seemed to notice or care.

Layla's swimming lessons are at a pool close to the town centre and we always drive there and park the car near to a pub and curry house. Driving there barefoot was not an issue, as I drove a campervan pretty much the entire length of Australia's east-coast with no shoes on, so the two miles to the swimming pool were no problem.

Walking the gauntlet of broken glass and vomit on Northampton's pavements was an altogether bigger challenge. I often take the children swimming on Sunday mornings - before the county council have had a chance to clear up Saturday night's carnage - and I physically have to guide Layla and Leo around giant puddles of chunder, splintered bottles and shattered pint glasses. Fortunately, Tuesday evening is not as apocalyptic as Sunday morning but I still had to tread carefully.

'Daddy, why is there always so much sick on this road?' asked Layla.

'Because some people who come out of this pub aren't feeling very well.'

'Then why did they go to the pub if they are not well?'

'They probably felt ok before they went to the pub.'

'So why does the pub make them poorly?'

'Sometimes if people drink too much, it makes them feel a bit dizzy and sick.'

'Is that the grown-up drink that you and Mummy have?'

'Yes.'

'Does it make you and mummy sick?'

'No. Well, not very often. Only very occasionally,' I said.

'Well, why do people drink that drink if it makes them feel dizzy and sick?'

'That's a very good question. For a while it makes you just feel happy, and it's only if you drink way too much that you feel sick.'

'I'm never going to drink that silly stuff. It sounds horrid.'

Coincidentally, it happened to be *Alcohol Awareness Month*, so I had certainly done my bit to help make Layla aware of the possible consequences of excessive alcohol consumption.

Layla had cried most of the week in fear and anticipation of this week's swimming lesson. Her usual teacher - a kind, smiley positive lady - had been off ill for a few weeks, and in her place was a large, strict, pushy, fairly scary... and particularly hairy man. I knew his methods probably worked well, but he was quite a change from what she was used to. Layla had been told that he would be taking the lesson this week and had been very upset about the prospect. I tried my best to explain to her that sometimes we have to do things that scare us in order to get better. It didn't really work, but a bribe of fish and chips on the way home seemed to help.

Midway through the lesson, the children all lined up at the end of the pool, holding onto the side in the deep end. They then took it in turns to see how far down the pool they could swim unaided. Layla, having previously never swam more than about four strokes without stopping, did her first ever five metre swim. I sat, poolside, with tears in my eyes and gave her a huge thumbs up and a subtle clap. Then minutes later, she managed a 10m swim. I was an emotional wreck at this point. Openly sobbing like a baby and clapping and whooping like a maniac. It's the proudest I have felt in a long time.

I was so excited for her the entire way home that I didn't even remember that I had no shoes on until I trod on a piece of battered sausage on the floor of the fish and chip shop. The other customers looked on in disgust as I peeled off the sticky sausage that had squelched between my toes.

April 17th

I ended my book's free promotion this morning after 13,000 free downloads in three days. I was still at number 1 in the free chart when I finished it, but it felt good to go out at the top. A few hours later, my book dropped back into the paid chart at number 4834. This was significantly lower than it had been before the promotion, but I heard that sometimes it takes a while for it to regulate and I hoped that things would pick up over the next few days. Rachel was less than impressed and had been somewhat dubious of the whole giveaway anyway.

'So you gave away 13,000 copies of your book and now it is further down the charts that it was before?' she said.

'Yes, but hopefully it will pick up. I reached as I high as I could and got to number 1 in the charts. That's pretty good, isn't it?'

'It's great, but it was the free chart. It was a bit pointless if the sales aren't as good afterwards, wasn't it?'

'Possibly. But it's still nice that 13 THOUSAND new people have downloaded my book. Even if they never read it. Isn't that pretty cool?'

'Yes, I guess you're right.'

It's strange how certain days just seem to celebrate themselves. An author friend of mine whom I met on Twitter (Tony James Slater, author of the brilliant *That Bear Ate My Pants*) uses the phrase *'as boring as bat shit'* quite regularly, and I picked him up on this in one of his Facebook posts. Is bat shit really that boring? He then told me he was in Malaysian-Borneo and about to go pot-holing in a bat-filled cave, presumably filled with bat shit. It happened to be *Bat Appreciation Day* today, so I recounted something to him that we had seen whilst visiting a petting zoo during our Easter holiday in Devon.

It had never occurred to me how bats actually go to the toilet. They spend the majority of their time hanging upside down, and if they did their 'business' in the upside-down position they would get a big face full of whatever came out the other end. I am excited to report that I got to witness first-hand how the process occurs. The bat (let's call him Dave), hanging by his feet, reached up with his hands (I'm not actually sure a bat has hands. Maybe its wings? You'll have to check) and then as he was hanging by his hands, Dave did what he needed to do, before swinging his feet back up to resume his upside-down position. It was a remarkable spectacle, and one that I would definitely recommend if you ever get the chance. Bat shit may be boring, but a bat shitting is anything but.

Ellis Island Family History Day proved to be a lot more interesting that it sounded. There is a website run by The Statue of Liberty - Ellis Island Foundation, which allows you to search the records by name.

I found 112 Mahoods listed as emigrating to the USA between the years of 1890 to 1924. These included two named George Mahood, one of whom was exactly the same age as me (33) when he arrived to start a new life in America. It was quite extraordinary to think about what a scary, unpredictable but exciting experience they would have had. They didn't have the luxuries that we do now of television and the internet, to help get an idea of what life was like on the other side of the world. All they had were stories, gossip and the occasional photograph. I'm not sure I would be brave enough to move to the other side of the world, knowing nothing about where I was going. We have been considering a move to Devon, to a town that I've been visiting a couple of times a year since I was born. It's only a couple of hundred miles away but the concept of that still terrifies me.

Reading all the details of families and individuals relocating to the other side of the world fuelled my desire to move. Not to America, but to another part of the UK. It would be another adventure, and one that I could share with Rachel and the children.

It was also *National Haiku Poetry Day* today. A Haiku - as you probably know - is a very short form of Japanese poetry consisting of 17 syllables, split into three lines of five, seven and five syllables.

A couple of 'famous' Haikus are this one by Basho Matsuo who is known as the first great (that's debatable) Haiku poet:

An old silent pond...
A frog jumps into the pond,
splash! Silence again.

by Basho (1644-1694)

And this one by Natsume Soseki who many (not me) consider the Charles Dickens of Japan:

Over the wintry
forest, winds howl in rage
with no leaves to blow.

by Soseki (1275-1351)

Another one that I found, that seems to have become an internet meme, is this one supposedly written by a school pupil to his teacher:

Five syllables here
Seven more syllables there
Are you happy now?
(anonymous)

I tried my own:

Writing haikus is
Extremely difficult and
Boring as bat shit

April 18th

Rachel and the children were out all day visiting friends. The sun was out and it was warmer than it had been in weeks. I decided to take advantage of the weather and do some work in the garden.

I got a little carried away, and a bit of trimming turned into a full-blown excavation of the largest shrub in our garden - the buddleia. The plant had developed into an alien life form, threatening to engulf our house. Complete removal was the only way to stop it. It took almost an entire afternoon of body destroying work to cut it down and dig up the roots. I snapped my spade, and almost my back, in the process.

I then decided to remove eight of the paving slabs, from our already small patio in order to make a modest vegetable patch. It was *National Garden Month*, so it felt like I was doing the right thing.

'What have you been up to today?' asked Rachel when she got home, in a way that actually meant: *'what pointless things have you done today, instead of having a proper job?'*

'Y'know, this and that,' I said, casually. 'Did some work. Did a bit of gardening.'

'Gardening? What sort of gardening?'

'Just a bit of pruning. Nothing major.'

She was already heading for the back door, which she opened to reveal a big hole in the patio where the buddleia had once been.

'Where has my buddleia gone?' she shouted.

'I dug it up. It was dead.'

'It wasn't dead. You kept moaning how it was growing so much.'

'Yeah. It grew so much that it died, suddenly.'

'Don't be stupid. Why did you get rid of it?'

'I told you I was going to trim it at some point,' I reminded her.

'Yes, but trimming doesn't tend to involve pulling up the roots too! What are you going to do with this big hole in our patio now?'

'That's going to be our very own vegetable patch.'

'Our garden is hardly big enough to incorporate a vegetable patch. Your veg patch looks like it is only big enough to grow A vegetable.'

'That's fine. It will be a particularly awesome vegetable then.'

'What made you think our garden was big enough for a vegetable patch? Are you going to plant an orchard next? Maybe a patch of woodland? Why don't you incorporate a fishing lake?'

She raised her eyebrows at me as though I was a mischievous pupil of hers, and strode back into the house. I felt very much like a naughty schoolboy. I did really want a vegetable patch, but the truth was that I HATED that buddleia. No matter how much I cut it back in the past, it kept on getting bigger and bigger. It had swallowed up our garden shed making it impossible for me to get anything in or out. I felt like this would be the year that it launched an attack on the house. I had to be pre-emptive and get rid of it before it got rid of us.

April 20th

One of the websites that I am using for these holiday listings included *Starman Day*, but there wasn't any further information about its origin or meaning. I wasn't able to establish whether this was in honour of the comic book hero, the David Bowie song... or maybe the Estonian Internet Service Provider. I concluded that as the latter was unlikely and the first one didn't interest me at all, I would listen to my copy of David Bowie's *Starman* which I have on a vinyl of *Ziggy Stardust* that I found in a skip in Leeds.

It took me nearly an hour to get my record player down from the attic and remember how to attach my speakers to it. My effort was worthless as just after the line *'Some cat was layin down some rock n roll'* the needle skipped right through the rest of the track. A giant scratch etched into the record gave a subtle suggestion as to why the album ended up in a skip.

April 21st

My book briefly broke into Amazon's overall Top 100 for the very first time, which is something that I never thought I would achieve. It peaked for an hour or so at number 82 and then started its inevitable long, slow slide down back down the rankings. Sales had dramatically increased though, and the free promotion was an undoubted success. I'm very pleased that I tried to *Reach As High As I Can*.

I received a phone call in the afternoon about Father Dougal.

'I've found a cat wandering the street outside our house. I think it might be yours.'

'Really?' I said, squealing slightly.

'Yes, although it looks a bit different to the one on the poster.'

'Ah, ok. Well it's not a very good photo.'

'This one has a blue collar.'

'Ah, right. Our cat's was definitely red. But maybe someone put a different collar on him. Does he look like the picture?'

'No. Your picture and description said your cat was black and white. This one is ginger.'

'Oh,' I said. 'Thanks anyway.'

As the days went by we knew it was more and more unlikely that Father Dougal would turn up. Because he had gone missing for a month before, we were still clinging on to a shred of hope that he would be found. I still looked for him whenever I went out for a run or bike ride, but I had started getting used to the fact that we may never see him again. Doug asked on a daily basis whether we had heard any news. It had clearly affected him and Chris very badly. I was used to seeing Father Dougal sprawled on their sofa whenever I called around to visit, and their house felt noticeably emptier without him.

April 22nd

Chemistry was a subject at school that I didn't have a great deal of fondness for. Sure, you got to make things go BANG, and make chemicals CHANGE COLOUR, but these moments of excitement were always padded out with pages and pages of boring method and analysis. Rather than simply being able to write *'I put the blue stuff in with the yellow stuff and it fizzed a bit,'* you had to draw boring diagrams to show your apparatus, and then a detailed write-up of the method, followed by what you expected would happen, and then an in-depth conclusion of what did actually happen. No amount of writing or analysis ever proved to be more conclusive or insightful than: *'I put the blue stuff in with the yellow stuff and it fizzed a bit.'*

Our school chemistry lessons were made slightly more exciting by our eccentric and well-over-retirement-age teacher Mr Mack. He was terrified of any sort of chemical reaction, which made being a chemistry teacher a strange career choice. He certainly looked the part though; always dressed in a white lab coat, large glasses and a shock of white hair that made him appear as though he had been electrocuted, which he probably had. He used to set up experiments - usually involving a bunsen burner - and as soon as he lit the flame he would rush off to the store cupboard where he would hide behind the door whilst a group of 30 eleven year olds sat waiting for something to happen. He would poke his head around the door occasionally to see if anything had happened, which more often than not it hadn't. On returning to the desk where the experiment was taking place, a fellow student named Andy would then shout a loud BANG in Mr Mack's direction. Mr Mack would jump out of his skin and scurry back to the store cupboard while the rest of the class howled with laughter. This happened on a weekly basis.

I still have a chemistry set in the attic that I was given for Christmas years ago. I was 13 and hoping for an electric guitar, like the ungrateful sod that I was.

Surely now, as a mature 33 year-old, I would be able to appreciate the chemistry set, and fully embrace today's official day - *Chemists Celebrate Earth Day*.

The chemistry set was three-quarters full, but all of the decent chemicals had gone. All that remained were a bunch of boring looking powders, and after a quick read of the instructions, it was clear that the most exciting thing I was capable of producing with what I had left was an 'odourless gas'.

I put it back in the attic and concluded that chemistry and I would never be great friends.

April 23rd

The name George was never fashionable when I was at school. In fact, it was particularly uncool. It was a name that completely bypassed my entire generation. When I was born, the doctor asked my mum what she was going to name me, and she told him 'George'. When he returned an hour later he asked: 'What are you really going to call him?'

There were 1200 pupils at my secondary school, and I was the only George. Having endured seven years at primary school listening to the constant chants of *'Georgie Porgie pudding and pie, kissed the girls and made them cry'*, I then moved on to 'big school' where the comedians there added the line *'when the boys came out to play, he kissed them too cos he was gay.'*

I'm not going to claim that I was traumatised or mentally scarred from this mild bullying. I became immune to it pretty quickly and it mostly washed over me. Or at least I think it did. No doubt in years to come, when I have some form of mental breakdown, a psychiatrist will probably trace this deep-rooted anxiety to these childhood chants.

The name George has made a comeback in recent years, however, and I would almost go as far as saying that it's slightly trendy. If you are a child, that is.

St George's Day has never been a big occasion for the English. As a nation, we could not be more self-deprecating if we tried. The idea of celebrating and embracing our heritage is fairly far from the mindset of most English people. The day usually passes by without as much as a mention. Whereas *St Patrick's Day*, on the other hand, is a very big deal and he's the patron saint of a different country.

Things felt slightly different this year. There has been a definite increase in the level of national pride in the last year. I think much of this is a hangover from the London Olympics, when there was a massive swell of patriotism. On the days leading up to *St George's Day* this year I noticed more in the way of build-up than I have ever seen before. Many pubs had red and white flags and bunting out and were advertising special food and drink deals on *St George's Day*, several houses along our street had their St George's flags in their windows, and Layla's school had a *St George's Day* activity planned to mark the occasion.

It was therefore with mild excitement that I read an article in the local paper, forwarded to me by a friend. It detailed a planned *'mass gathering of Georges'* at a local leisure park called Billing Aquadrome (which is nowhere near as cool as it sounds).

They wanted as many Georges as possible to gather together, in an attempt to break a world-record for the most Georges ever assembled together in one place. I've always wanted to be a world record holder at something, and this seemed like the perfect opportunity.

It gets better. They also offered a free cup of tea or coffee to all Georges, and a voucher for a free Sunday lunch, providing the George came with a dragon. I asked Rachel if she wanted to come along with Leo and Kitty, as I felt like I needed some moral support. She jumped at the chance of watching me make a fool out of myself, and despite my protests, spent half an hour searching for the cuddly toy dragon that I had bought the children on *Appreciate a Dragon Day*.

Billing Aquadrome is a fairly rubbish caravan park, foolishly built on a flood plain in Northamptonshire. We arrived at the manned barrier by the entrance at about 9.50am.

'Hi. I'm here for the *St George's Day* gathering,' I said to the man at the gate.

'What *St George's Day* gathering is that?' he asked.

'There was an article in the paper asking for Georges to turn up here today. Am I in the right place? It said something about a free tea or coffee.'

'That's the first I've heard about it. I assume it's in the cafe/restaurant building just there,' he said, pointing to a cafe/restaurant building, which was just there. 'Hold on, I'll just check for you.'

The man phoned through and had a vague conversation with the person on the other end who clearly seemed to know as little about it as he did.

'The guy from the bar said it sounded familiar but he would speak to his boss. He said you should head on down there and he would sort you out with a free cup of coffee anyway.'

The huge, modern, purpose built hub was deserted. All of the Georges were asked to arrive between 10am-11am. It was only 10.01am, and I was obviously the first one there.

The confused barman gave me a free coffee when I showed him my ID (the first time I have ever been ID'd getting a coffee) and I paid for one for Rachel.

'I hadn't heard anything about this until my boss told me about it two minutes ago,' he said. 'I imagine there'll be lots of others along soon if it was mentioned in the local paper.'

'I hope so,' I said.

Leo and Kitty had a brilliant time pretending to play in a car arcade machine, whilst Rachel and I sat and laughed at the absurdity of driving somewhere five miles away just for a free coffee.

After about 40 minutes the place was still empty and it was clear that no other Georges were going to make an appearance. I did feel slightly embarrassed about being the only George in the entire county that had made the effort to attend. I was also quite proud that their 'gathering' hadn't been a COMPLETE disaster. Although, as far as mass gatherings go, I am not sure ONE George even constitutes a small gathering. Even the organiser, who had been quoted in the paper, hadn't bothered to turn up.

It had been a fun hour, and no real embarrassment caused. We lured Leo and Kitty away from the arcade machines and were just about to leave when I felt a wave of panic flow through my body. I had looked up to see a man enter the building carrying two big SLR cameras. He looked slightly confused as he made his way to the bar, and I watched as he had a discussion with the manager before she pointed over towards me in the corner. It was the local press, and they had come to photograph this historic occasion. I was mortified.

The photographer had driven down from Milton Keynes especially for the event, and after a lot of persuasion, I agreed to have my photo taken for the paper so that his trip wasn't completely wasted. I had to pose with the manager whilst holding my free cup of coffee in one hand, and my dragon in the other, with a St George's Flag wrapped over my shoulders. Rachel looked on, unable to control her laughter.

My embarrassment and shame was going to be put into a newspaper and delivered for free to every household in Northamptonshire.

On the way out, the manager Clair stopped me.

'Thanks so much. It was really good of you to make the effort to come,' she said. 'You and all the family can come back for a complimentary Sunday lunch and a free swim on us any time you like.'

Every cloud...

The only George at Billing Aquadrome - '... like a knight in shining armour'.
(photo courtesy of Northants Herald and Post)

It was *World Book Night*, and I had been sent an email from a radio station based on the south coast that I had never heard of. One of the producers had read my book and thought that I might be an interesting person to interview as part of *World Book Night*. I told them I wasn't a very interesting person, but I would be happy to speak to them. At 3pm the phone rang and I was put through to the DJ. We had a good interview and then he asked me whether I was going to be celebrating *World Book Night*.

I hadn't even thought about it. How WAS I going to be celebrating *World Book Night*? I had been so pre-occupied with *St George's Day* that I hadn't even considered it. But I was supposed to be celebrating as many of these holidays as possible so I couldn't really say no. Especially seeing as someone had asked me specifically.

'OF COURSE I will be celebrating *World Book Night*,' I said, enthusiastically. 'It's one of the HIGHLIGHTS of my year.'

I realised I had perhaps gone a little too far with that second statement.

'Fantastic. So what will you be doing to celebrate this momentous day?'

'Well... I... er...' I stuttered. 'I am planning on giving free copies of my book to... er... random people in the street.'

'That sounds like a great idea. Good for you.'

'Well, it's nice to be able to give something back.'

I received a tweet later in the afternoon:

'Free pint today at Behind The Bus Stop if you can prove you're a George.'

Behind the Bus Stop is a new independently run bar in Northampton, and, despite my earlier humiliation, a free pint seemed like too good an opportunity to miss, so I met a friend (not another George) at the bar after he had finished work to claim my freebie. Thankfully, this time, there were no local press present.

True to my word, I took five paperback copies of my book with me. I was running late so rather than stop random people and hand them out, I left them on the seat at the bus stop which is right in front of the bar (the bar is called Behind the Bus Stop for a reason). Within half an hour of us being there, all five books were taken. We watched as one by one people picked up a copy, looked around to see if they belonged to anyone, and then walked off. I have no idea if any of the people will ever actually read them, but it made me feel good. It also helped clear some crap from my desk. Not that my book is crap. Oh, never mind.

Despite the incident with the local press, *St George's Day* was one of the most fun days I have had in a long while. It's awesome being called George.

April 24th

Forming the focus of *National Secretaries Week*, *Administrative Professionals Day* was created in 1952 by Harry F. Klemfuss. His aim was to promote the importance of administrative assistants, and encourage people to show appreciation to theirs. The day is fairly popular in the US nowadays, and bosses are encouraged to buy their secretary a gift.

'I'm sort of your Administrative Professional,' said Rachel, when she found out what day it was.

'In what way?' I asked.

'I assist you in things. Like helping in the kitchen or helping you find the car keys.'

'Yes, but this is *Administrative Professionals Day*, not *Helpful Wife Day*.'

'But you don't have an Administrative Professional.'

'No, but that doesn't mean that you are my Administrative Professional by default.'

'I make you cups of tea sometimes,' she said.

'You ask me if I want a cup of tea and then put the kettle on and nothing else ever happens. I end up making the tea, but because you offered and put the kettle on, you think that means you can take the credit. Besides, making tea is hardly administrative.'

'Well I'm as close to an administrative assistant as you've got.'

'Ok fine. Do you want a cup of tea?' I asked

'Yes please. I have already boiled the kettle.'

I considered hiring an administrative professional.

I would love to have an employee to help me with the long and dreary procedure of processing wedding photos. I would also like someone that I could pay to do the other boring bits of work that I do. Unfortunately, I can barely afford to pay our own bills, let alone the wages of someone else.

I decided to post an advert on a Jobseekers website:

ADMINISTRATIVE PROFESSIONAL
For Photographer/author

Duties to include:
Processing digital photos
Boring computer work
Book promotion
Maintaining a website
Making tea

Benefits include:
Pleasant(ish) home-office environment
All the tea you can drink
Toast
Flexible hours

Salary: Non-existent
Location: Northampton

I received two responses. The first was from a guy named Greg. He wrote:

Dear Sir/Madam
I am interested in the Administrative Professional job advertised on 24/04/13. The salary description on the advert says 'non-existent'. Could you possibly clarify what you mean by this?

Kind regards,
Greg Davids

I wrote back…

Dear Greg
Thank you for your interest in the Administrative Professional job. Unfortunately, it is an unpaid position as I am currently not able to afford to pay anyone. The job may, in time, lead to a fully paid position, but this is unlikely.
If you would like any more details, or would like an informal chat then please don't hesitate to contact me.
Kind regards
George Mahood

I never heard from Greg again.

The other response simply said:

You tight-arsed prick.

April 25th

Rachel likes to pick and chose which days she is enthusiastic about. *Take Our Daughters & Sons to Work Day* was one that she was particularly keen that I celebrate.

'But I'm only working upstairs. I'll be sitting at the computer all day editing wedding photos. I don't think Leo and Kitty would enjoy that,' I pleaded.

'I think it's important that they get to see what Daddy does at work,' argued Rachel with a grin across her face the size of Texas.

'I think this day is designed for older children really. A sort of work-experience thing.'

'So you're just going to turn down an opportunity to celebrate this one are you, simply because you think they'll get in the way?'

'I didn't say that. I said… fine… whatever… they can both come to WORK with me for the day.'

'Great, see you later then. I'm going shopping'.

I have had some pretty unproductive days in my time, but this one topped them all. I sat Leo and Kitty on the small sofa in the study, and I perched next to them and tried to go through the photos from the wedding last weekend; deleting some photos, converting others to black and white, cropping out ugly guests, that sort of thing. Leo twanged the strings on my guitar incessantly, and Kitty just sat there banging her hand on the keyboard as hard as she could. I spent ages searching for several key group photos only to discover them in the Recycle Bin. She then sneezed all over the screen and wiped her snotty fingers over my laptop's scroll pad.

After a while I encouraged them both to get off the sofa and I let them roam around the two square metres of office space that I have. They were both fascinated to explore new things in a room that they never usually get to play in. The downstairs of our house is fairly child proofed, but the study is far from it. At one point I looked up to find Kitty perilously close to the paper shredder which I hastily moved. Leo then started fiddling around with a guillotine and a tangle of battery chargers.

I appreciate that *Take Our Daughters & Sons to Work Day* has the potential to be a great opportunity for children. Providing that your children are at an age when they can either observe or help out, and learn something, and that your job is a little more stimulating than sitting in a cramped upstairs bedroom.

My working day was over by 9.45am.

We went to the park instead.

The Red Hat Society is a social organisation for women over 50. It was created in 1998 in California by Sue Ellen Cooper after she gave her friend a red hat for her birthday, with the opening lines of a poem by Jenny Joseph:

When I am an old woman I shall wear purple
With a red hat that doesn't go and doesn't suit me.

The group has about two million registered members worldwide, but the entry requirements seem somewhat lax. I was accepted as a member of the *Red Hat Society* despite being a 33 year-old male. I didn't even need to lie on my online application.

This holiday challenge was slowly and subtly making me a part of middle-aged American feminism. I was already a big supporter of *Women in Blue Jeans*, and now here I was encouraging the *Red Hat Society*. Surely the groups could combine to form one supergroup: *The Women in Blue Jeans and Red Hat Society*. World domination would be inevitable.

I'm still waiting to see the benefits of being a member of the *Red Hat Society*, but it's only a matter of time.

April 26th

Today was *Hug an Australian Day*.

There are only a couple of Australians that I would go out of my way to hug. The first, and most obvious, is Kylie. After several phone calls I managed to get to speak to one of Kylie's agents or representatives.

'Hello, I was wondering if it would be possible to give Kylie a hug today.'

There was a long pause.

'I'm sorry, is this a joke?' said the woman at the other end of the phone.

'Er, no, it's *Hug an Australian Day* today and she's my favourite Australian.'

'Sorry no, that's not going to be possible.'

I was about to ask why, but she'd hung up. I resisted the temptation to call her back.

Alan Fletcher, who plays Dr Karl Kennedy in the Australian soap *Neighbours*, was next on my list. This may seem like a huge step down from Kylie, but he's a true legend in my eyes. Not only is he *'Australia's finest actor'* (George Mahood, 2013) but he is also a talented musician and a photographer. He tours student bars across the world with his band *Waiting Room* and is a renowned photographer in Melbourne.

I sent him an email.

Hi Alan

It's Hug an Australian Day today, and you are my second favourite Australian. Kylie wouldn't hug me and I was wondering whether you would? Are you by any chance in the UK at the moment so we could meet for a hug?

Thanks

George

I clicked *Send and Receive* on my email all morning, despite the fact that if he was in Australia, which was highly likely, then he would probably have been asleep. I eventually had a reply in the afternoon.

Dear George,
Unfortunately I am not in the UK. Maybe next year.
Good on you for your generosity of spirit.
Cheers, Alan

I take Leo to his swimming lesson on Friday afternoons and his teacher is a fairly scary Australian lady. As he is only three, I go into the pool with him during the lesson. She's very nice, but very strict and not the sort of person who I could ask for a hug from. Especially not whilst partially clothed in the middle of a swimming lesson. But I was getting desperate. I didn't know any other Australians in Northampton.

I find it mildly amusing that an Australian lifeguard ended up in Northampton, so far from the sea. Shark attacks in Northampton swimming pools are fairly uncommon, so I guess it is a slightly less stressful place to work than Bondi Beach. I was going to try and incorporate a hug subtly into conversation somehow, but I knew that would make it far more awkward. I decided just to be honest about it.

'It's *Hug an Australian Day* today,' I said, at the end of the lesson as we were wading towards the steps at the side of the pool.

'Is it?' she replied.

'Yes. Any chance of a hug?' I asked, apologetically.

'Really? Well, ok then,' she said and we had a very awkward and brief hug at the edge of the pool.

'You are Australian, aren't you?' I asked as I climbed up the ladder.

'No, I'm a Kiwi.'

'Oh God, I'm so sorry,' I said, mortified.

'Nah, I'm just kidding. Of course I'm an Aussie, you daft Pomme.'

'Phew, because that would have made it even more weird. See you next week.'

'Hooroo. See you later.'

April 27th

National Rebuilding Day is a day when volunteers throughout America team together to rehabilitate and improve homes of low-income Americans at no cost. It would have been a little impractical for me to get on a plane and fly to America to help build houses for free. I think hugging Kylie would have been a more achievable goal.

I ignored the genuine origin of this holiday, as well as the 're' prefix and used it as a reason to build the raised vegetable patch that I had been fantasising about since digging up the patio.

I had never bought a brick before and was somewhat overwhelmed by the choice at the local builders' merchants. I was given some truly useless assistance from a truly useless assistant, and decided on some cheap red engineering bricks. I bought 60 and a bag of idiot proof mortar.

Bricklaying was more difficult than I thought, but as I was only building a two brick high wall, and not any sort of structure, I had little concern for accuracy, stability, safety or tidiness.

'You've got cement all over the patio,' said Rachel over my shoulder.

'I know, sorry. It'll come off though. It's impossible to keep it all on the bricks.'

'Do you not think it would've been better getting someone who knows what they're doing?' she continued.

'You can talk. What about your attempt at plastering?'

I once came home to find Rachel attempting to plaster the spare bedroom, because a useless assistant at a DIY store had told her that plastering was easy. We had to rip out the entire carpet because she managed to get more plaster on the floor than the walls.

She didn't bother answering my question and disappeared back inside the house.

For a first attempt at bricklaying, I did a fairly decent job. The wall, although small, stayed standing and looked reasonably tidy, too. All we needed was some more soil... and some vegetables, and we would have a fully functioning vegetable patch.

April 28th

I remember being extraordinarily excited as a child when I made my first pinhole camera with my parents. It was such an amazing experience to be able to turn a humble shoebox into a piece of technology, and one that enabled us to produce instant images. I remember it clearly and think that is possibly what first stirred my love of photography.

Today was *Worldwide Pinhole Photography Day* and I wanted to recreate this level of excitement and magic for my children, as I hoped it was something that would stick with them forever, too. Whilst Layla was at school, Leo, Kitty and I made a pinhole camera out of an empty tube of Pringles (other stackable snack chips are available) from some instructions that we found on the internet.

We waited until Layla was back from school before the momentous occasion when we used the camera for the first time. I made sure to give it a dramatic build-up, but it is fair to say that they were a little underwhelmed. Producing a faint upturned image on the lid of an empty tube of crisps was, to me, still a spectacular thing. The children were less than impressed.

'But it's upside-down,' said Layla.

'Yes, but we made that picture using a tube of crisps.'

'What is the picture?' asked Leo.

'It can be whatever you want it to be. Point it at whatever you like.'

'Why don't you just take pictures with your phone, Daddy? They look much better,' he said.

'But this is a camera that we made out of a TUBE OF CRISPS! Isn't it AMAZING? This is state-of-the art. In my day we didn't even have Pringles. We had to use a shoe box.'

Layla and Leo were right, though. I couldn't argue with them. As incredible as it was to be able to take a picture (sort of) using a tube of Pringles, it was even more astounding that I could take beautifully sharp, brightly coloured photographs using the phone in my pocket.

Kids today. Pah! They don't know how lucky they are.

April 29th

Kitty is now 20 months old and has started to take an interest in her nappy 'goings-on'. She tends to say 'poo' or 'wee' when she has some action, and then insists on washing her hands after she has done whatever she was doing in her nappy. We have used reusable nappies for all three of our children and have been excited about the prospect of potty training Kitty, so that we never have to wash a dirty nappy ever again. Now seemed as good a time as any to try potty training. It was also *National Scoop the Poop Week* which made it even more appropriate, although I don't think the creators of this week intended it to be the human kind.

Things didn't go quite as well as we hoped, but there was plenty of poop scooping to do which meant that this holiday was well and truly honoured, although perhaps not celebrated.

April 30th

Rachel and I were fortunate enough to have a family holiday with my parents, sister and brother-in-law in South Africa soon after we were married. We travelled around the Western Cape with a guide, staying in different accommodation each night. Our evening meals were always cooked outside on a braai - which is a South African barbeque. These came in many forms; sometimes a purpose built brick structure, other times an open pit, or occasionally a shop-bought metal barbeque. But by far the most memorable was an empty washing machine drum. The drum - removed from the washing machine, obviously - forms an almost perfect incinerator. It is metal, and therefore fireproof, and covered in holes, which makes for great air circulation. Vegetables such as potatoes, onions and butternut squash were wrapped in foil and then dropped onto the embers. A rack was then mounted on top of the drum on which a variety of meats were cooked. Our guest chef for one night - a South African named Theo - asked us each how we would like our steak cooked.

'Medium rare.'

'Rare.'

'Rare.'

'Medium,' we each said in turn.

We then watched as Theo barbecued the steaks for over 20 minutes ON EACH SIDE over a blazing fire. We all looked on in disbelief as he cremated our dinner.

He then removed the 'rare' steaks, before cooking the medium-rare and the medium for another ten minutes. And South-Africans are supposed to be the King of Barbeques?

'Thank God we didn't ask for them well-done,' muttered my dad.

Although not overly impressed by the actual food, I was still incredibly amazed by the washing machine drum and vowed to get hold of our own as soon as we got home.

So, the day after returning to the UK, I headed off to the local tip and picked up an old washing machine for £5 which I then took back to our house.

Removing the drum from the washing machine was an unexpectedly difficult task, requiring hammers, spanners and a huge amount of brute force and swearing. My Mum then asked for one for Christmas so I had to go through the whole process again.

We mounted the drum on our patio on some bricks and lit a ceremonial fire, and then the following day we put it to one side and have not used since.

That was until the joint celebrations of today's *Beltane* and *Walpurgis Night*. Both amount to pretty much the same thing. They are spring festivals exactly six months after (or before) Halloween, and involve dancing around a bonfire. It was actually quite good fun, and the children got very into it. There was a lot of curtain twitching going on from the neighbours at the sight of five people dancing randomly around a blazing washing machine drum. It certainly renewed my love for my trusty braai, and it will now remain a regular feature on our patio. I think the dancing was a one off, though.

MAY

May 1st

Today was *Great American Grump Out*, and I had my own resident grump in the house. She wasn't American, but I was determined to out her grumpiness.

I'd had an argument with Rachel about clothes and she didn't speak to me for most of the morning. Girls have a habit of saying things like, *'I've got nothing to wear'*, or *'none of my clothes fit me'*. Six years of a rolling cycle of maternity, pregnancy and then post-pregnancy multiplies these comments by ten.

'You don't understand at all. There's no point in even discussing this with you. My clothes DON'T FIT,' she said. 'Last summer I was still breast feeding so all my summer clothes were suitable for that.'

'But what about your clothes from the summer before that, and all the summers before that?' I asked.

'You're not listening to me! All of my other non-maternity clothes that I have are too big for me. I wore them just after having babies, and I'm not the same size that I was then.'

'But surely your clothes from before we had kids now fit you?' I suggested.

'My God, you are sooo annoying. But they are six years old!'

'But you haven't worn them in six years so it'll be like they are new again.'

'Just because you are happy wearing the same clothes that you wore years ago doesn't mean I have to.'

She had a point. I have couple of t-shirts that I consider my 'Sunday best'. I will only ever wear them when we are going out, or for very special occasions. I would NEVER consider wearing them on a normal day. They are my NEW special t-shirts. Reserved for important days. Or so I thought. I recently worked out that they are each at least four years old, and both were bought second-hand from charity shops. What does that say about my normal clothes? I'm probably not the best person to be dishing out fashion advice.

I couldn't win. If I agreed with her then she would claim I thought all her clothes were horrible and that she looked fat and ugly. If I disagreed with her then she thought I was trying to piss her off.

The truth is that I think Rachel looks lovely in whatever she wears, regardless of whether her clothes are too big or too small and whether they are six years old or not. I'm not sure I would even notice, but that doesn't mean that I don't care.

The Great American Grump Out has been running since 2002. The idea is that you completely banish grumpiness for 24 hours. I was in a fairly chirpy and non-grumpy mood all day. Rachel, however, wasn't, and I saw it as my challenge to rid her grumpiness, seeing as I had seemingly caused it in the first place.

'Let's not argue. I'm sorry for suggesting that you did have clothes that were suitable,' I said to her, with doe eyes whilst she tidied things away from the sides in the kitchen in the frantic manner in which she does when she's in a bad mood.

'You're always doing that, questioning everything I do.'

'I'm sorry, I really am. It's *Great American Grump Out* today, so we need to make you happy,' I said, leaning in for a cuddle.

'Don't, I'm not in the mood,' she said as she pushed me away.

'*Choosing to be un-grumpy could result in strengthening your immune system, diminish tension in your central nervous system, relax your body, improve circulation, reduce your stress hormones and, possibly, make new friends,*' I said, reading directly from the official *Great American Grump Out* website.

'Seriously, I'm not in the mood. And I'm certainly not American.'

'Let's move house,' I said.

'What? Today?' she said, smiling for the first time.

'Well, maybe not today, but as soon as we can.'

Since *Ellis Island Family History Day*, I have been thinking more and more about relocating. There is no doubt that we have outgrown our current house and Rachel and I are both still keen on the idea of moving down to Devon. Rachel is much more proactive than I am about the whole thing, and I always seem to come up with an excuse to delay the proceedings. I don't even know why. It just seems like quite a daunting prospect and I am generally not fond of change. Today was *New Homeowner's Day* and it was definitely the motivation I needed.

So far, all of the holidays that I have celebrated have been fun, or interesting, but nothing has been life changing. I wanted this project to change me - hopefully in a good way - and the only way to do this would be to embrace the days that allowed for a more radical life change. *New Homeowner's Day* would certainly do that.

Obviously it's not practical, or possible, to sell, buy and move house in a day, but it was enough to start the wheels in motion. Rachel phoned up three local estate agents to arrange for a valuation of our house and I booked a mortgage appointment with our bank for later in the day.

I had not seen Rachel so excited for a long time. The Grump was well and truly gone.

As it was also *Loyalty Day* I booked the mortgage appointment with the bank I have been with since the age of 10. I figured they were most likely to be on our side and have faith in our ability to keep up repayments. I could not have been more wrong. I don't want to name and shame them (HSBC) but the lady I had a meeting with looked at me with contempt as soon as I mentioned the word 'self-employed'. I understand that banks are going through an extremely tough time at the moment and that all of their rules have tightened up, but there was no glimpse of empathy or understanding from the mortgage advisor whatsoever. Being self-employed obviously has some risk attached to it, and wages can dramatically fluctuate from year to year. Wedding photography, however, because it is generally booked so far in advance, does come with a level of security that even people in full-time employment don't have.

I then have the bonus of the additional revenue that I receive from book sales, which I felt slightly embarrassed to even mention.

'And is that amount declared as part of the tax return that you have just submitted?' she asked, slightly aggressively.

'Yes, of course.'

'So next year you won't have that additional income, so your wages will have reduced even further?'

'Well, not necessarily. My book is still doing ok, and hopefully that will continue,' I said. 'And I'm writing another book at the moment which will be out early next year.'

'And did you receive an advance from a publisher for the new book?'

'No. I'm going to publish it myself.'

She sniffed a little patronising laugh and banged away at her computer keyboard.

'What is the new book about, just out of curiosity?' she asked.

'It's called *Every Day is a Holiday* and involves me celebrating different quirky holidays each day. It's a sort of mildly humorous memoir.'

'It sounds a bit random to me. Isn't that more of a blog? I don't know if that would work as a book.'

'You're not the first person to say that, but I think it will be good.'

'And I assume that if you move to the south west, your wife will have a job to go to?' she asked.

'Well, no. Not to start with. She only works for one day a week at the moment, because we have two children who are not at school or nursery yet.'

She gave another little smirk.

'Well that means she becomes your 4th dependant as you will be supporting her as well as your children.'

'But I've been doing that for the last six years anyway,' I argued.

She carried on banging at her keyboard.

She eventually told me the total that we would be allowed to borrow. It was significantly less than we are borrowing for our current house.

'So, if we moved house, we wouldn't even be able to borrow what we are borrowing at the moment?'

'That's correct.'

'But we got our current mortgage when we were both working in minimum wage temping jobs. Are you suggesting that we are in a significantly worse financial situation than we were ten years ago?'

'It would appear so, yes. Sorry,' she said, with the manner of someone who was not in the least bit sorry.

'Well, thanks for that,' I said, and left the bank fairly abruptly.

I returned home and broke the news to Rachel. The Grump made a swift return.

May 2nd

Layla's school was closed as it was being used as a polling station. As Rachel was at work, I had all three kids to look after. I was extremely excited about the prospect, as although I often do things with all three of them on my own, it's quite rare for me to have all three for the entire day. I looked at my holiday list to try and find an appropriate celebration to incorporate into our plans.

Martin Z. Mollusk Day is an event celebrated in Ocean City, New Jersey during which a hermit crab named Martin makes an appearance. In the manner of Punxsutawney Phil on *Groundhog Day*, if he sees his shadow it means that summer will come a week early. As exciting as it sounded, Martin was in Ocean City, USA and we were in Northampton, UK.

It was also *National Day of Prayer* which was introduced by US Congress in 1952 as a day to encourage Americans to pray to God. The day has had its fair share of criticism from atheists over the years, and, in 2003, the American Humanist Association created the *National Day of Reason* to fall on the same date each year. It was in direct opposition to the *Day of Prayer*, and a protest about the close relationship between religion and politics.

That was decided then. I would spend the day with my children debating the positive and negative connotations of religion becoming entwined into US politics. It would be interesting and enlightening for them and undoubtedly a whole heap of fun.

'What do you think, guys? Do you think it's right that religion should have found its way into US politics?' I asked them over breakfast.

'What are you talking about, Daddy? Can we go to the farm today, because I didn't get to go on Mummy's birthday?' said Layla.

'Yeah, faaaarm!' shouted Leo.

'Faaarrrm,' repeated Kitty, knocking her bowl of Cheerios all over the floor.

'Ok, let's go to the farm then,' I said.

It was one of the warmest days of the year so far, and a much more enjoyable day than any scheduled holiday celebration could have provided. We were the first to arrive when it opened, and the last to leave as it was closing. Apart from one moment when I lost Kitty in a giant soft play structure, it all went really well. She emerged head first at the bottom of a purple corkscrew slide. Then Leo appeared a few seconds later with a guilty look on his face. Kitty spent the rest of the day repeating the phrase: 'Purple slide. Leo push me. Bump head. Scary. Purple slide. Leo push me. Bump head. Scary.'

May 3rd

I came downstairs to find Rachel shouting at her laptop.

'What's wrong?' I asked.

'I don't understand the stupid bidding on eBay?'

'What do you mean?'

'If I put in a maximum bid what happens if I don't want to pay that much?'

'Then you don't put in that as a maximum bid. You bid the maximum you are happy to pay.'

'I want to win it. I just don't want to pay what it will probably go for.'

'Well that's sort of the whole point of the bidding system. What are you bidding on anyway?'

'A rain coat.'

'A second-hand raincoat? Why? How much for?'

'They seem to go for about £80.'

'£80? For a second hand rain coat? Why on earth would you pay that?'

'It's really nice.'

'What's wrong with your other rain coat?'

'It doesn't go with my summer dresses.'

'Why would you be wearing a rain coat at the same time as a summer dress?'

'I don't know. I might need to.'

I didn't know how to respond, and I didn't want to annoy Rachel again with another argument about clothes, so I walked straight on through to the back door where all our shoes are kept.

National Two Different Coloured Shoes Day was surprisingly fun. I wore one blue trainer and one green walking shoe. Although they were slightly different heights, I soon got used to the limp. This wasn't the first time I had spent the day with two different coloured shoes on. I once photographed a wedding wearing one brown shoe and once black shoe because I had put them on in the dark. Nobody seemed to notice.

May 4th

May 4th has become known in recent years as *Star Wars Day*, due to the phrase *'May the fourth be with you'* being a reference to the classic Star Wars line *'may the force be with you'*. Nowadays you can't escape people tweeting, speaking and texting the phrase *'May the fourth be with you'* thinking they are the most clever and original person in the world, and the only person to have thought of such an astute and witty pun. The truth is, I invented the phrase. Way back in 1996, which was 15 years before *Star Wars Day* was even created. That's correct; the whole phenomenon (perhaps that is slightly over-hyping it?) is because of ME.

A good friend of mine from school called Sam, decided to have a party at his house whilst his parents were away. I was given the task of designing and producing the invitations, for no other reason than my mum had a laminator and some coloured paper. She was a teacher.

The party was due to be held on Saturday 4th May, and, in a stroke of genius, I invented the phrase *'May the Fourth be with you'*, and from this innocent party invite, the phrase has spread across the world.

Or so I thought. Having just done some extensive research (Wikipedia) I have discovered that perhaps I didn't invent the phrase after all. References go as far back as 4th May 1979 when the Conservative Party took out an advert in the London Evening News with the message *'May the Fourth Be With You, Maggie. Congratulations.'* That was a week before I was even born! DAMN YOU, Tory party.

Sam's party was a great success (because of my invitations, presumably) although somebody did do a piss in the punch.

May 5th

Kitty's potty training still wasn't going very well, but we had decided to stick at it. As with Layla and Leo, we decided to go for the all or nothing approach, and opted for pants instead of a nappy from Day One. She was great most of the time, but had regular accidents. I had taken to carrying a spare pair of her knickers in my pocket for emergency situations when I didn't have any other spare clothes handy.

Today, I was buying some bread and milk from the local Co-op. I was at the till and I went to retrieve my wallet from my trouser pocket, and as I pulled it out, a pair of pink girl's knickers flew out onto the edge of the conveyor belt. The cashier, a middle-aged Asian man, looked at the underwear and then at me with a look of horror across his face.

'POTTY TRAINING,' I blurted. 'They're in case of an accident.'

He raised one eyebrow at me with a look of confusion.

'Oh, no, not ME! They're my daughter's. SHE'S potty training.'

He looked to either side of me and then straight back to me when he could see that I was alone.

'She's at home. Oh, NEVER MIND!' I said, hastily snatching the knickers and stuffing them quickly into my pocket.

I can't shop at that branch of Co-op ever again.

'You pulled out a pair of girl's pants in the shop?' laughed Rachel when I told her what had happened. 'That's brilliant. You must have looked like such a dirty old man.'

'Thanks a lot! The more I tried to explain it to him the less convincing it sounded. It was so embarrassing.'

'Oh well, does it fit in with any of your holiday celebrations today? It's not *National Paedo Day* or anything, is it?'

'It's *World Laughter Day*,' I said. 'But it wasn't funny in the slightest.'

'It's the funniest thing I've heard in a long time. I'll celebrate this one on your behalf.'

May 6th

To celebrate *No Diet Day* I needed to be on a diet in the first place. I have never been on a diet before. In the past, I have always been lucky enough to stay at a fairly constant weight, usually through exercise - playing football, running occasionally and walking or cycling, instead of driving, whenever possible. Since having children things have changed. The weight has gradually piled on. I'm not going to try and blame old age or metabolism or 'my glands'. I can't even really blame a lack of exercise, as although I now only play football once a week instead of twice, and rarely run or cycle, I am kept active with three children; a trip to the park is a work-out in itself. The real reason why I have put on weight is simply because I eat too much. I eat SHIT LOADS of food. The kids wake early so we tend to have breakfast before 7am. We are then all hungry by late morning so lunch tends to be at about 11.30am. I then have my 'proper' lunch at about 1pm. Most nights we try to eat as a family at about 5pm, but I'm then hungry later in the evening so have another full dinner at about 9pm. Having FIVE meals a day, it's no wonder I've put on weight.

It didn't bother me at all until recently when Rachel and I were on a rare night out at a restaurant.

'I'm getting fat, aren't I?' I said to Rachel as I bit into a huge cheese and bacon burger, as the fat dribbled slowly down my chin.

'No you're not,' she said kindly.

'I am. Be honest, you can tell me the truth.'

'You're not fat,' she said again, this time slightly hesitantly. 'You're just... biggishly built.'

'BIGGISHLY BUILT?' I said, spitting chunks of burger across the table. 'What do you mean?'

'Did I say that? I don't think I said that. No, I didn't say that.'

'You did! You just said I was BIGGISHLY built.'

'I don't think I did. What does that even mean? Is biggishly even a word.'

'No, but you still said it. And it's a polite way of saying I'm fat.'

'I didn't say you were biggishly built.'

'What did you say then?'

'Nothing. I just... I just... I don't know what I said.'

Further confirmation that I was biggishly built came when I went to read the dessert menu and I looked down and something was blocking my view. I then realised it was my cheeks. I had never been able to see my own cheeks before, and there they were impeding my line of sight.

There had been other clues too, that I had conveniently ignored. I had recently received my final stamp on my loyalty card at Embers Grill takeaway. It was a landmark achievement that I was very proud of. Most weeks, after photographing a wedding, I would call into Embers Grill for a shish kebab and chips to eat whilst watching *Match of the Day*. I had received ten stamps on my loyalty card in the space of a couple of months. The reward for completing the card was a free kebab. You would have thought that the alarm bells should have sounded when I first got a LOYALTY CARD at a FUCKING KEBAB HOUSE, but oh no, it seemed like the most natural thing in the world.

I had also noticed an issue with a pair of trousers that I wore for photography jobs. They had been slipping down around my waist whilst I was working, and for a while I assumed that I must have just been skinnier than when I bought them. I then had the shocking realisation recently that they weren't slipping down my waist; they were actually being PUSHED down by my stomach. Rachel was right. I was getting bigger and I needed to do something about it.

That was over a week ago and I had totally forgotten about the idea of dieting until it was *No Diet Day*. But as I said, to celebrate *No Diet Day* properly, I needed to be on a diet in the first place. So I decided, there and then, to go on a diet... the following day.

Every year a different dieting fad comes along, which claims to be completely different to all the others: Atkins, Dukan, South Beach etc. This year's craze is the Fasting Diet. It comes in various guises, and is not a new concept as such, but it is certainly new to me. The idea is that for five days of the week you eat pretty much whatever you like, but on the other two days you reduce your calorie intake to 500 for women or 600 for men - usually spread between two meals (breakfast and dinner). I have genuinely never looked at calorie information before in my life, so I have got no idea how many calories are in what, but I am prepared to give it a go. I like a challenge and, although tiresome, a diet is basically just another challenge.

As it was *No Diet Day*, today was to be one of my non-fasting days. I celebrated by eating an entire Toblerone. Tomorrow I would fast.

May 7th

The Falcon was the trusty little racing bike that I used during my Land's End to John O'Groats trip. It was a bike completely unsuitable for a full-grown man, but it's fair to say that I became more than a little obsessed with it. I kept it after the trip and it takes pride of place... in my shed. I don't ride it very often because, well, it's ridiculously uncomfortable and incredibly unreliable.

But in September of last year I was persuaded to sign up for a triathlon (by a friend who subsequently decided not to enter) and I realised a few days before the event that I didn't have a road bike. Sure, I did have another bike, but that was a big, ugly, unwieldy thing that would not look the part in a triathlon. Not that The Falcon did either, but it was at least a road bike. I decided to dust off the cobwebs and give it a bit of oil, and it looked almost as good as it did when I got it - which was pretty shit looking, to be honest.

The triathlon itself was brilliant fun. It was only a *sprint* distance which involved relatively short stages of the swim, bike and run. The Falcon was even more uncomfortable than I remembered and I heard lots of sniggers and comments from the marshals and other competitors along the route. However, its erratic chain, which used to fall off every few hundred metres throughout the length of Britain, stayed on the entire way. I then put it back in the shed where it has remained ever since.

May is *National Bike Month*, and it seemed only fair to allow The Falcon out of confinement for some fresh air, in order to honour this celebration. I swapped my usual breakfast of a bowl of cereal and a couple of pieces of toast for a small bowl of yoghurt and a chopped banana. I was fasting.

I then spent the morning out and about, exploring the beautiful countryside around Northampton on my bike. The gears creaked and the cogs grinded through neglect and resentment at coming out of retirement. But The Falcon definitely still had it. Despite being bent over in my hunchback position, with my arse already suffering from the bike's inhumane saddle, I was ripping up the miles.

I got back home at midday having cycled about 30 miles, which was the most I have cycled in a long time. I was ravenous, and was just about to dive into the sweets drawer (yes, we have a sweets drawer) when Rachel interrupted:

'I thought you were fasting today,' she said.

'Oh, bollocks. I'd forgotten.'

'Does that mean you're not allowed any sweets?'

'Yes. Not only that. It means I can't have anything for lunch at all.'

'Ah.'

I spent the entire afternoon in a dreadful mood, because of the hollow, gnawing feeling in my stomach. I watched as the clock ticked through until 5pm, which I decided was an acceptable time for dinner.

A small bowl of soup briefly eased my hunger, until it returned half an hour later.

'I fucking hate this stupid fucking fasting diet,' I said. 'What a load of shit.'

'Why don't you just stop it then?'

'Because I'm biggishly built.'

'No you're not. Stop being silly.'

'I am. You were right. I'm going to stick at this until at least the end of the month.'

'Oh dear. These next few weeks are going to be fun,' she said.

May 8th

I didn't like the sound of *Cranmere Day*.

Cranmere, I imagined, would be a boring American politician who established some pointless act many years ago, and has now been given a holiday in his honour.

I did a quick internet search, just to humour him, and was pleasantly surprised; *Cranmere Day* had nothing to do with any American politicians. It was, in fact, a day to celebrate an exciting pastime that I didn't even know existed – Letterboxing.

In 1854 a guide, named James Perrott, left a bottle at Cranmere Pool on Dartmoor to encourage walkers to this remote site to leave calling cards to show they too had visited the place. The bottle was later replaced with a box, and various other boxes started appearing across Dartmoor. Clues were circulated to the whereabouts of these boxes, and the leisure pursuit of Letterboxing was born.

Nowadays, there are over a thousand letterboxes on Dartmoor. Each waterproof box contains a log book and a unique rubber stamp. The person who discovers the letterbox then stamps their own log book to prove they have visited it, and stamps the log book in the letterbox to show they found it. The letterbox is then placed back where it was found. There is even a 100-club for enthusiasts to join once they have found 100 boxes.

I was frustrated that such an exciting and fun activity had passed me by. I got the impression from reading the letterboxing forums that it is quite an exclusive club, and that they are happy for it to be a largely unknown sport. It's a bit like *Fight Club*. I almost feel guilty for giving away the details that I have. The first rule of letterboxing is DO NOT TALK ABOUT LETTERBOXING.

I wanted in.

Letterboxing has gained popularity in the US in recent years, but outside of Dartmoor it is relatively non-existent in the UK. I found a site devoted to Urban Letterboxing, which is basically what it implies. There were a few boxes listed in London, York, Bath and Brighton but that was all.

It was time to put Northampton on the Letterboxing map.

I walked into town with Leo and Kitty and bought a plastic container, some cheap kids' rubber stamp pens and a small hardback notebook. When we got home I wrote in big letters on the container.

OFFICIAL LETTERBOX – PLEASE DO NOT DISTURB

Inside the logbook, I listed my details and instructed anyone who found the box to stamp the logbook with their stamp, and leave some contact details in case of a Northampton Letterboxing get-together (you never know). I planned to encourage other people around the town to hide their own boxes and hopefully in time Northampton would become the new Dartmoor.

I was extremely excited already. I was the creator of a new regional Letterboxing movement. Admittedly it was a movement with me as the only member, and a box that was still sat on my kitchen table, but it was a start.

I left the box where it was, and planned to spend the next couple of days scouting for a suitable hiding place.

Then, just to confuse things, I came across the sport of Geocaching, which I had heard of but didn't know too much about. Geocaching is basically the same as Letterboxing but using GPS and a series of co-ordinates. This sounded far too high-tech for me. I preferred the old-skool method of following a clue from a bit of paper. Besides, Northampton isn't quite ready for GPS yet. We have only recently got Channel 5.

May 11th

Today was my birthday, but I didn't have time to celebrate it at all. I had to photograph a wedding all day, but before I left the house I had several other days to try and celebrate.

International Migratory Bird Day celebrates the incredible journeys of migratory birds between their breeding grounds in North America and their wintering grounds in Mexico, Central, and South America. Woo hoo! Party time!

Were they expecting me to put on a welcome party for the birds? What happened if they didn't arrive on the second Saturday of May, as scheduled on the calendar? All that preparation would go to waste. I subscribed to the official *Bird*

IQ Newsletter which would give me a monthly dose of birding news. I could hardly wait for my first issue.

Then I had to celebrate *Letter Carrier's Food Drive Day*. This is another specifically American one. The idea is that you leave some non-perishable food in a bag on your doorstep and the postman collects it and takes it to a food bank, which is then sent off to places that need it.

It sounded like a brilliant idea to me, and it was one that I'm sure the British public would embrace, if only our postal service offered it.

I sent an email to Royal Mail asking why they didn't have an equivalent, and I had a reply waiting for me at the end of the day:

Dear Mr Mahood

Thank you for your email regarding the Letter Carrier's Food Drive Day.

Unfortunately here at the royal mail we do not have Letter Carrier's Food Drive Day but your comments have been taken on board and if there is any change we will advertise it on the website.

If you have any other queries or problems in the future don't hesitate to contact us again.

Regards

Derek Allan

Customer Service Advisor

Why not send your own email to Royal Mail, encouraging them to start *Letter Carrier's Food Drive Day*? Together we can make this happen! Although, imagine how long our postman Jason's round would take, if he had to lug a bag of groceries around with him too. On second thoughts, forget it.

The wedding went well and once I got home I sat down (without a kebab) to watch the highlights of the FA Cup Final that I had missed, and upload the wedding photos to my laptop. Photographing weddings always tires me out. It's not a particularly physical job as such, but 12 hours on your feet carrying heavy camera equipment does take its toll. I felt drained and weary and was ready to head up to bed when I clicked on my emails and opened an intriguing one.

Love the idea of Stay up All Night Night. I'll be celebrating it here in Florida. What have you got planned?

Oh SHIT! I had completely forgotten. It was *Stay Up All Night Night*. The holiday that I created. It was out there. It was official. Other people were going to be observing it, too (well, one at least). I didn't have a choice but to celebrate it as well.

It was 11.30pm and I wanted nothing more than to crawl into bed, but if I couldn't even celebrate my own holidays then what hope was there for me for the rest of the challenge?

I made myself a cup of coffee and watched a bit more TV, but it was a real effort just to keep my eyes open. There was no way that I would see it through until morning at that rate. I decided to go for a run. My shorts and socks were all in the bedroom and I accidentally woke Rachel as I attempted to retrieve them.

'Hello. How was the wedding, Birthday Boy? What are you doing?' she asked, half-asleep and straining her eyes towards the alarm clock on the other side of the room.

'The wedding was fine thanks. I'm just going for a run.'

'Why are you going for a run? It's 12.30am.'

'Remember that holiday I made up? *Stay Up All Night Night*? Well I had forgotten it's tonight. I need to do something that'll keep me awake.'

'Have fun,' she smiled, and then rolled over to sleep again.

I ran into the town centre, which seemed like a good idea at the time, as I didn't fancy the idea of the local parks at night. Northampton town centre can be an unpleasant place at the best of times. At 1am on a Saturday night, when you are sober, there can't be many worse places on Earth.

I ran down the main pedestrianised street to a chorus of abuse and insults. I have never felt more awake. I then ran all around the streets near to where I live, still secretly hoping that I might spot Father Dougal.

I made it home alive after a run of about 50 minutes. It was 1.30am and morning was still a long way off. I cooked a pizza, and opened a bottle of wine (thankfully today was not a fasting day). I watched some awful late night television. I then made a start on editing the photos from the day's wedding. This wasn't how I had hoped my birthday would pan out; drinking alone at 2am whilst working and watching the shopping channel.

I watched a film whilst pacing around the room trying to stay awake. I went on Twitter and Facebook, but as most of the people I follow or am friends with are from the same time zone as me, there was nothing happening at all.

At about 4.30am I started to hear the dawn chorus of the birds, which was followed shortly after by the sunrise. I decided that the sunrise signified the end of the 'night' and so crept up to bed at 5.10am. My *Stay Up All Night Night* had not been as fun as I hoped, but maybe I hadn't gone into it with the best preparation.

May 12th

As luck would have it, I couldn't get to sleep once I tried, and by 6.15am Leo, Layla and Kitty were all awake too, so there seemed little point in persevering. Today was to be my 'pretend birthday' and we planned to go to the zoo, which, for some reason, has become a tradition on my birthday since Layla was born.

It was *Hug Your Cat Day*, which, although a cruel reminder that Father Dougal was missing, was also a pleasant reminder that we did still have Batfink, who is a very loving and affectionate cat. So I hugged the SHIT out of her. Not literally, that would be rank.

We spent the day at Twycross Zoo and I walked around in a zombie-like state due to my lack of sleep. The predicted bad weather had put most people off, and despite it being a Sunday, we had almost the entire place to ourselves.

Once home, we put the kids to bed, and Rachel and I sat in the garden by the braai (no dancing this time) and took it in turns to throw a ball into an empty flowerpot whilst eating huge chunks of the birthday cake that she and the children had made whilst I was working on my actual birthday. The phone rang, which was unusual for 9pm on a Sunday, and we initially planned to ignore it but I then decided to answer it before it woke up Kitty.

'Hello, have you lost a cat?' said the well-spoken lady on the other end.

'Yes, we have. Father Dougal. He's a big black one.'

'I've found him.'

I grabbed the car keys and headed straight over. The lady lived a few streets away and she had noticed a cat sneaking through her cat flap for a couple of weeks to eat her cat's food. She had not been able to get close enough to read his collar but had managed to lock the cat flap on the most recent occasion. Father Dougal was in quite a bad way. He had lost a lot of weight, and had somehow got one of his front legs through his collar so that he was now wearing it across his body like a beauty sash. Maybe that's how all the cool cats wear them on the street these days. The collar had cut deep into his skin and the wound was dirty, matted and severely infected. It was so amazing to see him, and he seemed very pleased to see me, too. The lady refused her cash reward so I dropped around a bottle of wine and box of chocolates the following day.

Doug was at our house too when I returned, as Rachel had knocked on his door to tell him the good news

'Oh, Basil! We're so pleased to have you back. We didn't think we would see you again. You had us all properly worried this time, you little tinker,' he said, rubbing the top of his head. The cat's head, that is. Not his own.

'Poor little fella, he looks like he's in a bad way. He needs to see a vet urgently,' said Rachel.

'I know, but it's 10pm on Sunday. They will all be shut,' I said.

'I'm sure there will be an emergency out-of-hours place,' said Doug. 'Don't worry about the cost. I'll pay for it.'

'That's very kind of you, Doug, but you don't need to do that. Do you not think we should just wait until the morning?'

'Doug's right. It might be too late tomorrow. How would you feel if he didn't make it until morning?' said Rachel.

'OK, you're right. I'll go and call them.'

'I'll come with you,' said Doug eagerly.

'Thanks Doug, but it might take a long time. You'd better stay and look after Chris. We'll be ok.'

'Ok, if you're sure. I'll be over first thing tomorrow morning.'

After finding an out-of-hours vet, I put Father Dougal back into the cat carrier and drove the three miles to the practice.

The vet was one of the most beautiful women I have ever seen in my life. I, on the other hand, looked like one of the roughest human beings ever to grace this planet. I had not slept at all the night before, and had not had time for a shower before spending the day shepherding three young children around a zoo.

'So he's been missing for tree months?' she asked in her lovely Irish accent.

'Yes. We didn't think we'd see him again. He's quite smelly as well since he got back,' I said, trying to transfer any suspicions she may have had for my hygiene problems over onto Father Dougal.

'Yes, he does whiff a bit,' she said, seemingly convinced.

'I tink what I'm going to do is try and cleanup dis here wound and hope that the wee fella then…' she continued, but I wasn't listening to a word she said. I was completely transfixed by her eyes and sexy hypnotic voice. I nodded, and said *yep* and *uh huh,* occasionally, to show I was listening. The strangest thing was that she was staring right back at me throughout, with a cheeky smile. Her name was Wendy, which was a name so at odds with her appearance that it almost tainted her beauty, but she somehow managed to pull it off.

'We'll keep him in overnight, but don't worry he'll be grand,' she said.

'What was that?' I said, being woken from my hypnosis. 'IT'S GOING TO COST US A GRAND?'

'Ach, no. I said he'll be grand. He's going to be ok. He's a lovely wee fella, isn't he?. I've got a cat that looks just like him.'

I left the surgery feeling relieved that Father Dougal was going to be ok. I got back in the car and caught a glimpse of myself in the rear-view mirror. It was at this point that I noticed a huge smear of cake icing across my upper lip and another on my chin. It was no wonder Wendy had been smiling at me. The cow.

As if today had not been action-packed enough, I still had to celebrate Limerick Day.

I have loved limericks from an early age. One of my greatest achievements in life was coming third in the Little Brington Village Fete limerick competition, at the age of eleven. Although, I doubt there were more than about four entries. Limericks had to be dedicated to Frank, the village postman, and were to begin *'There once was a postman named Frank'*.

My prize-winning entry went like this:

There once was a postman named Frank
Who went to Iraq for a prank
He changed his name
To Saddam Hussein
Now delivers the mail in a tank.

At the time, I remember thinking how clever it was. And SO topical. Looking at it now, it is clear that it is silly and rather insulting. It posed some questions, too. Why did Frank go to Iraq? What sort of prank did he do in Iraq, or was the prank just the fact that he went to Iraq? Why would he change his name to Saddam Hussein, during the Gulf War, when Saddam Hussein was firmly rooted as the most hated man in the world? That would be IDIOTIC. And after changing his name, why the fuck would he then return to England and drive around a quiet rural village in Northamptonshire, delivering mail in a TANK? It just didn't make any sense.

I decided to write a limerick about Wendy the vet and Father Dougal, for the simple reason that it felt topical. I soon discovered that my limerick writing abilities have improved very little in 23 years. This was my first effort:

There was a young vet named Wendy
Father Dougal she did try to mendy
She stitched up his neck
So I wrote her a cheque
Because she didn't take my flexible friendy

For any readers under the age of 30, *'flexible friend'* was a phrase used by the credit card company Access in its advertising before it was taken over by Mastercard. It sounds like it was a euphemism for my penis, but that was not my intention. Honest. There just aren't many words that rhyme with Wendy. Yes, I know that 'friendy' and 'mendy' aren't even proper words, but it was the best I could do. And, no, I didn't really try to pay with an Access credit card that became defunct in 1996. I didn't even write a cheque. Oh, leave me alone, I'm doing the best that I can.

I then tried taking the name *Wendy* out of the equation as I have proven that it's not the easiest of names to rhyme with. This was my second attempt, which was even worse than the first:

There once was a beautiful vet
Who stitched up our poorly old pet
'Whatta good looking chap',
She said to the cat.
And she left us one hell of a debt.

The oldest poem written in the metrical pattern of a limerick can be traced back to Thomas Aquinas (1225-1274). His limerick, when translated, went as follows:

Let my viciousness be emptied,
Desire and lust banished,
Charity and patience,

Humility and obedience,
And all the virtues increased.

It makes my Frank the postman effort look worthy of a Poet Laureate accolade. His wasn't even slightly funny. So what that he wrote it 800 years ago, and that limericks didn't have to be funny back then? That's no excuse for such a boring effort. And since when did *increased* rhyme with *emptied?* What a loser!

According to the American social critic Gershon Legman, a true limerick must be OBSCENE. He stated that a limerick was not a proper limerick unless it contained some rude or vulgar content. Perhaps my 'flexible friend' was not misplaced after all. Legman described clean limericks as being a fad, and solely for magazine contests (and village fetes presumably).

I tried one last effort.

Father Dougal the cat was quite fussy,
And Wendy, she was quite the hussy
She said 'He'll be fine,
He looks just like mine.'
Oh I wished that she'd show me HER pussy.

May 13th

I was fresh, clean and cake icing free when I returned to pick up Father Dougal the following morning. The receptionist handed him to me in the carry basket, and I didn't even get a chance to show Wendy how well I scrubbed up.

'Wendy wants to see you next week,' said the receptionist.

'Really? Does she? What does she want to see *ME* for?' I blushed.

'She wants to check Father Dougal's stitches and make sure the wound is not re-infected. It's standard procedure.'

'Ah, Father Dougal! Oh, yes of course.'

It was great to have Father Dougal home, and needless to say Doug was delighted.

'The vet has asked that we monitor what he eats over the next few days, just to check that he's recovering,' I said to Doug. 'Would you mind not feeding Basil for a few days just so that we can keep track of what he's eating?'

'Of course, absolutely,' he said.

It was *Leprechaun Day* and *Frog Jumping Day*, two completely unrelated days which both coincidentally involved small strange green things hopping around. There was no other way to celebrate than to put on my trusty lime-green Oakley 20 hoodie and hop around the garden. I can't say that I gained anything from the experience but it certainly brought a smile to Rachel and the kids' faces.

May 14th

During breakfast I could hear Doug whistling for Father Dougal. Father Dougal had not eaten much at our house since coming home, so I decided to politely mention it again.

'Doug, would it be ok if you didn't feed Basil for a couple of days?' I said, when I saw him out in the garden later.

'Yes, that's fine. I'm not feeding him at all. Just the odd snack here and there.'

'Please could you not feed him any snacks either? It's just for a couple of days. We need to check he's eating enough and we can't do that if he's eating at your house, too.'

'Oh, ok. Fair enough,' he said.

Later in the day I heard him whistling again, and again I saw Father Dougal emerging from Doug's cat flap a while later licking his lips. Again I had another chat with Doug.

'I haven't been feeding him,' he said. 'I've only been giving him cat biscuits. That doesn't count does it?'

'Yes!' I said, getting slightly frustrated, before a feeling of guilt hit me. If Doug didn't feed Father Dougal then there was a chance that he might not go into their house. This would be a huge loss to him and Chris - even if only for a few days. Did I really want Doug to stop feeding him because of what the vet had said, or was I just getting excited about the idea that Father Dougal would be exclusively our cat again, albeit temporarily? As important as the instructions from the vet were, I realised that it was more important for Doug and Chris to see Father Dougal/Basil, and it was clearly obvious that Father Dougal was eating properly, that was for sure.

'No, you're right,' I said. 'Biscuits are fine. In fact, he's looking a lot better now. Carry on as you were.'

'Ok then. If you insist.'

'It makes me sad that Father Dougal spends all of this time next door, rather than with us,' said Rachel, back inside our house.

'If you were a cat, would you choose a house with three loud children that chase you around all day and try and pick you up, or a nice warm house in which you have a choice of rooms and nobody disturbs you?'

'I suppose I'd choose Doug's house. It still makes me sad though.'

'I know what will cheer you up. It's *Dance Like a Chicken Day* today. Come on, you know you want to.'

'No I really don't.'

'Yeah, you do.'

The *Chicken Dance Song*, or *The Birdy Song*, as it is more famously known in the UK, was composed by Swiss accordion player Werner Thomas in the 1950s. The original Swiss song was called *Der Ententanz (The Duck Dance)* and it gradually spread across Europe in many different versions. The dance was introduced to the United States by a German group called The Heilbronn Band at an Oktoberfest celebration in Tulsa, Oklahoma. The band wanted to demonstrate the dance in costume, but there were no duck costumes to be found. A local TV station provided a chicken costume and so the *Chicken Dance* was born.

In 2000 it was voted the *'most annoying song of all time'* in a poll commissioned by an online music site. As a child I remember the song being a staple at any Christmas party, wedding or school disco, but it has been years since I have heard it.

'Here we go. Let's have a little dance,' I said to Rachel as I typed in *'Chicken Dance'* into YouTube on the laptop.

'Seriously, there's no way I'm dancing,' she said.

And then the song started, and I saw a little smile creep across her face. She was reading a book on the sofa, but couldn't help but give her arms a little flap and her bottom a little wiggle.

'That's the spirit. I knew you'd love it.'

'That wasn't a dance. It was just a twitch,' she said

May 15th

As part of *National Employee Health and Fitness Day* I decided to try and take some steps to improve the health and fitness of the employees of my photography business (me). I found a list of suggestions on the internet. As I am the only employee, some of the suggestions were a little impractical.

1. Partner up with a nearby gym and offer an employee discount

I think the gym is unlikely to offer me a discount if it's just me. Plus I hate gyms.

2. Start intramural athletic teams like softball, kickball or soccer and compete against other companies in your area.

A one man team? That could be interesting. And then challenge other companies?

'Hey, do you fancy a game of Kickball?' I would say to other companies in my area.

'What the hell is kickball?'

'I've no idea, but it sounds fun. If you get a team together we'll have a match.'

'Ok, do you have a team?'

'Nope, it's just me. BRING IT ON!'

3. Encourage biking or walking to work if employees live nearby

Rachel doesn't like it when I cycle indoors.

4. Post signs to take the stairs instead of the elevator
We have an ELEVATOR in our house? WTF? I had no idea. Sod the stairs; I'm going to use our elevator from now on.

5. Bring in your health insurance provider to the office to give employees physical exams
Er, ok then.

6. Form lunchtime exercise groups – go to the gym with some co-workers or take advantage of a walk or run if weather permits
Yes, I could do that. Although I would be on my own, and I'm not sure that counts as a group.

7. Establish healthy meal clubs that share recipes and healthy snacks throughout the day
Again, I'm not sure that one person constitutes a 'club' but I'm happy to share recipes and snacks with myself. It just means I end up eating more. I'm supposed to be on a diet!

(Susanne Ross - Senior Product Marketing Associate at Cvent.com)

After going for a quick run at lunch time, and sharing my snacks with myself, I then ate chocolate chips whilst wearing nylon stockings and a straw hat. As you do. *Chocolate Chip Day, Nylon Stockings Day* and *Straw Hat Day* all celebrated in one bizarre, slightly creepy moment.

May 16th

My first book (did I mention I had written another book?) has spent some time since being released occupying the number one spot in the *Cycling* chart on Amazon UK. It's quite exciting to be number one in a chart, and even more so when the books below it are written by people like Sir Bradley Wiggins, David Millar and that cheating fucking SCUMBAG Lance Armstrong. Admittedly, their books all sold a ridiculous number of copies when they were released, but still.

I have been extremely happy having a 'best-selling' cycling book, but there were two issues that were slightly bothering me about the whole thing. Both of which I had chosen to ignore.

Firstly, my book is not really a cycling book. Yes, it is about a bike ride, but it's not really about bikes, or cycling in any way.

Secondly, the fact that my book is number one in a category, suggests - although I don't like to admit it - that's it's not a very popular category. The problem with being in a not very popular category is that not many people browse for books there.

I had debated switching to a more popular category in the hope of it becoming more visible for browsers, but that would mean losing my number 1 spot. The only other vaguely suitable categories that I could switch to would be *'Memoirs'* or *'Humour'*. I'm not sure my book is technically either of those. Surely a memoir should be based on more than a three week trip? And humour? Well, that's very debatable.

It was *Biographer's Day* today so it seemed like as good a day as any to swap. I instantly dropped from the Number 1 *Cycling* book on Amazon UK to the number 32 *Biography and Memoir*. It didn't have quite the same ring to it, but hopefully it would open my book up to a brand new audience.

'What are we going to do about the house?' said Rachel, after we had put the children to bed, in a voice that signified that she wanted a proper 'talk'.

'I don't know. There's not much we can do, is there? If we move then we wouldn't be able to buy anything nearly as big as this house, and you think this house is too small.'

'It's not just that it's too small. I just feel that we need a change. I feel like we've been here long enough.'

'I agree completely. But if we can't afford to buy anywhere else then moving isn't really an option.'

'We could always rent somewhere else,' she suggested.

'We wouldn't be able to afford that as well as paying the mortgage on this place?'

'I know. I mean sell this house and then rent somewhere in Devon.'

'Really? Would that not be a bit of step down seeing as we own our own house?'

'Maybe. But it might be our only option, though.'

The idea was warming to me for the first time.

'And I suppose it does give us a bit of flexibility if we decide we don't like it down there and want to come back,' I said.

'Exactly.'

'Yes, I think that might be a good solution. I would be happy renting.'

'Then in a year or two, if I've got a job down there, and I'm no longer your 'dependent' then maybe we'll be able to get a mortgage again.'

'Ok, let's do it. Let's put the house on the market.'

'Really? Do you mean that?'

'Of course I do. Let's move house this summer, one way or another.'

'YEAH,' she said, giving me a big hug.

May 17th

As previously mentioned, Rachel disapproves of me cycling indoors. She's SO unreasonable. Today, though, was *National Bike to Work Day* so she couldn't really complain. My office

(Kitty's bedroom) is five metres from my bedroom. My bike lives outside which is 18 metres from my bedroom (yes, I measured it). To bike to work I had to walk 18 metres past where I work, retrieve my bike from the garden, carry my bike back upstairs past where I work and then cycle the five metres along the upstairs hallway, which involved a step and a tight turn around the top of the stairs. The bike then wouldn't fit into the already full study so I had to carry it back down the stairs and into the garden, before returning back up the stairs.

It wasn't the most practical of commutes to work, but I certainly felt physically energised by the whole experience. I don't think I'll make it a regular thing, though.

May 18th

Our local football team - Northampton Town - are currently languishing in League Two which is the fourth tier of the English football league system. I've been to watch them a few times over the years, but I am certainly more of an armchair fan. I check their results whenever they play, read the match reports and discuss their progress (or usually lack of) with Doug throughout the course of the season. Our discussions usually involve whether The Cobblers (as they are known, as Northampton was famous for its shoe manufacturing) will survive relegation.

This season, however, they have done surprisingly well and have somehow found themselves in the play-off final at Wembley with a chance of securing promotion to the dizzy heights of League One. The Cobblers have reached the play-off finals on two previous occasions (1997 and 1998), one of which they won, and the other in which they lost. I went to watch their last final at Wembley in 1998 when they lost 1-0 to Grimsby.

Today I had a very rare Saturday without a wedding booking, so it seemed like an ideal reason to head to Wembley to support my local team. I sent messages to a group of friends a few weeks ago as soon as the tickets went on sale to see who was keen to come. Responses ranged from an understandable *'I'm looking after the baby all day'*, to the dubious *'I'm away that weekend'* to the vague *'sorry I'm busy'*, to the honest *'I don't want to.'* A couple of friends didn't even bother replying. I couldn't find a single friend to come to Wembley with me to support The Cobblers. I even asked Doug if he would like to come, but he was, quite understandably, not able to leave Chris for an entire day.

'Do you think Layla and Leo would like a trip to Wembley to watch The Cobblers?' I asked Rachel.

'Probably not,' she said. 'You took them to that Olympic football match and they didn't like that much.'

'This is different, though. It's at WEMBLEY and it's NORTHAMPTON!'

'I'm not sure a five year-old and three year-old would appreciate that subtle difference. Remember what happened last time?'

During the London Olympics I somehow ended up with a shit load of tickets to watch obscure football matches at Coventry City's stadium to watch matches involving random teams like Gabon and Honduras. When I applied for Olympic tickets, I thought that Coventry would be a nice convenient place to visit from Northampton. I hoped that I might get to watch the likes of Brazil playing Team GB. It turned out that I was probably the only person who applied for these matches, as I got all of the tickets that I put my name in the ballot for. For one of the matches I thought it would be fun to take Layla (aged 4), Leo (aged 2) and Rachel's granddad (aged 90). It turned out not to be the best idea I've ever had. We had to park the car in a bramble bush in an overgrown plot of land next to a disused pub, and gave a man £5 and he promised to 'look after' the car for us. We then had a mile long walk to the stadium where we discovered that our seats were in row WW, which was the second row from the top of the stadium's tallest stand. Navigating those ridiculously steep stairs with two young children and a very unsteady 90 year-old was an unbelievably nerve-wracking experience. After about ten terrifying minutes - during which a retired nurse who had seen us struggling, came and helped Rachel's granddad up the last section - we eventually made it to our seats. Leo then got bored after the first five minutes of the match. Thankfully we had a spare seat next to us so I suggested that he lie down on the two fold down seats and have a little sleep. He duly obliged but after a further five minutes he moved slightly and one of the chairs flipped up and his head slipped into the gap and became wedged in the seat. This was during a particularly quiet point in the match and he howled in terror. Hundreds of people turned around to see where the commotion was coming from as I tried frantically to prise his head from the seat and calm him down.

On the way back to the car after the match, we then got caught in a severe thunderstorm. We all arrived back at the car completely drenched and exhausted but with massive smiles on our faces about what a ridiculous and strangely exciting day it had been. Walter, Rachel's granddad, had to spend the next couple of days in bed because he was so sore from all the activity, but he still talks about the day with great fondness. The heroics from the likes of Mo Farah, Jessica Ennis and Greg Rutherford over the following days paled into insignificance compared to my feat. Yet where was MY Olympic gold medal?

'Yes, you're right. It didn't go as smoothly as I hoped,' I said. 'I think it will be much easier this time though. I won't take your granddad.'

'Ok, but don't say I didn't warn you.'

'Layla, would you like to come to another football match, like the one we went to with Walter?'

'No thanks. I don't really like football.'

'Leo, how about you? You like football. Do you want to come?' I asked.

'I don't like WATCHING football. I like playing football, and watching telly.'

'Oh, that's a shame. I'll have to eat all the sweets by myself.'

'I'll come!' shouted Layla.

'And me!' shouted Leo.

I then phoned my sister who lives in London to suggest that we drive and park the car at her house and commute from there. There were two reasons for this. Firstly, it would mean avoiding the trains from Northampton that would be crammed full of Cobblers fans, and secondly, I knew it was going to coincide with *Visit Your Relatives Day*, so it seemed like a good excuse to call in to see her.

'Sounds great. Have you bought your tickets yet?' she asked.

'Not yet. Why?'

'Can Guy and I come too?'

'Of course. Since when have you liked football?'

'I don't, but I've never been to a live game, and Wembley sounds fun. And Guy is always up for anything remotely sporty.'

'Sounds great. We'll drive to yours and then we can all go together from there.'

The Cobblers put on a shocking performance and were thrashed 3-0 by Bradford City. Leo moaned most of the way through it, but he and Layla seemed to enjoy the whole experience of the crowds, the train, and the big foam hands that I bought them as souvenirs. I also took along some Reese's Peanut Butter Cups as it was *I Love Reese's Day*. They are quite hard to get hold of in the UK, but it's worth the effort because they are amazing. What was even better was that Layla and Leo didn't like them, so I had to eat them all myself.

Leo had a major tantrum on the way back when I had to break the news to him that when I had said we were getting the train from Wembley Park to Queens Park it was, in fact, one train station to another train station, rather than two different playgrounds.

May 19th

Of all of the headless chickens in the world, Mike The Headless Chicken is definitely the most famous. He's head and shoulders above the rest. No, wait, that was a bad choice of words.

Mike The Headless Chicken became an American celebrity in the 1940s. He was minding his only business - with his head intact at the time - at his home in Fruita, Colorado, when his owner Clara Olsen sent her husband Lloyd out to choose a chicken to kill for their evening meal with her mother. Lloyd, wanting to preserve as much of the neck meat as possible - to keep his mother-in-law happy - did the deed with his axe, but then the chicken continued to roam around as if nothing had happened.

Lloyd was a bit confused and so left the chicken alone. When he returned the next morning, 'Mike' - as he was at some point named - was still alive. Lloyd and Clara decided that despite having no head, Mike deserved to live due to his fighting spirit and so set about devising a way to give him food and water by means of an eye-dropper. A week later, the Olsens drove Mike 250 miles to the University of Utah where he was studied by scientists. They concluded that the axe had somehow missed the jugular vein and a clot had prevented him from bleeding to death. Most of his head was now in a jar, but some of his brain stem and one of his ears remained on his body and so he remained remarkably healthy.

Mike The Headless Chicken spent the next 18 months touring across America as *The Headless Wonder Chicken* with a dedicated manager and Lloyd and Clara Olsen. He was featured in Time and Life magazine and valued at $10,000.

Unfortunately, all of this success went to his head (sorry, I did it again) and Mike suffered the fate of many celebrities before and since. He choked to death in a motel room.

His legend lives on, though, and the *Mike the Headless Chicken Festival* is celebrated every year on the third weekend of May in Fruita, Colorado.

It sounds completely crazy and irrational, but the main reason that I have been reluctant to put the house on the market is not because I don't want to move, not because I am scared or apprehensive about the prospect of relocating, and not because I have been too busy with other things. It's because I'm terrified about breaking the news to Doug and Chris. I would feel awful telling them that we are going to be moving away. And what about Father Dougal? The prospect of Doug and Chris losing another cat - albeit one that isn't actually theirs - would be unbearable for them. Losing Basil would mean taking a huge part of their life away from them, and the thought made me feel physically sick.

But the feelings of a neighbour shouldn't shape the way we make decisions as a family. As much as I didn't want to upset Doug and Chris, I knew that I couldn't let the uncomfortable feeling inside delay me telling them. I hated the idea that they would find out first from a *'For Sale'* sign going up outside our house. We had to tell them.

It was going to be hard, but I needed to be the one to break the news. Doug would prefer it to come from me.

'Rachel?' I said, wimping out. 'Would you be happy to tell Doug today about us putting the house on the market?'

'Sure,' she said.

Either Rachel was a lot braver than me, or she didn't have the same level of compassion about the situation.

An hour later I could hear her in the garden. Doug had come outside to hang the washing.

'Hi Doug.'

'Hi Rachel. Bit warmer today, isn't it?'

'Yes, it's lovely. Doug, we've decided to put our house on the market,' she said, quite bluntly.

There was a slight pause.

'Ok, well good luck,' he said, which was followed swiftly by the sound of his backdoor closing.

'That didn't go too well,' said Rachel in the kitchen.

'I know, I heard. It sounded very awkward. Poor Doug. Don't worry, I'll talk to him.'

I saw Doug outside the front of his house later in the day and so nipped out to have a chat with him. We had a long conversation about the move, and he told me how he and Chris had been in tears when he had told her. But he understood that we had outgrown our house, and he knew that we couldn't live there forever.

'We will both just miss you all so much if you moved,' he said. 'You're like family to us.'

'We would miss you both too. But we'll still keep in contact, and come and visit.'

'Would you really visit?'

'Of course we would. If we move to Devon then I will have to come back to Northampton regularly for work, so I'll always call in to see you both when I'm up here.'

'We'd love that. You're welcome to come and stay any time. There's always a bed for you here, kiddo.'

'Thanks Doug, I really appreciate it. We'll be here for a good while yet, though. It might take a long time for the house to sell.'

'Come here, kiddo,' he said, putting his arms around me and squeezing me tightly. 'Don't you forget about us, will you?'

'There's no chance we'll ever forget about you. This is certainly not goodbye, that's for sure.'

I felt so much better after our conversation. A huge weight had been lifted. Moving house is no longer a secret plan that Rachel and I are hatching. It is something that is now out there. It is real, and other people know about it. It is actually going to happen... providing we can sell the house, and find somewhere to live.

May 21st

I woke in the morning at 6.15am. Or should I say, I was woken at 6.15am by Kitty, who had been woken by Layla going to the toilet, who had been woken by Leo snoring. Either way, it was my turn to get up with them. I was greeted downstairs by a flooded kitchen. The washing machine had leaked its contents all over the floor. After getting the children their morning milk and sitting them in front of CBeebies, I then soaked up the excess water with some towels before mopping the rest up.

I traced the leak to a hole about an inch and a half long in the rubber seal around the washing machine door. It looked like someone had taken a huge bite out of it. Despite Kitty's tendency to try and eat most things, even this seemed beyond her. I managed to find the missing piece of rubber inside the drum and it was clear that it had just perished.

I looked on the internet and found out that it was possible to buy a new seal, but it looked quite fiddly and complicated to fit. Washing machine maintenance is not my specialty. No form of maintenance is my specialty in fact.

'We'll just have to buy a new washing machine,' said Rachel, when she came downstairs an hour later.

'That's your answer to everything, isn't it? We can't afford to buy a new washing machine just because one small bit of it is defective.'

'One small bit that makes it leak all over the kitchen floor. That's quite a significant small bit, don't you think?'

'I'll fix it. There must be a way.'

'Oh good. I've heard that before.'

Why am I writing about a leaky washing machine? Bear with me, there is a point to this story. Kind of.

It was the day we decided to finally put our house on the market. We phoned the estate agents to say that we would like to go ahead, and they appeared on the doorstep within minutes. The property market is obviously fairly slow in Northampton.

It took them half an hour to measure up and hastily take some photographs. We then signed the contract and that was that.

Then my phone rang. It was 3.30pm.

'Hi George. It's Josh,' said Josh.

Josh? I knew that name. But where from?

'Hi Josh,' I said. 'How are you?'

'Er, yeah, I'm ok thanks. We were supposed to be meeting you at 3.15pm in Thrapston to discuss our wedding?'

I had an overwhelming feeling of nervousness in my gut.

'What? Really? I'm so sorry. I thought that wasn't until next week?'

'No, it was definitely today. We've both got it in our diaries.'

I blurted out a load of unconvincing excuses and sincere apologies. I offered to drive straight over to them, but Thrapston is 40 minutes away and they had somewhere else to be. I made a new appointment to meet them next week and highlighted it in my diary with big fluorescent exclamation marks.

I was so cross and angry with myself. I have several of these meetings each week, either with brides and grooms who are thinking of hiring me, or couples who have already booked me and are going through the details. I'm very occasionally a few minutes late but I never miss appointments. The small consolation was that this couple had already booked me, so I wasn't missing out on a potential new booking, but in a way it made things worse, as not only had I wasted their time, but I had instilled a niggling thought into their heads that I was unreliable.

'Aw, don't worry about it,' said Rachel. 'These things happen. It's been a bit of a crazy day with the estate agents and the washing machine.'

'I know, but I feel so awful about it. I hate letting people down.'

'Have you done any holiday celebrating today? What day is it?' she asked.

'I've no idea. I haven't even looked.'

I went upstairs and half-heartedly checked my list, secretly hoping fate would have worked its magic and it would be *National Miss a Meeting Day* or *International Piss Someone Off Day*. Unfortunately it was neither of those. I was too miserable to consider *National Endangered Species Day, World Day for Cultural Diversity for Dialogue and Development* or *American Red Cross Founder's Day*.

Then I spotted *We Need a Patch for that Day*. Patches are a quick-fix option for many things; holes in clothing; holes in bicycle inner-tubes; pot-holes are patched with tarmac; smoking is cured with a patch; travel sickness is cured with a patch.

Then, from the depths of my sadness and despair at missing my meeting, a eureka moment rose from the flames. Yes I know I'm mixing my metaphors. WHO CARES? I was THAT excited!

The washing machine had a hole. It was *I Need a Patch for that Day*. It needed to be patched. I could patch it using a bicycle puncture repair kit. Now this may not seem like the most logical use of a puncture repair kit, but it seemed like a wonderful idea at the time. I no longer cared about the meeting I had missed. I had a washing machine to patch.

The gap in the seal was a LOT bigger than the standard sized patches that I had. Undeterred, I glued several of the patches together and then glued the whole thing to the section of the rubber seal that had the gap in it. I then stuck several more patches on the other side and a few random ones on various edges to try and make it watertight. I was very proud of my handiwork. I had repaired a washing machine with a bicycle puncture repair kit.

I left it an hour for the vast quantity of glue that I had used to dry and then decided to give the machine a try. It took an extra push to get the door to close because of the mountain of patches that I had added, but I figured that this just made the seal even more effective. I started the machine up and for the first few minutes as the drum began to fill things looked good. And then a few drips started to seep from the door. I put down a tea-towel assuming it would be sodden within minutes, but by the end of the machine's cycle, parts of the tea-towel were still dry. My repair had been a partial success.

'So, did your puncture repair job work?' laughed Rachel.

'Sort of. We'll have to put a tea-towel under the door every time we use the washing machine but it doesn't leak too badly.'

'I can live with that. Well done, I'm impressed.'

May 22nd

I enjoy celebrating days that don't require any research into their meaning. Some days are so easy to follow as they are simply an order or instruction. Today was *Buy a Musical Instrument Day*. I didn't just by A musical instrument. I bought THREE.

I bought Layla, Leo and Kitty a cheap harmonica each from a local discount shop. It was the worst decision I have ever made in my life. A harmonica played well is not a particularly pleasant sound. THREE harmonicas played badly by young children breaches all sorts of human rights.

May 23rd

It was *World Turtle Day* and I was looking after the children. There is not an abundance of turtles in Northamptonshire, so we went to the park, because we hadn't been to the park for at least a day. However, as a special treat I decided to take them to the park with the springy wooden turtle instead.

'Why can't we go to the other park?' moaned Leo.

'Because the park we are going to has a springy wooden turtle.'

'I don't like the springy wooden turtle.'

'Kitty does. It's her favourite. Isn't it Kitty?'

'Kitty not like it,' said Kitty.

'Well, it's *World Turtle Day* today.'

'What does that mean?' asked Leo.

'It means it's the springy wooden turtle's birthday today,' I lied. 'And he's having a birthday party. Would you like to go?'

'Okaaaay,' conceded Leo.

The park was fun, and the kids enjoyed themselves as usual, but I don't think they will be rushing back for the springy wooden turtle's birthday next year. It was a pretty shit party, to be fair.

May 28th

San Juan Capistrano is a busy place for animals. I've already celebrated the swallows returning to Capistrano, and today it was the turn of the slugs. Legend has it that slugs spend their winter in Capistrano before returning to their summer dwellings on May 28th, which is the catchy titled *Slugs Return from* San *Juan Capistrano Day*.

I hate slugs. I like to think that I am kind and caring to nearly all animals and will try to save them rather than kill them. There are a few exceptions; fleas, wasps and slugs. I used to be quite caring to slugs too, and would make an effort to 're-home' them, rather than kill them. This involved flinging them into the garden that backs onto ours. I have since hardened and become a bit more ruthless. I set up a beer trap a few years ago, using a plastic bottle cut in half and filled with beer. It was incredibly effective but I think it actually attracted more slugs to the area, like a sort of sadistic slug disco. I then resorted to good old fashioned slug pellets. These were fine until we had children and they started to poke around in the flowerbeds.

My aunt and uncle live in north Cornwall and have a large vegetable plot and a couple of polytunnels. They are largely self-sufficient for fruit and vegetables. My aunt is a big advocate of organic gardening, so whilst being given a tour of her garden last year I asked her how she dealt with the issue of slugs, seeing as she was unable to use pesticides. She is also a vet, so I was intrigued to find out her humane, organic, non-suffering slug prevention method.

'Like this,' she said, bending down and picking up a slug from one of her lettuces. She then took a pair of kitchen scissors from her pocket and cut the slug in half, before throwing the severed parts into the grass behind her. 'Problem solved.'

Sure enough, the slugs had returned to our garden on May 28th (although admittedly I hadn't checked in recent weeks. They had probably been back for ages, for all I knew) and they had already feasted on the hosta that my mother-in-law had grown me for my birthday. I couldn't bring myself to try my aunt's slug control method, slug pellets were still out of the question, and I didn't want to waste more beer on a beer trap. Instead I crept out at night with a torch and picked off the slugs one-by-one. I then threw them into the neighbour's garden. I made sure to throw them three doors down, as we liked our immediate neighbours on either side. We were fairly sure that the residents of the house three doors down had left an old fridge outside our house recently because they couldn't be bothered to dispose of it themselves. This was revenge. Ha! That'll teach 'em!

May 29th

I used to be pretty obsessed with my compost bin. I'm not ashamed to say it. I was very proud of it and treated it well. Worms loved it, and the compost looked great. Almost TOO GOOD to use. But then things started to change. The nice looking compost became a soggy, wet, soupy slime that smelled so bad we started to avoid that part of the garden. Our garden is so small that more than half of it became a no-go zone because of the odour from the compost bin. I know my own complacency was to blame. I added too much cut grass which apparently wrecks the balance. Secondly, our county council started collecting food waste, so it became easier to empty stuff into the kitchen caddy rather than fight with the dirty, stinking compost bin at the bottom of the garden, and... WHY THE HELL AM I WRITING ABOUT COMPOST? My God, what has happened to me? What has happened to this book? I'm supposed to be celebrating 'quirky' holidays, not discussing fucking composting techniques. Look, it was *Learn About Composting Day*, OK? I don't make the rules.

So I spent some time, as you do, learning about how best to make compost, and how to avoid the rookie mistakes that I made last time. The problem is that our house is for sale. There was a time that I was so obsessed with my compost that I genuinely planned that if we ever moved house I would bag up all the precious compost and take it with us. I think I saw it as a symbolic act. All of the prized rotten fruit and vegetables that I had spent years laboriously creating, would then be used in the garden of our new house to promote new beginnings and new growth. Or some bullshit like that. There is no chance in HELL that will happen anymore. I can't wait to see the back of it. There seems little point in getting obsessive about compost again if I'm not going to be here to reap its rewards.

Instead, I dug a big pit in my newly-built vegetable patch and emptied the entire contents of the compost bin into the hole. The fumes of the toxic sludge made me gag and caused my eyes to stream. Any viewers shown around the house would have to be provided with breathing apparatus and safety goggles. This would not have been a great selling point. I hastily covered over the mush with more soil from the far end of the garden. I then sprinkled a packet of rocket seeds into the vegetable patch. As it is such a fast growing leaf, I hoped to at least enjoy something home-grown in my new patch before our house sold. The soil/sludge I had created was pure energy; a seed's paradise. It was surely the soil equivalent to a can of

Red Bull, and we would be feasting on home-grown rocket in no time.

May 30th

Mahlon Loomis was a dentist. But he was not just any old dentist. He was a dentist with unbelievable sideburns. That's not his only claim to fame, though. As well as inventing artificial teeth, he is also credited with discovering wireless communication way back in the 1870s. I don't understand technology. It really confuses me and I try not to think about it too much. I can't comprehend how a song, a photo, a conversation, a film or a video of a cat playing a piano can travel through the air in perfect quality from one device to another. How anyone could have had the foresight to conceive of wireless communication nearly 150 years ago, when I am still none-the-wiser now, is completely beyond me.

Loomis proved his theory by flying two kites at equal heights several miles apart in Virginia and was able to complete a DC circuit through the atmosphere. At the time he was dismissed as a fraud and was denied funding for further research by the US government, but he stuck to it and his discoveries paved the way for much of today's technology. Loomis Day, on May 30th, celebrates the day in 1872 on which Mahlon Loomis was finally granted his patent.

To celebrate, I made two kites with copper wires and flew them both into an overhead electricity power line. I'm KIDDING! Don't try this at home, kids!

JUNE

June 2nd

Over the last few years Father Dougal has started regularly spraying urine in our house. He tends to favour things made of plastic: the vacuum cleaner, plastic bags, and, unfortunately, buggies and children's toys. The smell and the cleanup really are disgusting. It sounds unbelievable, but it all stems from my Land's End to John O'Groats trip (it may seem as though I squeeze a mention of this bike ride in at every possible opportunity, but I promise this is genuine). Before that, he was a happy, loving, affectionate cat who never sprayed at all. Whilst I was away for three weeks, Rachel noticed that he started to mark his territory in the house. She said he was more agitated and nervy than before I left. She was convinced it was because of the change in dynamics in the household, with him becoming the alpha male in my absence. I maintain - secretly - that it was probably more likely a reaction to spending three weeks with Rachel. After living with Rachel for 12 years I'm surprised I haven't started urinating everywhere because of the stress. It's only a matter of time.

Today was *Pet-stress Awareness Day*, so I finally decided to look into the issue properly and see if there was anything that could be done.

There are various spray deterrents, tablets and soothing music CDs available to buy, all of which I had dismissed in the past because they all had lots of negative reviews and hefty price tags. One product that did sound hopeful was a plug-in pheromone diffuser. I have to confess that it sounded like a load of bullshit to me, but I was happy to give it a go. It was basically a Glade Plug-in that releases a cat pheromone, which calms and de-stresses the cat, therefore stopping it from urinating. It stops the cat urinating INSIDE the house, obviously. I didn't want it to stop urinating completely. That would be unhealthy and he would likely explode. I had ordered the plug-in a few days ago (see, I told you I would try to be more pro-active) and it arrived on time. I plugged it into a socket near to where we feed the cats, turned it on and hoped for the best.

June 4th

Rachel is very efficient with her tidying. By 'efficient' I mean 'annoying'. You have to be physically holding onto something if you want to prevent it being put back where it came from. Very often when I am in the kitchen, I will get out a knife from the drawer to chop an onion, I will then bend down to pick an onion out of the cupboard and in the time it takes me to stand back up, Rachel will have washed up the knife, dried it, and put it back in the drawer.

It was then no surprise that I was searching in the back of a cupboard for an empty plastic pot to put some leftovers in, when I found the letterboxing tub, complete with stamp and notebook, that I had assembled almost a month ago. I had completely forgotten about it, as Rachel had obviously stored it away, right after I left it on the side.

I headed off to the park with Leo and Kitty to find a suitable place to hide it. We settled on a thorny bush next to the pond at one of the local parks. Later in the evening I posted a clue as to its whereabouts on a letterboxing site:

Head to this popular Northampton park. Stand in the spot for feeding the ducks. Take ten paces backwards (mind the tree) and three to your right. You might need to wear gloves.

It is only a matter of time before the whole of Northamptonshire is going letterboxing crazy.

June 6th

Tomorrow is my friend's son's 1st birthday.

I had been incredibly organised and bought him his present over a month ago. It was one of those red and yellow bubble cars; the kind that have been around since I was a child. I ordered one on the internet despite reading several reviews from people moaning about how it took almost three hours to assemble.

'THREE HOURS to assemble a plastic car? Yeah right. You bunch of LOSERS!' I thought to myself. I see those cars at baby groups all the time and they are clearly just a couple of pieces of plastic slotted together. There is no way that they could take any time or effort to assemble.

Seeing as his birthday is tomorrow, I thought I should probably open the box and slot those bits together just so that it was ready. Rachel was working and so Leo, Kitty and I spent the morning at the park (for a change) and then when I put Kitty down for her nap in the afternoon, I suggested to Leo that he could help me build the car.

I opened the box confidently and was shocked to discover that there were in fact more than just a couple of pieces. There were HUNDREDS. The assembly instructions had 32 different stages and the *equipment required* list included a hammer, screwdriver and a drill. A DRILL? To slot together a plastic car? I don't think so.

Leo and I set to work, and it soon became clear that his assistance was quite limiting. He climbed into the wheel-less, roofless chassis and then moaned that it didn't have a steering wheel. He then got one of the car's axles stuck in the wrong hole, and rolled one of the crucial washers under the fridge. I had to leave one of the screws protruding by a couple of centimetres because I was unable to hand-screw it through three layers of plastic. I should have used a drill.

The whole process took us just over three hours. Leo got bored halfway through and wandered off to watch TV, but I was then joined by Kitty after she had woken from her nap.

We picked up Layla from school and she was excited to see the new car gracing our living room floor. Having spent the entire afternoon building the stupid thing, I couldn't really deny the children a play in it. But I didn't want them to mark it in any way.

I then had a genius idea. It was *Drive-In Movie Day*

'How would you like to sit and watch a film in the car?' I suggested.

'YEEAAAAAH!' they all shouted together.

'But we won't all fit,' said Layla.

'I know, but whoever is not in the car gets to watch the film from sitting in this GIANT CARDBOARD BOX,' I said, producing my trump card - the large box that the car pieces arrived in.

'Who wants to sit in the car and who wants to sit in the box?'

'BOX!' they all shouted.

'But who wants to have a go in this brand new, never-before-used, shiny car?'

'BOX!' they shouted again.

'Ok, well Leo, as you helped build it, you get to go in the car first and Layla and Kitty can go in the box. Then we'll swap around after a few minutes.'

'Ooooooh, that's not fair. I want to go in the box,' shouted Leo.

'You get to choose the film, Leo,' I said.

'Okaaay.'

Rachel's return home from work on a Thursday is usually greeted by a completely trashed house, screaming children and me frantically doing my best to try and get everyone and everything under control. On this occasion, she walked in through the door and instantly said a suspicious 'Helloooo?' before poking her head around the corner into the nice tidy sitting room.

Leo was sat quietly in the newly built car, whilst Layla and Kitty were both squashed next to each other in the cardboard box watching the film. I was sat on the sofa.

'What's going on?' she asked.

'It's *Drive-In Movie Day*,' I replied.

'Looks like fun. Can I watch too?'

'Sure,' I said. 'Hop into my passenger seat.'

'The car looks good. Did it take long to build?' asked Rachel as she squashed up next to me on the sofa.

'Nah, about ten minutes,' I said.

June 7th

Hi George. Loved the book. If you ever want to turn it into a feature film then get in touch.

As far as Twitter messages go, it was definitely the most interesting I've received. The idea of a film version of my first book had been suggested to me a few times over the last few months.

'Your book would make such a great film.'

'Have you sold the film rights yet?'

'I'd love to see Free Country: The Movie.'

But never by a REAL filmmaker. It had never really occurred to me, to be honest. Still, who was I kidding? FUCK

YES! Of course I was interested in turning my book into a film!

I sent him a casual reply.

'Feel free to drop me an email'

An hour later I received a long email from the producer with details about his vision for the film of my book and how he pictured it as *'The Full Monty, meets Withnail and I, with a bit of The Hangover thrown in.'* I loved the sound of that. It definitely sounded like my kind of film. He sent me details of his previous work and experience and he came across as a very well respected and genuine filmmaker.

I did have one small concern. A friend of mine has also been desperate to turn my book into a film. He has spoken to me about all of his great ideas and visions. I really love and admire his enthusiasm but I keep trying to put him off. He has no experience whatsoever of filmmaking or the industry, just bags and bags of energy. Because I didn't ever consider that anyone else would ever want to make a film of it, I told him he could go ahead if he really wanted to and that I wouldn't get in his way. I did also advise him that I didn't think it was a very wise idea.

I decided to tell the producer about my predicament. He replied instantly.

'Concerning your pal aspiring to do this as a first foray in featureland, for your sake and his, run for the hills. I say that regardless of whether we get to work together. Making even the smallest feature is a long and fraught process (in my experience take the worst moments of the publishing experience and multiply by ten).'

He echoed my fears exactly. It was time to contact my friend.

I gave him a call and broke it as gently as I could, and told him that I would try - if possible - to get him involved in the whole filmmaking process and that it could be a useful learning experience for him. I tried to tie it into a holiday celebration and so wished him a Happy *National Doughnut Day*, too. I don't think that helped.

He was understandably gutted and I did feel very guilty about the whole thing. He hadn't yet invested any time or money in pursuing it, but he had been so excited about the idea. I logged onto Facebook later in the day and saw he had updated his status:

Sometimes moments of inspiration can be sucked away as if they were never inspired in the first place :'(

What had I done? I had destroyed his dreams. I had sucked away his inspiration. I had broken him. And all for purely selfish reasons.

Just to rub salt into the wound, I went to comment on his status but clicked *'like'* by mistake.

'George Mahood likes this'. I quickly clicked *'unlike'* and sent him an email instead telling him that I honestly thought it was for the best, for his sake too, and that it would save him a lot of grief, stress and money in the long run.

In the evening I had a much more positive email from him, saying that he had thought about it and decided that rather than being a door closed on his dreams, it was opening up a new opportunity for him to learn from the professionals and gain experience. He was excited and enthusiastic again about the project, and I felt a huge sense of relief.

June 8th

I used to love mornings. As a child, getting up early was the best thing EVER. For years I wanted to be a milkman when I grew up, simply because it meant getting up ridiculously early and starting work whilst everyone else was still asleep.

Then I became a teenager and mornings were then the worst thing in the world. It didn't matter how much sleep I got, my excitement for getting up early was gone for good. There was a brief respite during my first year at University when my halls of residence (that's a very posh name for a building full of grubby student beds, isn't it?) provided breakfast every morning. I never missed a breakfast during my whole time there. Every morning I would be up at 7am, walk the 50 metres down the corridor to be served breakfast and I would then crawl back into my bed for the rest of the morning. Those were the days.

Then, after university, when my working life began, mornings took on a far more sinister connotation when I would be woken by an alarm clock each morning to signify that I would have to go off to WORK at a job that I hated.

Then I became self-employed and mornings were filled with guilt about trying to feel productive about my day, and feel like I did actually have work to do, even though I often didn't.

And then, finally, the worst stage of all. Babies. I love my children more than anything, but after nearly six years with young children I still can't get used to being woken early every single morning. What makes things even harder is that the morning is their most happy and enthusiastic time of the day. They wake up in a great mood, ready to start another day, full of life and energy, just like I used to do. I wake up miserable that my day has started by having to wipe someone's bottom, empty a potty, change a nappy or clean-up spilled Cheerios from every corner of the kitchen. Once the grumpiness has worn off, and my body and head have slowly accepted the fact that it is daytime, I am then fine, and I promise myself that I'll be in a good mood when the same thing happens tomorrow morning. But then tomorrow morning comes and it's like it's the WORST DAY OF MY LIFE all over again.

Today was *Upsy Daisy Day*. To begin with, I assumed it was a day to celebrate the irritating, and clearly sexually-frustrated, character from the children's TV show *In The Night Garden*, but then I discovered that it was unconnected.

Upsy Daisy Day encourages people to face the start of each day positively, and to wake up *'gloriously, gratefully and gleefully'* each morning.

That all sounds great in principle but it didn't actually address the fundamental problem. *HOW?*

I Googled *'how to wake up feeling fresh'* and discovered hundreds of sites offering the 'secrets' of how to feel better in the morning. These ranged from avoiding coffee, sleeping with the window open, not eating after 8pm, not drinking alcohol, not having any confrontation with your partner, sorting out the feng shui of your bedroom. They were all things I had tried at various points in the past, but to do them all at the same time would require a lifestyle change that was so extreme that it was unrealistic.

A couple of other suggestions that did stand out were, firstly, to get up at the same time each day. Our children don't have a set time that they wake up. It can be anywhere between 5.30am and 7am. Thankfully it's usually after 6.15am. The only way for me to get up at the same time each day would be to set an alarm to get up before them. It was worth a try, though.

The other, more morbid technique is to go to sleep imagining the possibility that you might die and never wake up. That way, when you do wake up (hopefully) you'll be grateful for the extra day you have been given and use it as an opportunity to do something meaningful. This is apparently a Buddhist method - and there was me thinking Buddhism was a calming and positive religion.

I decided to give it a go.

I kissed the children goodnight again on my way to bed, and lingered longer than I normally would by their bedside imagining that this might be the last time that I would see them. I then lay in bed thinking of all the possible scenarios of what might happen to me in the night. I got up several times to check that I hadn't left the gas hobs on and to make sure those scented candles of Rachel's were definitely extinguished. I checked the batteries in our smoke alarm. I looked at the carbon monoxide detector to see if it had changed colour. I double checked that ALL the doors were locked, in case of an intruder. It was without a doubt, one of the worst night's sleep of my life. I did wake up feeling glad to be alive, but on many, many different occasions throughout the night. When I eventually did get up with the children at 6.15am, I was so tired and grumpy that death was almost preferable.

June 10th

We have hundreds of pens in our house. I genuinely mean HUNDREDS. They are everywhere. About 95% of them don't work though. But for some reason, whenever we find one that doesn't work we put it back in the drawer and try another, rather than taking the logical and pro-active step of throwing it away. I've lost count of the number of times I've had an important phone call and needed to write down a number in a hurry, and then spent several minutes frantically searching for a bloody pen that works. In most cases I have to give up and then scratch the number or details onto a bit of paper with the blunt tip of an empty biro, in the hope that I will be able to decipher the information later.

Today changed all that. Today was the highly anticipated *Ball Point Pen Day*. I know I have already slagged off pens on *Pencil Day*. It was all about the pencils then, and I was very critical about pens. I'm a hypocrite, I admit it. The pencil let me down at the wedding, and it was a ball point pen that came to my rescue. It was only fair that I celebrate their day too. However, the celebration of *Ball Point Pen Day* was tinged with sadness as I decided to actively dispose of many of them. I got the kids to help me.

'Who wants to play the *Pen Hunt Game* and the *Pen Test Game*?' I asked.

'MEEEE!' they all shouted.

'Great. So the rules of the *Pen Hunt Game* are simple. I have hidden lots and lots of pens all around the house, and you have to see if you can find them all,' I said.

'How many pens are there?' asked Layla.

'Lots. I'm not sure exactly.'

'Are they everywhere?' asked Leo. 'Even the toilet?'

'Er, I don't know. Maybe. You'll have to see.'

'What sort of pens?' asked Layla.

'All sorts. Collect any pens that you can find. Ok... ready, steady... GO!'

We searched in drawers, on desks, in cupboards, down the back of the sofa, in the car, in coat pockets, in the garden and behind curtains. We piled a huge mountain (more like a small molehill actually) of pens onto the floor in the sitting room and surveyed our treasure.

'Did you really hide all these, Daddy? Or did you just want us to find them for you?' asked Layla suspiciously.

'Well, I sort of hid them. Just not today. It was a fun game anyway, wasn't it? Now it's time for the *Pen Test Game*!'

'How do we play that?' Layla sighed.

'You pick up a pen. Give it a quick squiggle on the paper and if it doesn't work you put it in this box. If it DOES work then you put it in this other box. Got it?'

'Got it!'

We tested each pen in turn. We were completely ruthless and operated a zero tolerance policy. If it didn't work then into the bin it went. NO second chances. It was incredibly therapeutic. By the end, we were left with just a handful of working pens. It felt extremely liberating, and the children had all enjoyed themselves immensely. *Ball Point Pen Day* had been a surprising success.

And then I found £50.

June 11th

With just over two weeks to go of this six-month challenge, I can feel the excitement building. I'm looking forward to being able to start a day without checking the diary to see what day I am supposed to be celebrating. I'm finding it a bit hard to get used to the 'me' that this project has created.

Take today, for example. It was *Corn on the Cob Day*. I love a good corn on the cob, so I was very happy to have another excuse to eat them. But Tuesday is also one of my fasting days, so my immediate concern was *'how many calories are in a corn on the cob?'* A month ago, I would not have been able to guess to within the nearest 500. I had absolutely no concept whatsoever of calories. Four weeks of the fasting diet have honed my skills considerably. *'Probably about 90-100?'* I estimated. There are in fact only 83. I was delighted. It meant I could have a corn on the cob for dinner, and still have 217 calories to spare for something else. Or I could just have 3.6 corn on the cobs. WHAT HAVE I BECOME? The old me would have eaten 3.6 corn on the cobs AND something else.

I have been sticking rigorously to my fasting diet and although I have found it difficult, it has not been nearly as hard as I anticipated. I would almost go as far as saying that I have enjoyed it. Yes, I did get a little grumpy and hungry on the fasting days, but these feelings were counteracted by the increased energy that I have felt, and, more importantly, the weight loss. I have lost over 10lbs in a month, without really doing anything. I am no longer biggishly built.

June 13th

I had been dreading this week from the moment I first noticed it on my list. It was *National Blood Week*.

I have always been terrified of needles and the thought of giving blood made me wince. I had tried once before when I was at university, but was rejected as they told me I was slightly anaemic. This is apparently common with many students, and was probably due to my diet of beer and toast. I knew that it was unlikely I would still be anaemic, but had been using it as my justification for not giving blood ever since.

This whole challenge was about making me a better person, and this was an observance I was not going to let slip by. Poor planning meant that although it was *National Blood WEEK*, I had to donate TODAY. Most of the week had already gone, and the next two days I knew I had back to back weddings. I had a photography job down in Hemel Hempstead in the early afternoon but had a bit of free time before and after, during which I could go and donate. I rang the blood donor helpline to find somewhere that I could give blood.

'Sorry, there are no donor sessions in Northampton today, I'm afraid. The next one is on Monday at the hospital,' said the lady from the National Blood Service.

'I need to go somewhere today really. I'm happy to drive. Is there anywhere else nearby?' I asked.

'If you can suggest some other places then I can look for you.'

'Err... Milton Keynes? Daventry?'

'Ok... let me see... no, Milton Keynes has a session on Monday too, and Daventry has one on Tuesday.'

'No sorry, it has to be TODAY, I'm afraid'.

I realised how strange it must have sounded to her. My local hospital, which is half a mile away, would happily take my blood in a couple of days, but I was demanding somewhere the same day.

'How about Hemel Hempstead?' I asked, remembering my photography job.

'Hang on... they've got a session tomorrow, but I guess that's no use?'

I tried desperately to remember places between Northampton and Hemel Hempstead.

'LUTON!' I shouted, as though I had just won at bingo. At a weird bingo hall in which they shout 'Luton' instead of 'house'.

'Let me see... Yes! Luton has a permanent donor centre on St George's Square in the town centre,' she said.

'Brilliant. What time does it close, and do I need to book an appointment?' I asked.

'It's open until 4.15pm, and there's no need to book an appointment, you can just turn up.'

And so I did.

After taking some pictures of Hemel Hemptead's Mayor opening an ugly new apartment building, I drove back up the M1 as quickly as I could (within the national speed limit, of course) to get to the session before it closed.

Luton has the most ridiculous one way system I have ever encountered. I swear that at one point I managed to become stuck in a loop in the town centre that seemed to have no exit roads. I passed under the same tunnel THREE times whilst I desperately looked for a way out. It was as though I was trapped in an ugly concrete whirlpool. Having spent a few hours driving around Luton, I would now choose the whirlpool every time.

I eventually spotted a parking space on a road that seemed fairly close to the main shopping area. It had a 1 hour maximum stay, but I was only giving blood, not donating an organ. How long could it possibly take?

I found the donor centre easily enough and the whole process of registering was quick and simple. I had a 'prick test' done on me. Not to see if I was a prick, but to test for anaemia. I was all clear.

The actual blood donation was a breeze, and nowhere near as scary as I had imagined. I got hooked up to a machine which then took the required amount of blood and then beeped when it was complete. My machine beeped less than 30 minutes after I had parked my car.

'As this is your first time, you'll need to just lie there for a few minutes before we sit you up,' said the young nurse as she labelled the bags of my blood. 'I'll come back in 10 minutes.'

She came back 10 minutes later and adjusted the bed up to a three-quarter sitting position.

'We have to sit you up in stages, as you can feel very light headed, particularly on your first visit,' she said. 'I'll go and get you a drink. Would you like orange or blackcurrant?'

'Orange please, but I feel fine... I... my car...'

But she was gone.

Another 10 minutes passed and she eventually let me sit up.

'If you go through to the relaxing area, Margaret will sort you out with some biscuits or crisps and you should have another drink. We ask everyone to sit in there for 15 minutes after giving blood, just in case,' said the nurse.

'But my parking ticket expires in about five minutes,' I pleaded.

'I'm sorry, but we have to be careful'.

Margaret gave me a cup of tea and a Wagon Wheel and I read a well-thumbed copy of Woman's Own. There was a great article on how to get that bikini body in time for summer. I was the only person in the room, and Margaret kept her eyes on me like a hawk. At one point I stood up and walked towards the door, but she caught my gaze and said 'where do you think you're going?' without even moving her lips. She was a ventriloquist hawk.

I sat back down.

'Hi Margaret. I feel absolutely fine, and I think I'm ok to go now,' I said a few minutes later.

'You're supposed to wait 15 minutes,' she said.

'I know, but my parking ticket has already expired and I really can't afford to pay for a fine.'

'Well, it's up to you. You can leave if you want, but don't say that I allowed you.'

I rushed from the donor centre, feeling great and wishing that I'd grabbed another Wagon Wheel on the way out, because they are so damn hard to find these days. As I reached my car there was a parking attendant writing out a ticket.

'Excuse me, I'm really sorry,' I panted. 'I've just been to give blood and I didn't realise it would take this long. Is there any way you can cancel the ticket?'

'Sorry Sir, it's in the system,' said the large, smiley Afro-Caribbean parking attendant, with braided hair and way too much lipstick. She was looking slightly sorry for me.

'Honestly, all I did since parking here was give blood. They just make you rest for a while afterwards, and I ran back here as quickly as I could. I'm only a couple of minutes late. Please?'

'Ok, ok. You're lucky you caught me on a good day. I haven't quite completed the ticket yet, so I'll cancel it for you, but maybe you should allow a bit of extra time in future.'

'Thank you very, very much. That's really good of you. I really appreciate it.'

'You're welcome. Well done for giving blood. I'm too scared of needles,' she said.

'I was too, but it was actually fine. You should do it. They even give you a free Wagon Wheel.'

'A Wagon Wheel? Jeez, I haven't had one of those in years. Thanks, I think maybe I will. Have a nice day,' she said as she walked off.

'You too. Any idea how I get back to the motorway?' I asked.

'Just follow the one-way system. It'll get you there eventually'.

I felt a huge sense of achievement. Not about overturning the parking ticket, but about getting safely out of Luton's one-way system. No, I mean about giving blood. I genuinely felt a sense that I had done something worthwhile and I now promise to become a regular donor. If it hadn't been for *National Blood Week* and this challenge of mine then I would probably have used the anaemia excuse for the rest of my life. To anyone, like me, that has a fear of needles, it really was a very easy and painless experience. And if that doesn't sway you, maybe the free drinks and the Wagon Wheel will.

June 14th

My surname has provided much confusion and amusement over the years. Apart from the frequent use of the word 'manhood' instead of Mahood, we more frequently have it confused with the surname Mahmood. Most sales calls that we receive ask to speak to Mr or Mrs Mahmood, and much of our post is addressed as such. Often when people hire me for a photography job they have a look of surprise when then meet me to discover that I'm not Indian.

'But your name, Mahood... isn't that, like Indian or Pakistani or something?' they often say.

'It does sound like it should be, but it's actually Irish. There's loads of Mahoods in Ireland. Just not many in Northampton.'

I say this to people because it is what I've always said. I've no idea if it is true. I just remember once when we visited my grandparents in Belfast that there were a significant number of Mahoods in the telephone directory. Back in Northampton there was just the one family.

It was *Family History Day* so I decided to do some research in order to have a more convincing response next time somebody asks. I phoned up my Dad but he wasn't much help.

'I think it comes from *McHood*, which is probably Gaelic for something. That's about all I know, I'm afraid.'

A quick search on the internet taught me more in ten minutes than I have learnt about my name in 34 years. I really do think this whole *'internet'* thing might catch on after all.

The first bit of information that I found stated that the name Mahood means *'maker of hoods'*. This seems like a bit of a strange occupation to me. A maker of HOODS? Is a hood even a thing on its own? Surely the hood of an item is just made by the same person that has made the rest of the garment? It's doesn't seem right that the people who make coats, dressing gowns, or hoodies do their bit and then have to call on the *'Maker of Hoods'* to do the hood part.

'My work is done. I have stitched the sleeves, the cuffs, the neck and attached all the buttons. Now it is time for the hood. QUICK! CALL MAHOOD!'

My mum has a running joke that she has done for longer than I can remember. Any raincoat or jacket that she has ever owned with a detachable hood, she removes the hood and puts it in her pocket. Then, with a part of it poking out of her pocket, she says 'Ask me what this is.' So we all have to ask, 'what is that?' and she says 'it's ma'hood', and we all roll around laughing on the floor for about an hour. Except we don't. I now do it all the time to my kids, and they look equally unimpressed with me.

I do wish my family were makers of hoods, though. It sounds like a very skilled and admirable profession. Surely there would be plenty of free hoodies too (or the hood part, at least), without having to run 20 miles.

The website also stated that the name possibly originated from the settlement of Hood in a village called Rattery in

Devon. Strangely, Rachel and I both already have a slight affinity with this village. For years we used to pass a lone sign on the A38 for Rattery when we were driving down to Devon on holiday. We were always very curious as to what it was. For many years we assumed it might be some sort of cattery, but for rats, but then decided there probably wasn't too much demand for a rat cattery. Then one year, I made a spontaneous decision and swerved off at the junction to find out once and for all what Rattery was. We were delighted to discover that Rattery was in fact a quaint little Devon village with a lovely looking pub, serving amazing sounding Sunday roasts. If it hadn't been for the fact that we had already stopped for our own roast dinner in the form of a McDonalds *Big Mac Meal* at Taunton Deane service station (my favourite on the M5), and if it hadn't been a Tuesday, then we would have definitely stayed in Rattery for Sunday lunch.

I also found another listing on an ancestry website that said Mahood was an anglicized form of the Gaelic Ó hUid meaning *'son of Ó hUid'* (the Ó hUid family being poets). So, I'm either the descendent of a hoodmaker from Devon, or related to some poets from Ireland. Either way I'm very happy with that.

It was also *Work @ Home Father's Day* - a day specifically for father's who have elected to work from home and spend more time with their family. Although I technically fall into this category, nobody else in the family seemed to be celebrating MY day so it passed by without a whimper.

I couldn't really protest too much as I was photographing a wedding and therefore not working from home, OR spending time with my children.

June 17th

Whilst we were at the park I decided to check on the letterbox that we had hidden, to see how many people had stamped the log book. I hoped that it might even be full and I would need to replace it with a new one. I traipsed into the bushes with Leo and Kitty and spent several minutes searching in and around the bush in which I had hidden it.

It was gone.

My beloved letterbox had disappeared without a trace. I was absolutely gutted (until I remembered that it was just a plastic box that I had dumped in a bush and nothing of any real importance). It's not as if it was of any financial value to anyone, and it could not have been seen by a passer-by. I concluded that it must have either been stolen by someone with an urgent need to keep food fresh, or it was cleaned up by an extremely efficient, off-piste litter picker.

When we got home I deleted my entry from the letterboxing website and removed Northampton from the world of urban letterboxing.

I had been keeping a close eye on my prized vegetable patch, which had been planted with just the one crop - rocket, which isn't technically even a vegetable. But it was all about quality, not quantity, and I knew it would be particularly awesome rocket, because it was fueled by my very own toxic sludge compost.

Sure enough, the shoots appeared within days and we now have a healthy crop. Today was *Eat Your Vegetables Day* - a day when people are encouraged to eat their vegetables. The vegetables that you eat don't have to be YOUR vegetables, though, but I chose to interpret it literally. I also chose to interpret rocket as a vegetable, and specifically MY vegetable. So there.

Even if it takes our house a few months to sell, I can safely say that, because of the vegetable patch that I created, our family will be completely self-sufficient... in rocket.

June 18th

Despite my cynicism, the pheromone spray that I bought for Father Dougal has worked wonders. It was a truly remarkable purchase. It felt like he was a new cat. Not only has he stopped urinating in the house, but he has become a very affectionate cat again. In the evenings, he now comes and sits on our laps, allowing us to stroke and cuddle him like he used to in the *'good old days'*.

'It's so lovely having the old Father Dougal back,' said Rachel.

'It's amazing,' I said, tickling him under the chin as he purred on my lap.

'I didn't think that Glade Plugin thing that you bought would be anywhere near as effective.'

'I know. Neither did I.'

'Who would have thought that a simple thing like that could calm him down so much and stop him being so stressed out and agitated all the time?' she said.

'Do you think they do them for humans?' I asked.

'What do you mean?'

'Perhaps they do human pheromone diffusers too. I would order one immediately and plug one next to your side of the bed. It might have the same effect on you as it has on Father Dougal.'

'You're such a dick,' she said.

June 19th

I am a competitive walker. I don't actually compete in official walking competitions. But when I walk, I really walk. I have my own little speed walking competitions with people. They don't know that I'm racing them, but I am. I'll spot someone further down the road, and see if I can catch them before reaching a certain lamppost. I usually make a point of crossing the road in advance so that I don't tear up behind them like a lunatic. Instead I just cast a casual smile their way as I fly past on the opposite pavement. *'Eat my dust, loser,'* I mutter to myself. Very, very rarely have I been overtaken by another walker. And on those few occasions, I'm fairly certain that performance enhancing drugs were involved.

I don't mind slow walkers. Providing they STAY OUT OF MY WAY. There's nothing worse than a slow walker who hogs the pavement. I do sometimes allow an exception for the young, elderly, overweight or disabled, but there is no excuse for a healthy able-bodied person to walk slowly.

Today was *World Sauntering Day*.

I hate sauntering. I hate saunterers. But today I had to be one of them.

I had a few things to do in town, and normally I would nip in on my bike and be there and back within 20 minutes. Today I set off at a very leisurely stroll; ambling casually down the street. It felt very uncomfortable to begin with, but I soon settled into it. I think I almost enjoyed it. I had travelled down this road most days for the last ten years, and I spotted lots of things I had never noticed before: buildings, shop facades, posters, signposts and amusing graffiti.

Although I quite enjoyed sauntering, I HATED people overtaking me. And EVERYBODY was overtaking me. They must have all thought I was such an idiot, strolling along at 1mph. I wanted to stop them all and tell them: *'I don't usually walk this slowly. Normally I walk VERY fast. You should see me when I really walk,'* but I couldn't because they had always disappeared off into the distance before I could even open my mouth.

'Where have you been? I thought you were just going to pay a cheque in?' asked Rachel.

'I was. But I sauntered there. And then I sauntered back.'

'You've been gone for nearly three hours. Let me guess. *National Sauntering Day?*'

'Actually it is *WORLD Sauntering Day*. This shit's gone global.'

'Oh, sorry. So how did it go?'

'It felt pretty good actually. I think I could get used to it. I feel really chilled out now.'

'That's great. So from now on you can devote entire mornings to paying cheques in. That's such a productive way to spend your time. Maybe you could spend the afternoon buying a loaf of bread or something. Or perhaps posting a letter? Actually, better not overdo it. Leave the letter posting for another day.'

'Ok, ok, I get the message. I'll just use my bike next time. No more sauntering from me.'

June 20th

Since *Upsy Daisy Day* last week, when I suggested ways to feel fresher in the morning, I have started setting an alarm clock. In order to beat the children I have been getting up at 6am. It did seem to be having a positive effect. I did curse the moment the alarm went off each morning and, as always, it felt like the worst day of my life every day, but once I was up, that feeling soon wore off, and I actually felt significantly better than when I was getting up at irregular times. It also gave me a chance to have a little time on my own in the morning to have a cup of tea, read a book, reply to some emails or watch some breakfast TV. It has also increased my productivity by having an extra hour or so in the day, and I didn't feel any worse off from the reduced amount of sleep.

This lasted for two days.

Then on the third day, despite my stealth-like tip-toeing down the stairs, Leo had heard me and was at the top of the stairs in a split second.

'What are you doing, Daddy?' he asked.

'Er... nothing. Go back to bed, pal.'

'Why are you going downstairs? Is it morning yet?'

'No, not yet. I was just going to get a glass of water.'

'Can I have one too please?'

'Just have some water from the bathroom.'

'But why are you having water from downstairs?'

'I... er... I like the downstairs water better.'

'So do I. Can I come too?'

'Ok, fine. You can come downstairs, too.'

Seconds later, Layla appeared at her bedroom door and I could hear Kitty shouting from her cot.

'Is it morning?' asked Layla.

'Yes, I suppose so,' I sighed. 'Come on downstairs.'

This pattern has been repeated every day since. So much for *Upsy Fucking Daisy Day*.

June 21st

'You do realise that there are thunderstorms forecast all weekend in Belgium?' said Damian, as we met at Northampton train station for the start of a two night stag weekend in the Belgian city of Ghent.

It was 6.15am and extremely cold and wet and I was standing in the train station in a pair of shorts and flip-flops, as all the London-bound commuters with their coffees and their papers bustled through the turnstiles.

'Really?' I said. 'I hadn't checked the weather.'

The truth was it was *National Flip Flop Day*, but I didn't want to draw attention to it.

A group of about ten of us boarded the early train to London, where we sat and swigged from cans of lager at 6.30am, surrounded by the sneers of suited businessmen and women. It's quite difficult to drink beer on a train before breakfast without feeling like a lowlife. However, it is the LAW when you are on a stag do. We then got the Eurostar to Brussels, on which we consumed a lot more beer, before getting a connecting train to Ghent, arriving just in time for a quick beer before lunch.

Ghent is a beautiful city. We had a brilliant three days and really soaked up the Belgian culture by doing lots of traditional Belgian things; such as watching the British & Irish Lions play rugby on TV against Australia, eating in Pizza Hut and drinking Guinness in Foley's Irish Pub. We did also drink more than our fair share of Belgian beer, and eat copious amounts of Belgian waffles.

The stag (let's call him Jim, because that was his name) was dressed as Dennis the Menace (long story). As part of his stag do challenges, he was required to take part in his own waffle eating contest to secure a place in the Guinness Book of Records. There isn't currently a world record for *'the most Belgian waffles eaten in ten minutes'*, so the bestmen had arranged to submit an official record attempt after Jim had completed his challenge. It all had to be filmed, and the rules read out beforehand, in order to make it official. Jim was so unbelievably hungover that it took him EIGHT minutes just to eat the first waffle. These waffles weren't particularly big either. They were about the size of a small piece of bread. Or a waffle, if you can get your head around that.

It was at this point that I reminded Jim that he was attempting to set a new WORLD RECORD; a landmark that other waffle-eaters would aspire to. Having only eaten ONE waffle, he was currently a joint world record holder, with every person who had eaten a waffle, ever. In between gagging, and regular sips of water, he managed to finish the second waffle off just as the timer hit zero. Ten minutes. Two waffles. It had been painful to watch.

The contest took place at an outdoor cafe and a small crowd of Belgians had gathered to witness this momentous occasion. They very quickly dispersed once Jim's feeble attempt was over. The bestmen had rather optimistically bought TWELVE waffles from the cafe. Once Jim had finished, the rest of us demolished the remaining waffles in a matter of seconds - a couple of people eating two in less than 30 seconds. We didn't tell Jim this because it was HIS moment. He was a WORLD CHAMPION waffle eater and we didn't want to steal his thunder.

After arriving back in the UK, the bestmen submitted an application to Guinness World Records, complete with the video footage. A few weeks later they received a response.

'Thank you for sending us the details of your proposed record attempt for 'Most waffles eaten in 10 minutes'. Unfortunately, after thoroughly reviewing your application with members of our research team, we are afraid to say that we're unable to accept your proposal as a Guinness World Records title.'

There were no further details as to why it had been denied, but the reasons were fairly obvious.

These weren't actual size.

June 22nd was also *Stupid Guy Thing Day*; a day when people are encouraged to recognise and accept that often guys do stupid things. Judging by the evidence in this book, I think it's fair to say that I have celebrated this on a daily basis.

June 24th

As I had been away in Belgium for three days leaving Rachel on her own with the children, I felt it was only fair that I should take Leo and Kitty out for the day. We walked to the park, for a change, and I did my best to stay awake. Stag Dos are incredibly exhausting. Three days of drinking, eating and not sleeping is a hardcore endurance event. We blokes don't get nearly enough sympathy for what we have to go through.

I was standing at the swings, pushing one child with each hand, when I heard a familiar voice behind me.

'Alright mate. How's it going?' he said.

I turned around and Ian Stewart - the Facebook 'jerk' that I deleted on *Dump Your Significant Jerk Day* - was standing there with his young daughter.

'Yeah, good thanks, Ian. How are you?'

'Not bad, not bad. Same old. You been up to much recently?'

'Not really. Just the usual.'

'I haven't seen you on Facebook for a while.'

I gulped and shuffled awkwardly.

'No, I'm not really on there much these days, to be honest. I haven't seen much of you on there either,' I said.

'Maybe you deleted me! Ha ha.'

'Ha! As if! Why would I do that?'

'Only kidding.'

'It is weird, though. I've heard Facebook sometimes has a bit of glitch and randomly removes friends.'

'Yeah?'

'Yeah. Apparently it's fairly common.'

'That's probably what it is then. Anyway, good to see you, mate. We should go out for a beer sometime.'

'Definitely. Great to see you too! See you again soon I hope.'

I sent a *Friend Request* to Ian Stewart - my new BFF - the second I got home.

June 25th

The film producer who had been interested in optioning the film rights to *Free Country* had been away on a shoot in

Nepal for a few weeks, but on his return had sent me a long email detailing his continued enthusiasm for the project. He starting talking figures, which would be minimal to begin with, but I understood that this was just a token gesture for him to show willing, and more significant payments would then follow if the film ever went into production.

He sent me over a contract which was 11 pages long and full of jargon that I didn't understand. I read through it extremely carefully trying to work out all of the details. The idea suddenly became very exciting and I even started having thoughts about who could play Ben and me in the film version. Sure, the book would be torn apart if it was made into a film, but I was happy with that. It needed a lot more action. Maybe a few explosions, a car chase, and definitely some love interest. But hopefully not between the two of us. Although, *Brokeback Mountainbiking* would be a damn good name for a gay porno version of my book.

I was all set to sign the contract and seal the deal, but decided I should get a second pair of eyes to look over it first. I emailed it to my sister, who is conveniently a lawyer, and asked her to have a read through for me.

She replied a little later and had picked up on a couple of things that were slightly concerning. She pointed out that the contract allowed him to *'exercise the option'* at any point. This means that the film rights to the book get passed over to him, but he wouldn't have to pay me a penny until the film actually went into production. Which might never even happen.

I had naively thought that if the film didn't get made then maybe someone else would buy it further down the line. Perhaps this was just an oversight or a mistake from the producer. Or maybe he does this for lots of different books? Options them for a nominal fee, exercises the right straight away, which means that he owns the film rights FOREVER, and then spends his time trying to get funding and interest together hoping one of his many projects will take off, whilst the rest of them spend forever in limbo.

She also highlighted another concern about the wording of a clause regarding 'sequels'. It appeared that he would also get film rights to any future books involving the same characters. So... er... that's ME then. As I have only ever written non-fiction, I am likely to be in every book I ever write. So, although this book is in no way a sequel to *Free Country*, it does feature the same character (me) so I would therefore be giving up the rights to this book too (not that I am in any way suggesting that this book could be ever made into a film. But if you are a producer/director and think it has potential, then, hey, get in touch!)

I sent him an email highlighting my concerns, whilst still trying to sound positive about the whole thing.

June 26th

I had a reply from the film producer first thing in the morning. He had addressed all of the issues that I had raised about the contract. Part of it, he claimed, 'got lost' somewhere, and he did rewrite it so that it answered my concerns. I did forgive him for the errors, as today was *Forgiveness Day*. It was possible that he was telling the truth but it still sat slightly uneasily with me.

I didn't quite know how to proceed. I really liked the guy and had a good feeling about his enthusiasm, but having never met him, I felt like I couldn't be rushed into making a decision. And the glaring omissions from the contract - that I, admittedly hadn't spotted - did not fill me with huge amounts of confidence. I asked Rachel for her advice.

'It would be foolish to miss out on the opportunity to have it made into a film, wouldn't it?' she said.

'Definitely. But I don't know enough about the industry or how it all works to know if this is a good deal. It might also be foolish for me to jump at the first person that shows any interest.'

'True. But what happens if he's the ONLY one who shows any interest?'

'Oh, I don't know. It's so tricky.'

During the stag-do in Ghent, in my drunken stupor, I spoke to my friends about the interest I'd had about a film.

'A film? That's fucking wicked. Definitely go for it. Why would you not?'

'Free money, for something you have already written. And just think how many new people would buy the book having watched the film?'

'Can you get me tickets for the premiere?'

'Who do you think they'll cast as you? Gerard Depardieu? He's the only actor with a nose as big as yours.'

To say that they were all enthusiastic was a vast understatement. Although, Belgian beer definitely had an influence on their passion. I still felt like it was a big decision to have to make without doing any research.

The producer had told me that he was fully booked with work for the next few months and would not make a start on mine until September. So I sent him another email and explained that I was still very keen on the idea, but needed to spend a few more days to think it over and consider the options.

This week is *National Mosquito Control Awareness Week*. I thought we had discussed this already? Wrap everyone in BUBBLE WRAP, for God's sake!

June 27th

Way back in 1893, two sisters named Mildred J. Hill and Patty Smith Hill wrote the lyrics and melody to a song for their kindergarten pupils.

Good morning to you,
Good morning to you,
Good morning, dear children,
Good morning to all.

Over the years the words were adapted into the *Happy Birthday* song that we all know and love today. It is the most widely recognised song in the English language, and, very likely, the world.

Happy Birthday to You
Happy Birthday to You
Happy Birthday Dear (name)
Happy Birthday to You.

Many people over the years have tried to claim copyright and ownership of the song. Warner/Chappell Music currently owns the copyright, and they claim that it is technically illegal for the song to be performed in public without royalties being paid to Warner. Even including the lyrics to *Happy Birthday* in this book I probably face a very lengthy jail sentence, or possibly the death penalty. It's a risk I am willing to take. Such is my dedication to this challenge.

Today was *Happy Birthday To You Day*. June 27th, 1859, is the date on which Mildred J. Hill, the song's original composer, was born.

June 27th is also Layla's birthday. Our first child has just turned SIX. It does feel like the years have whizzed by, but I also can't remember what it was like not having children. It feels like they have always been there. This, I guess, is a good thing.

Layla had lots of her friends over for a birthday party. It was a lovely sunny day, and they all played games and had a nice picnic in the garden. There were a few noticeable winces from the grownups about the compost smell that was still emanating from the vegetable patch, but the children didn't seem to mind. We had breathing apparatus on standby if required.

We sang *Happy Birthday* as loud as we could. Although we were on private property, the voices of 20 shouting children and adults would have been heard all over the surrounding area, violating all sorts of copyright laws. I'm such a badass that I didn't get authorisation or pay a single penny in royalties. So see you in court, Warner/Chappell Music!

June 29th

We had a couple of viewings for our house in the first few days after it went on the market - probably the estate agents' friends - but nothing since. Not only did we feel that they had valued the house too highly, but the photos they had taken were shit. I thought at the time - as the young work-experience guy rushed around the house, snapping away with his little compact camera - that he seemed remarkably efficient. We hadn't even tidied the house as he had just said he was coming to get a few details. I offered to do a quick tidy and move things out of the way that were obstructing his photos, such as piles of toys, cereal packets... and children. He told me not to bother, and, as it was his profession, I trusted him to do a decent job of it. The results were disappointing. Rachel had suggested that I take my own photos instead, but I felt that would be a bit weird and I didn't want to tread on their toes.

Today was *Camera Day* so I decided that maybe she was right. It was, after all, our house, and if better photos increased the likelihood of more viewings then it had to be worth a shot.

I took some nicely composed, well-lit photographs of all of the rooms, put them on a CD and dropped them over to the estate agent mid-morning. The young work-experience kid was at the reception desk.

'Hi. I've taken some new photos of our house. Any chance you could update the listings on your website and Right Move?' I asked, handing him the CD and hoping that I wouldn't offend his photographic skills.

'Of course. No problem. I'll get that done right away for you, Mr Mahood.'

The phone rang just as we were putting the children to bed.

'Hello, Mr Mahood. It's Stuart the estate agent,' said Stuart the estate agent.

'Hi Stuart. How are you?'

'Very well thanks. Listen, we've had a couple of calls this afternoon about arranging viewings for your house. Is it ok if we schedule two in for Monday? Probably between 1-2pm.'

'Sounds perfect. We'll make sure we're out to give you all a bit of space.'

'Ok, great. It looks like those photos that you dropped in earlier today might have done the trick.'

'That's great. Fingers crossed. Have a good weekend, Stuart.'

'Thanks, you too.'

June 30th

I had reached the final day of my six month holiday challenge. I had mixed emotions. I was extremely happy and relieved that I had made it through to the end and not given up completely when things got boring *('that was on January 2nd,'* I hear you say). But, I was also sad that it was over. As time-consuming and exhausting as it had been, I had enjoyed the thrill at looking through my list each morning to see what excitement the day had to offer.

I was hoping for a big finish in the way of holiday celebrations, but June 30th was a little disappointing on that front. I spent a little time in the morning reading some facts about meteors (it was *Meteor Day*, by the way. I'm not that much of a geek). We then decided to take advantage of our free family swim and Sunday lunch at Billing Aquadrome, which I had been offered as part of my *St George's Day* humiliation in April. We invited my mum and dad along too, so that we could pay for their meals and feel less like a bunch of cheapskates.

After an enjoyable swim in the pool, we sat outside in the sunshine eating a delicious free Sunday carvery that had been made possible simply because I had decided to celebrate my name. Surrounded by my six favourite people in the world, I could not have asked for a more fitting end to the challenge.

When I set out on this quest, I didn't expect it to transform me into a stronger, wiser, more intelligent, and more confident individual... and it certainly hadn't.

But I did feel different. I felt more energised. I felt more zeal and gusto about the unpredictability that each day offered. My normal life had been able to carry on pretty much as usual, yet I was able to add a little bit of spice to each day simply by observing the eclectic mix of celebrations that these holidays provided.

It certainly hadn't panned out as I anticipated. Although, I'm not quite sure what I had expected from it. I think I assumed that I would be travelling around the country, or perhaps even jet-setting off to the other side of the world to celebrate obscure events. If I'd had more time and money then it could have been very different. Not necessarily better. Just different; more glamour, more exotic locations, more special effects, more celebrity cameos perhaps. This was certainly a low-budget production (apart from the Viagra). One produced almost exclusively in Northampton and the surrounding area. Not that that is a bad thing.

But it wasn't possible to devote more time to each day. I had completely underestimated the magnitude of the task, and of how many *'official'* days there actually are. It's a relentless stream, and they just kept on coming. I couldn't even pause for a second as they ended up swamping me. The only way to keep on top was to ride them like a wave and try to stay afloat; celebrating and writing, celebrating and writing.

I enjoyed the whole experience immensely. I have learnt so many new things, encountered new people and expanded my knowledge more than I could possibly have imagined. Some of it useful. Most of it less so. I learnt about moths. And penguins. And Finnish saints. I've learnt about dimpled chads, plug-in developers and I have learnt just how adaptable bubble wrap can be.

My cooking repertoire expanded considerably. I am now a seasoned expert at cooking with canned food, and I also have a wealth of knowledge of ham related dishes. And I certainly appreciate the versatility of mushy peas.

I have had so many great experiences too, that were only possible because of this challenge. I have joined societies, started (and disbanded) a regional letterboxing movement, fixed a washing machine, written limericks and haikus. I've been defeated by children in a pillow fight (although that was an experience I would rather not repeat), I've cruised around *Second Life* half-naked, and I was the only George at Billing Aquadrome. I have lost a cat, found a cat, been unable to help save another cat, and, in the process, grown even fonder of our neighbours.

There have been many other benefits, too. I am no longer biggishly-built; I have lost weight and feel so much healthier for it (I no longer have an Embers Grill loyalty card either). My office, and my life, have been tidied, untied, re-tidied, and I'm probably much better off for it. I even had my own room for one day.

Most importantly of all, I have learnt about the people closest to me, and about how much fun we can have together, even in the strangest of circumstances. This year I have worked harder than I have ever worked before; cramming each day full of activity, as well as my normal day-to-day duties. But I have also spent more quality time with Layla, Leo, Kitty and Rachel than ever before; balancing my time so that they were always the top priority. The most fun holidays to celebrate were undoubtedly the ones involving the rest of the family. Holidays SHOULD be celebrated with others, and for too much of this challenge I kept the celebrations largely to myself. That is my only regret. That, and the time I took a pair of girl's knickers out of my pocket in public.

Has it changed me for the better? I honestly don't know. I'm not sure I would be the best judge of that. I certainly feel happier than I did at the start of January, and I think a great deal of that can be attributed to this challenge

There is so much to look forward to for the rest of the year. Our house is for sale and we will be moving to Devon one way or another, there is a good chance that my first book will be made into a film, and there is every possibility that Ben and I will be heading off on our first hashtag microadventure at some point soon. I am enormously excited about the next few months.

We finished our lunch and my mum and dad then took the children inside to play on the arcade machines. Whilst they were gone, Rachel passed me a gift-wrapped present across the table.

'What's this?' I asked.

'You'll have to open it,' she said.

I eagerly tore back the paper to reveal a 2013 diary.

'A diary? Cool, thanks. What's this for? It's the end of June!'

'Look inside,' she said.

I opened the book and slowly flicked through the pages. The diary entries were all blank.

'What am I looking for? There's nothing in it.'

'Keep going.'

I carried on turning the pages. May - nothing. June - still nothing. And then I got to the first week in July and each day had handwriting on.

'What the...' I started, and took a closer look. Rachel had handwritten all of the holiday celebrations into the diary for each day. I flicked through the rest of the year and every single one of the days between July and December had different official days written on them.

'What is this?' I asked

'You're not really going to stop now are you?' she smiled.

'What do you mean?'

'You've completed your six month challenge, but that means that there is still another six months of holidays that you haven't yet celebrated. You can't miss out on those, surely? You're only at the halfway point.'

'But I thought you were fed up of this whole thing? I thought you would be desperate for me to finish it?'

'Not at all. I think it's been really good for you. I've loved seeing your enthusiasm over the last few months. You've had your moments when you've been pretty annoying, but you have those all the time. I don't think I've seen you this happy in ages.'

'Do you really want me to continue?' I asked.

'Absolutely! Besides, it's *Creative Ice Cream Flavours Day* and *U.S. Postage Stamp Day* tomorrow. We can't miss out on those now, can we?'

'This is amazing. It is really kind of you. Thank you so much,' I said, hugging her tightly.

'You're welcome.'

'I'm so looking forward to the rest of this year. It will make it much easier having it all written down in a diary, rather than the stupid print-outs I've been using.'

'I know. I thought you needed to be more organised in your approach for the second half of the year. Speaking of which, have you found anyone for the Administrative Professional job that you advertised for?'

'No, not yet. Why, do you know someone?'

'I might be interested in applying for the role.'

'Really? Fantastic! When can you start?'

'Tomorrow.'

The End... for now

HUGE thanks to you, dear reader, for making it this far. It's been a very strange, but really enjoyable book to write. I hope that you gained some pleasure from it, too.

If you did like it, I would be extremely grateful if you would consider leaving a short review on Amazon or Goodreads. Self-published authors rely almost exclusively on your reviews and recommendations to friends and family, so please help spread the word as much as you can. Thank you!

Life's a Beach (Every Day Is a Holiday - Part 2) is out NOW!

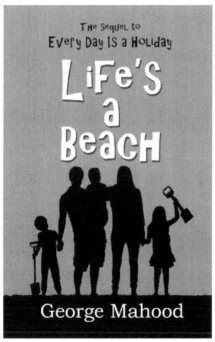

All of the photos in this book are available to view in high-resolution on Facebook.

www.facebook.com/georgemahood

You can also follow me on Twitter for general ramblings:

@georgemahood

Feel free to drop me an email with any comments, feedback or criticism. It's always great to hear from readers and I respond to every email.

george@georgemahood.com

I have a website, but there is not much to see there.
If you sign up to the newsletter you will be the first to hear about any new releases
http://www.georgemahood.com/newsletter/

As you have probably gathered from the subtle mentions in this book, I have also written another book –

Free Country: A Penniless Adventure the Length of Britain.

Here's what others have said about it:
"...spent last night laughing so much my coffee came out my eyes..."
"...this book is quite simply the best I've read in years..."
"...a completely bonkers challenge and a brilliantly funny read, I couldn't put it down..."

Free Country is available on Kindle and in paperback on Amazon.

I also published a brand new book at the end of 2015 –
Operation Ironman: One Man's Four Month Journey from Hospital Bed to Ironman Triathlon

You don't need to have any interest in triathlons or sport to enjoy it. It contains plenty of the nonsense that is in my other books.

Here's what others have said about it:
"…it won't fail to entertain, enthral and motivate…"
"…hilarious and heart-warming…"
"…I laughed, I cried, and am proud of a man I have never met…"

Operation Ironman is available on Kindle and in paperback on Amazon.

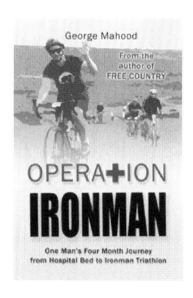

Acknowledgements

Firstly, I would like to thank Rachel, Layla, Leo and Kitty for everything. Thank you for all of the support, for putting up with me being so annoying, for all of the laughs and for the vital help with the editing (Rachel, not the children). This challenge would have been nowhere near as much fun without you.

Special thanks to Miriam and Damian for their kind words of encouragement. Massive thanks also to Tony James Slater for his feedback and valuable words of advice about publishing and writing in general.

Thanks to beta readers Julie Freed, Nancy Lynch, Karen Knight, Susan Jackson and Jennifer Bendriss for their important input.

Additional thanks to Jim - the waffle-eating disappointment - for just being Jim.

Big thanks also to those responsible for running the holiday listing sites. In particular: Chase's Calendar of Events, Brownielocks and Holiday Insights

I would also like to thank all of the amazing people that created these weird and wonderful holidays in the first place. Thank you for believing in your celebration enough to make a day out of it. Without you guys, this book would have been very, very short.

Thank you all again,

BIG love,
George

www.facebook.com/georgemahood
www.twitter.com/georgemahood
www.georgemahood.com

Printed in Great Britain
by Amazon